Public Life and Public Lives: Politics and Religion in Modern British History

Essays in Honour of Richard W. Davis

Edited by

Nancy LoPatin-Lummis

Wiley-Blackwell

for

The Parliamentary History Yearbook Trust

Editorial organisation © 2008 The Parliamentary History Yearbook Trust
Chapters © 2008 The Parliamentary History Yearbook Trust

BLACKWELL PUBLISHING
350 Main Street, Malden, MA 02148–5020, USA
9600 Garsington Road, Oxford OX4 2DQ, UK
550 Swanston Street, Carlton, Victoria 3053, Australia
Blackwell Publishing is now part of Wiley-Blackwell

First published 2008 by Blackwell Publishing Ltd

Library of Congress Cataloging-in-Publication Data
1   2008

Public life and public lives : politics and religion in modern British history : essays in honour of Richard W. Davis / edited by Nancy LoPatin-Lummis.
    p. cm.
    Includes bibliographical references and index.
    ISBN 978-1-4051-8160-0 (acid-free paper)   1. Common good.   2. Religion and politics–Great Britain–History.   3. Great Britain–Politics and government.   4. Great Britain–Colonies–Administration.   I. LoPatin-Lummis, Nancy.   II. Davis, Richard W.
    JC330.15.P83 2008
    261.8′30941–dc22

                                                                        2007048806

ISBN: 978-1-4051-8160-0

A catalogue record for this title is available from the British Library
Set in 10/12pt Bembo
by SNP Best-set Typesetter Ltd., Hong Kong
Printed and bound in Singapore
by Hó Printing Pte Ltd

The publisher's policy is to use permanent paper from mills that operate a sustainable forestry policy, and which has been manufactured from pulp processed using acid-free and elementary chlorine-free practices. Furthermore, the publisher ensures that the text paper and cover board used have met acceptable environmental accreditation standards.

For further information on Blackwell Publishing, visit our website:
http://www.blackwellpublishing.com

CONTENTS

PREFACE

In 2003, after 40 years of university teaching, Richard W. Davis retired from his position as professor of history and director of the Center for the History of Freedom at Washington University in St Louis. He was honoured with a reception from his colleagues in the history department. A few months later, his first graduate student, Richard W. Cosgrove, distinguished professor of history emeritus at the University of Arizona and then president of the Western Conference on British Studies, invited him to give the plenary at the Western Conference on British Studies in October 2004. He reminisced about his career in 'Confessions of a Political Historian'. But plans had been in the works for some time before that to pay tribute to Richard's career, celebrate his achievements and honour him as a teacher, colleague and friend. Those plans have finally turned into a reality, thanks to Clyve Jones, editor of *Parliamentary History*, Richard's sometime collaborator and longtime friend. Without his willingness to support this *festschrift*, we, the contributors, would not be able to truly celebrate Richard's career in the way that would show him how instrumental he has been in the profession at large, and central to our own professional lives: through our scholarship and his profound influence on it. This collection of essays, mostly by his former graduate students, but also by colleagues with whom he studied, taught and worked, is the sincerest celebration we can think of to honour our mentor and friend. It is with our greatest respect and abiding admiration that we dedicate this volume to Richard W. Davis.

LIST OF CONTRIBUTORS

Derek W. Blakeley is an assistant professor of history at McNeese State University in Lake Charles, Louisiana. He completed his dissertation on Lord Curzon's political career after 1905 at Washington University in St Louis under the supervision of Professor Richard W. Davis.

Richard A. Cosgrove is university distinguished professor emeritus at the University of Arizona. He is the author of *The Rule of Law: Albert Venn Dicey, Victorian Jurist* (1980); *Our Lady the Common Law: An Anglo-American Legal Community, 1870–1930* (1987); and *Scholars of the Law: English Jurisprudence from Blackstone to Hart* (1996). His most recent book (with Anthony Brundage), *The Great Tradition: Constitutional History and National Identity in Britain and America, 1870–1960*, is forthcoming from Stanford University Press.

Richard R. Follett joined the Covenant College faculty in autumn 2001 and was promoted to associate professor in summer 2003. He received his BA in history from Arizona State University in 1986, and his MA and PhD in modern British and European history from Washington University in 1996. His first book, *Evangelicalism, Penal Theory and the Politics of Criminal Law Reform in England, 1808–30*, was published in 2001. His current research includes the life and times of the British law-reformer and anti-slavery activist, Sir Thomas Fowell Buxton (1786–1845), and European economic and political integration since 1945.

Edwin Jaggard one-time dean of the faculty of arts at Western Australia's Edith Cowan University, formerly lectured in modern British and Australian history. His *Cornwall Politics in the Age of Reform, 1790–1885* was published in 1999. Articles on British electoral politics have appeared in various journals including *History, Australian Journal of Politics and History, Journal of British Studies, Albion* and *Parliamentary History*.

Padraic Kennedy is currently an assistant professor at York College of Pennsylvania. He received his PhD in 1996 from Washington University under the guidance of Richard W. Davis.

Denys P. Leighton studied at the Universities of Virginia, Freiburg (Germany) and Oxford and completed his doctoral dissertation under the supervision of Richard Davis at Washington University. He presently teaches history at Tulane University, New Orleans, and had previously taught at the University of Delhi, India. His major recent publication, developed from his doctoral thesis, is *The Greenian Moment: T. H. Green, Religion and Political Argument in Victorian Britain* (Exeter and Charlottesville 2004). He is currently working on the arts and crafts movement in relation to Indian nationalism, and temperance, social reform and gender in India, c.1880–1940.

Nancy LoPatin-Lummis is professor of history at the University of Wisconsin-Stevens Point. She is the author of *Political Unions, Popular Politics and the Great Reform Act of 1832* (1999) and co-general editor of *The Lives of Victorian Political Figures by their Contemporaries* (2005–). Her articles on parliamentary reform in the early 19th century appear in *Parliamentary History, Journal of British Studies, Journal of Victorian Culture, Midland History* and *Victorian Periodicals Review,* among others. She is currently working on a political biography of radical reformer, Joseph Parkes.

Michael A. Rutz (BA, MA, University of Michigan; MA, PhD, Washington University in St Louis) is assistant professor of history at the University of Wisconsin–Oshkosh. He is the author of 'The Politising of Evangelical Dissent, 1811–1813', which appeared in *Parliamentary History,* and 'The Problems of Church and State: Dissenting Politics and the London Missionary Society in 1830s Britain', which appeared in the *Journal of Church and State.* His research interests include 19h-century religion and politics, the history of christian missions, and cross-cultural exchange in the 19th- and 20th-century British empire.

Susan Mitchell Sommers is an associate professor and department chair in history at St Vincent College in Latrobe, Pennsylvania. She earned a BA and MA at Southern Illinois University at Carbondale, and an MA and PhD from Washington University in St Louis. Dr Sommers is the author of *Parliamentary Politics of a County and its Town: General Elections in Suffolk and Ipswich in the Eighteenth Century* (2002) as well as several articles and book reviews. Her current book project is *The Radical Brotherhood: The Society of the Gentlemen Supporters of the Bill of Rights.*

Andrew Muldoon received his PhD from Washington University in 1999. He has taught in the history and literature programme at Harvard University and is now an assistant professor of history at Metropolitan State College of Denver. His current work focuses on cultural influences on British policy making in India.

Timothy Parsons holds a joint appointment as an associate professor in the history department and African and Afro-American studies programme at Washington University in St Louis. He is the author of *The African Rank-and-File: Social Implications of Colonial Service in the King's African Rifles, 1902–1964*; *The 1964 Army Mutinies and the Making of Modern East Africa*; *Race, Resistance and the Boy Scout Movement in British Colonial Africa*; and *The British Imperial Century, 1815–1914: A World History Perspective.*

Reba Soffer professor of history, emeritus, at California State University, Northridge, has written extensively about 19th- and 20th-century British intellectual history. A Guggenheim fellow and past president of the North American Conference on British Studies, she is the author of two prize-winning books: *Ethics and Society in England: The Revolution in the Social Sciences, 1870–1914* and *Discipline and Power: The Universities, History and the Making of an English Elite, 1850–1930.* Her latest book, *History, Historians, and Conservatism in the Twentieth Century* is forthcoming.

R.K. Webb is professor of history, emeritus, at the University of Maryland, Baltimore County, and formerly professor of history at Columbia University, where Richard Davis was his student. He was the editor of the *American Historical Review* and is the author of *Harriet Martineau, a Radical Victorian* (1960), *Modern England* (1968, 2nd edn, 1980), and a number of articles on English unitarianism.

ACKNOWLEDGMENTS

The editor and publishers would like to thank the following for grants, or donations, which made publication possible: Nancy Bayne, associate vice chancellor emerita, University of Wisconsin-Stevens Point; Hillel Kieval, chair, department of history, and Robert Thach, dean of graduate studies at Washington University, St Louis; and The Parliamentary History Yearbook Trust.

The photograph of Richard was kindly taken by his son, Ben Davis.

BIBLIOGRAPHY OF THE PUBLICATIONS OF
RICHARD W. DAVIS

1966:
'The Strategy of "Dissent" in the Repeal Campaign, 1820–28', *Journal of Modern History*, xxxviii, 374–406.

1971:
Dissent in Politics, 1780–1830: The Political Life of William Smith, MP (Epworth Press).
'Buckingham, 1832–1846: A Study of a "Pocket Borough" ', *Huntington Library Quarterly*, xxxiv (1970–1), 159–81.

1972:
Political Change and Continuity, 1760–1885: A Buckinghamshire Study (David and Charles; Archon).

1973:
Somers: The History of a Connecticut Town (with Fred. C. Davis) (Somers Historical Society).

1974:
'The Whigs and the Idea of Electoral Deference: Some Further Thoughts on the Great Reform Act', *American Historical Review*, lxxxi, 532–9.

1976:
Disraeli (Hutchinson; Little Brown).
'Deference and Aristocracy in the Time of the Great Reform Act', *American Historical Review*, lxxxi, 532–9.
'The Mid-Nineteenth Century Electoral Structure', *Albion*, viii, 142–53.

1978:
Review of Trygve Tholfsen, *Working Class Radicalism in Mid-Victorian England* (Columbia University Press, 1977), *Business History Review*, lii, 445–7.

1979:
Contributed to the section on the house of lords, 1660–1800, in *A Register of Parliamentary Lists, 1660–1800*, ed. David Hayton and Clyve Jones (University of Leicester History Department; Anglo-American Associates).

1980:
'Toryism to Tamworth: The Triumph of Reform, 1827–1835', *Albion*, xii, 132–46.
Review of Keith Robbins, *John Bright* (Routledge and Kegan Paul, 1979), *Journal of Modern History*, lii, 512–13.

1981:
Review of Leslie Mitchell, *Holland House* (Duckworth, 1980), *American Historical Review*, lxxxix, 391–2.

1982:

'Committee and Other Procedures in the House of Lords, 1660–1685', *Huntington Library Quarterly*, xlv, 20–35.

'The Tories, the Whigs and Catholic Emancipation, 1827–1829', *English Historical Review*, xcvii, 89–98.

1983:

The English Rothschilds (Collins; University of North Carolina Press).

1984:

'The "Presbyterian" Opposition and the Emergence of Party in the House of Lords in the Reign of Charles II', in *Party and Management in Parliament, 1660–1784*, ed. Clyve Jones (Leicester University Press; St Martin's Press), 1–35.

1987:

Review of J.C.D. Clark, *English Society, 1688–1832: Ideology, Social Structure and Political Practice During the Ancient Regime* (Cambridge University Press, 1985), *American Historical Review*, xcii, 412–13.

1988:

Review of Wendy Hinde, *Richard Cobden: A Victorian Outsider* (Yale University Press, 1987), *American Historical Review*, xciii, 700.

1989:

Review of Angus Hawkins, *Parliament, Party and the Art of Politics in Britain, 1855–1859* (Stanford University Press, 1987), *American Historical Review*, xciv, 1096–7.

1990:

'The Politics of the Confessional State, 1760–1832', *Parliamentary History*, ix, 38–49.

1991:

' "We Are All Americans Now!": Anglo-American Marriages in the Later Nineteenth Century', *Proceedings of the American Philosophical Society*, cxxxv, 140–99.

Review of Robert Hale, *Pulpits, Politics and Public Order in England, 1760–1832* (Cambridge University Press, 1989), *Journal of Modern History*, lxiii, 766–7.

Review of Albion M. Urdank, *Religion and Society in a Cotswold Vale: Nailsworth, Gloucestershire, 1780–1865* (University of California Press, 1990), *Journal of Economic History*, li, 971–2.

Review of E.A. Smith, *Lord Grey, 1764–1845* (Clarendon Press of the Oxford University Press, 1990), *American Historical Review*, xcvi, 1195–6.

1992:

Religion and Irreligion in Victorian Society: Essays in Honor of R.K. Webb, co-editor with R.J. Helmstadter (Routledge).

'The Whigs and Religious Issues, 1830–1835', in *Religion and Irreligion in Victorian Society*, ed. Davis and Helmstadter, 29–50.

1993:

'Whigs in the Age of Fox and Grey', *Parliamentary History*, xii, 201–8: a review article covering John W. Derry, *Charles, Earl Grey: Aristocratic Reformer* (Blackwell, 1992); and L.G. Mitchell, *Charles James Fox* (Oxford University Press, 1992).

Review of Ian Newbould, *Whiggery and Reform, 1830–1841: The Politics of Government* (Stanford University Press, 1990), *Journal of Modern History*, lxv, 402–3.

1995:

Lords of Parliament Studies, 1714–1914, editor (Stanford University Press).

Origins of Modern Freedom in the West, editor (Stanford University Press).

'The Duke of Wellington and the Resurgence of the House of Lords', in *Lords of Parliament*, ed. Davis, 97–115.

Contributor to the section on the house of lords, 1660–1800, in *British Parliamentary Lists, 1660–1800. A Register*, ed. Grayson Ditchfield, David Hayton and Clyve Jones (The Hambledon Press).

1996:

'Disraeli, the Rothchilds, and Anti-Semitism', *Jewish History*, x, 9–19.

1997:

'Wellington and the "Open Question": The Issue of Catholic Emancipation, 1821–1829', *Albion*, xxix, 39–55.

1998:

Review of Paul Smith, *Disraeli* (Cambridge University Press, 1996), *Victorian Studies*, xli (1997–8), 307–9.

1999:

Contributed six articles to *An Oxford Companion to the Romantic Age: British Culture, 1776–1832*, ed. Iain McCalman (Oxford University Press).

'The Duke of Wellington and the Ultra Peers', *Wellington Studies*, ed. C.M. Wollgar, iii, 35–55.

'The House of Lords, the Whigs and Catholic Emancipation, 1806–1829', *Parliamentary History*, xviii, 23–43.

2000:

Review of Theodore K. Hoppen, *The Mid-Victorian Generation, 1846–1886* (Clarendon Press of the Oxford University Press, 1998), *Journal of Modern History*, lxxii, 190–2.

Review of K.D. Reynolds, *Aristocratic Women and Political Society in Victorian Britain* (Clarendon Press of the Oxford University Press, 1998), *Victorian Studies*, xliii (2000–1), 181–3.

2001:

'A Last Blast?', *Parliamentary History*, xx, 359–62 [on catholic emancipation; a reply to Peter Jupp].

2002:

Wellington, Peel and the Politics of the 1830s and 1840s (University of Southampton, 14th Wellington Lecture).

Contributed six articles to the *Oxford Dictionary of National Biography* (Oxford University Press): John, 1st Baron Crewe of Crewe (1742–1829); Thomas Grenville (1755–1846); George Nugent-Temple Grenville, 1st marquess of Buckingham (1753–1813); Ferdinand Rothschild (1839–98); Joshua Scholefield (1774/5–1844); and William Smith (1756–1835).

2003:

Leaders in the Lords: Government Management and Party Organization in the Upper Chamber, 1765–1902, editor (Edinburgh University Press); also issued as *Parliamentary History*, xxii, pt 1.

'Introduction. Leaders in the Lords', in *Leaders in the Lords*, ed. Davis, 1–12.

'Wellington', in *Leaders in the Lords*, ed. Davis, 43–55.

Review of F. David Roberts, *The Social Conscience of the Early Victorians* (Stanford University Press, 2002), *Victorian Studies*, xlvi, 142–4.

Review of Philip Salmon, *Electoral Reform at Work: Local Politics and National Parties, 1832–1841* (Boydell and Brewer; Rochester University Press, 2003), *Albion*, xxxvi, 153–4.

2005:

Partisan Politics, Principle and Reform in Parliament and the Constituencies, 1689–1880: Essays in Memory of John A. Phillips, co-editor with Clyve Jones and Philip Salmon (Edinburgh University Press); also issued as a supplement to *Parliamentary History*, xxiv.

'Wellington, Peel and the House of Lords in the 1840s', in *Partisan Politics, Principle and Reform in Parliament and the Constituencies*, ed. Jones, Salmon and Davis, 164–82.

2007:

Review of *Unrepentant Tory: Political Selections from the Diaries of the Fourth Duke of Newcastle-under Lyne, 1827 38*, ed. Richard A. Gaunt (Parliamentary History Record Series 3, 2006), *Parliamentary History*, xxvi, 255–7.

2008:

A Political History of the House of Lords, 1811–1846: From Regency to Corn Law Repeal (Stanford University Press).

A PUBLIC LIFE: RICHARD W. DAVIS, HISTORIAN, MENTOR AND GENTLEMAN

NANCY LOPATIN-LUMMIS (with DENYS LEIGHTON)

Richard W. Davis was born on 8 December 1935 in Somers, Connecticut. He was the youngest of four sons and was introduced to history by his father who taught the subject at Hartford Public High School. Richard graduated from that school in 1953, and attended Amherst College, where he graduated in 1957, *magna cum laude* with a degree in history. Opting to ignore the advice of friends who suggested the study of his favourite subject matter, British history, would suit him well in a career in the CIA, he left New England at the age of 22 years to start his graduate studies at Columbia University under the direction of R.K. Webb. Richard tells that his time spent at Columbia was memorable for many reasons. First and foremost, it established his lifelong scholarly connection to, and remarkable friendship with, Bob Webb. Second, it introduced him, when Webb was on sabbatical, to J.H. Plumb. The two were an enormous influence on Richard. Webb helped him 'discover' the role of dissenters in creating liberal opinion in early 19th-century British high politics. Plumb was there for the dreaded 'orals'. They were dreaded because several graduate students (seven, I recall) had taken – and all failed – their comprehensive exams in modern British history. Richard, in fact, performed well in the orals, so impressing Plumb that the latter arranged for Richard to receive scholarship money to support his research and teach at Christ's College, Cambridge the following year. Richard spent two years at Christ's College, and received an MLitt in history in 1962. He taught American history to the athletes of the university while researching his dissertation. He returned in 1962 to defend his dissertation.

Richard loved recounting his memories of the Columbia years to his graduate students. The stories he most delighted in retelling concerned bizarre characters and events totally unrelated to his career as a student. With the kind of dark humour that we have come to appreciate from Richard, we all learned of his neighbours, the young and constantly bickering couple in an apartment across the hall. Richard enjoyed delivering the chilling details of the apparent disappearance of the young woman, signaled by the abrupt halt in the couple's endless fighting. But the silence coincided, Richard related, with grizzly bemusement, with his neighbour's sudden accumulation of excess garbage – requiring its removal from his apartment in several large black garbage bags. The pressures of graduate school need not, Richard assured us all, turn one into an axe murderer. We were not so much relieved as intrigued as to why Richard found this story so delightful.

While still at Cambridge, where the most bizarre personalities seemed to be his fellow instructors of American history at Christ's, Richard accepted his first American teaching post at the University of Rhode Island (URI). Richard faced new challenges, this time in the form of the Roman catholic church and the bishop of Rhode Island. Richard, so

xviii   *Nancy LoPatin-Lummis (with Denys Leighton)*

the story goes, was asked to participate in an alumni event at the university that would look at the freedom of speech. He was asked to talk about something 'controversial'. Richard made a mock syllabus listing some potential 'controversial' readings. The day after the event, Richard woke up to headlines in the *Providence Journal* proclaiming 'URI Professor Requires *Fanny Hill*'. The state's attorney general, as well as the Roman catholic bishop had denounced him. Hounded by the media for interviews, Richard enjoyed, for a time, rock star status, and was asked his opinion on the first amendment and numerous political hot topics. When the president of Brown University, Barnaby Keeney (who had successfully fought infringements on academic freedom by the state before), took up Richard's 'cause' (and *Fanny Hill* as required reading on the Brown campus), the bishop and the attorney general backed off. Richard was hailed a hero and protector of free speech, which, he always told us, translated into being the champion of URI fraternities caught screening 'blue films'.

Perhaps the shock of the experience, perhaps the need for better weather, or simply out of the desire to get back to research and leave star status behind him, Richard accepted a position at the University of California-Riverside in 1964. His many triumphs at Riverside included receiving one of the first National Endowment for the Humanities Fellowhips (NEHF). He mentored his first PhD candidate, Richard Cosgrove (who has contributed an essay to this collection), who remembers that even so early in his career, Richard had mastered the art of graduate advising, combining adherence to the rigours of scholarship with personal concern for individuals and their families. Richard also met his wife, Elisabeth. As Elisabeth tells the story, she had left England to be with California relatives, was working as a bank teller and trying to get over a failed romance back home, when Richard came in to do some banking and, after some polite conversation, asked her to dinner. In a move that is vintage Elisabeth, she checked his balance to make sure he could actually afford to pay for the dinner before accepting. That partnership of quiet intellectual pursuit, dignity, as well as quirky, inured pragmatism, has sustained Richard's academic career (and aided dozens of graduate students) with great devotion and humour. Richard publicly acknowledged this to the academic community when he dedicated his book on Disraeli to Elisabeth, 'the perfect wife'.

In 1969, Richard accepted a position at Washington University in St Louis and left the sunny skies of California for the humidity of the midwest. He joined a department distinguished by its dedication to the study of British history, that included J.H. Hexter and J.G.A. Pocock. He was, at different times, chair of the department (1974–7) and served as the director of the graduate programme in history for several years. As is well known, this was a period of crisis for US graduate studies in history and many other disciplines. During the 1970s and 1980s, many talented PhDs in British history were unable to find secure academic employment. However, the good track record of the history department at Washington University established in part by Hexter and Pocock, as well as the opportune recruitment of Richard and his younger colleague, Derek Hirst, to guide students of British history, meant that British history at Washington University did not fare badly in comparison with other leading American departments in that area. While the department could not recruit so many graduate students in British history as, for example, the considerably larger departments at Yale, Princeton, Columbia or Chicago, it was able to tap a stream of able American students and even attracted students from Britain, Australia and Canada. Two other distinguished historians of Britain, Richard Helmholtz and Gregory Claeys, also taught in the department at various points between 1970 and 1990, and the historians of Britain during Richard's tenure at Washington University enjoyed cordial relations with faculty in the English department, so that history graduate students were able to benefit from the guidance of faculty in both disciplines. Although only a medium-sized department by American standards, history at Washington University often had as many as three *bona fide* British historians at once, as well as American historians knowledgeable about Britain. The university was able to command other valuable assets as well, including extensive library resources relating to the history and culture of Britain. Richard was one of the most attractive parts of the package. Nor was Richard's impact at Washington University limited to graduate teaching. Known as an excellent lecturer, Richard taught undergraduate courses on a variety of modern British topics and instilled in many students a love of history. Undergraduates enjoyed the content and sophisticated style of those classes. Richard won the university's award for outstanding teaching in 1988.

The following year, Richard's academic position changed. In 1989, while continuing as professor of history, he became the director of the Center for the History of Freedom. Funded by Washington University and numerous foundations such as the National Endowment for the Humanities, the Liberty Fund, and The Exxon Education, Mellon, John M. Olin, and Lynde and Harry Bradley Foundations, the centre produced 15 volumes. Richard served as general editor of *The Making of Modern Freedom* series (1992–2003), which, inspired by the lead of Lord Acton, sought to trace the development of modern freedom from the 17th century to the present. It was never Richard's intention to become the director of the centre. The idea for the project had been Jack Hexter's. After retiring from Yale, Hexter had returned to St Louis and Washington University and started working on raising funds to house such a research centre. Richard worked with Hexter in conceptualising the centre and grant writing. When the centre opened in 1986, Hexter was the director and Richard the associate director. As Hexter's health declined, it was agreed that Richard would chair the search committee that was to hire his replacement. The search was not successful despite the fact that by that time (1989), the centre was well-funded and an attractive place for scholars. Real plans for conferences and publishing needed to begin. A publisher needed to be selected and negotiations started. Washington University asked Richard to take over as director. He refused. They insisted. He reluctantly agreed.

The Freedom Center, at least at the beginning, enjoyed an uncertain reputation at Washington University. It was well known that it received funding from 'right wing' sources such as the Liberty Fund and the Bradley Foundation. There was also some notoriety produced by the centre's location in the Reserve Officers' Training Corps (ROTC) building (renamed the Academy Building), which had, during the Vietnam wars, been damaged in a fire set by protesting students. However, Richard was in no position to be choosy about the centre's neighbours on the edge of the university. (The US poet laureate, Howard Nemerov, was a regular passerby on his way through university city to the Olin library or the English department.) As for the issue of funding, Richard pointed out that the centre received financial support from various sources and was in no way obligated to toe any kind of ideological line in the work it did. He was sometimes irritated by ill-informed criticism of the centre, but this did not in the least deter him in his activities as director. Richard brought many fine scholars into association with the centre and the History of Freedom series, who did admirably balanced work. The centre had, for most of its existence, a small permanent staff of two Elisabeths and a Rebecca to oversee its administrative and publishing activities – namely, Mrs Davis, Elisabeth Case and Becky Rauvola. It is no secret that a small fraction of the centre's budget went towards coffee and cookies that sustained more than a few regular 'visitors' to the centre, principally Richard's graduate students.

Richard claims that the only volume of the History of Freedom series for which he was responsible intellectually was the second one, 'Liberty Secured? Britain Before and After 1688'. This was, he said, a response to the first volume that, in his view, focused too heavily on the early part of the 17th century and the causes of the English Civil War. He did, however, contribute as an essay writer to other volumes and was the editor and head of the advisory board that published all 15 volumes. He modestly cast his role at the centre as 'chairman of the board' and not the 'presiding genius that Jack was and would have been'. Nonetheless, the Center for the History of Freedom provided Richard the opportunity to direct and publish new interventions into historical debates that went well beyond the limits of the Glorious Revolution or English history, for that matter. He was able to see, first hand, distinguished and dedicated scholars debate, reject and revise each other's work. Richard was part scholar, part editor, part diplomat. In 2003, he retired from the centre and from teaching. The centre's final volume came out soon thereafter.

During his 34 years at Washington University, Richard wrote or edited nine other books and numerous articles and book reviews. He was a Guggenheim, NEH and Huntington Library Fellow. He received several grants from the NEH and the American Philosophical Society. He served as the chair of the American editorial committee to *Parliamentary History* from 1981 until just recently, and was an engaged member of the emerging North American Conference on British Studies, serving on its council from 1990 to 1992 and chairing its nominating committee in 1997–8. He also served as president of the Southern Conference on British Studies (1985–7) and as president of the Midwest Victorian Studies Association (1997–9). He was the placement secretary for the Anglo-American Associates (1978–81) and is a fellow of the Royal Historical Society. Richard has served the larger scholarly community as a consultant for the NEH. Just before his retirement, he was named the Wellington lecturer at the University of Southampton. In 2005, he was awarded the Andrew W. Mellon emeritus fellowship for his latest research on the house of lords in the early 19th century.

Richard W. Davis, a self-described political historian, devoted his career to understanding, in his own words, 'the play of power and influence and how they are mobilized to get things done'.[1] As a scholar, his work was in the areas of political reform and its electoral ramification for Victorian politics, the interconnection between non-anglican politicians and their newly assimilated role in electoral politics and court, and most recently, the role of the hereditary aristocracy in the house of lords.

The central questions he asked have remained constant from his earliest publications to the present: how did individuals envision the public good in modern Britain, and how,

---

[1] Richard W. Davis, 'Confession of a Political Historian', Western Conference on British Studies (Tucson, 2003), 8.

through religious and moral beliefs, coupled with wisdom and political savvy, could they improve the public good through the ever-changing 19th-century political institutions? Whether it was dissenter, William Smith, the duke of Wellington, or Lionel Rothschild, the campaign against the Test and Corporation Acts, a regional study of the electoral outcome of post-Reform Act elections, or the significance of religion and personality in creating party leadership in the house of lords, Davis changed the focus, but never the substance of his historical inquiry. For those who like consistency in their historians' interests and keys to unlocking the hidden meaning of why things happened as they did, Richard has never disappointed.

Richard began his significant publication record with *Dissent in Politics, 1780–1830: The Political Life of William Smith, MP* (1971), arguing that the world of 18th-century politics, as depicted by Sir Lewis Namier, Norman Gash and H.J. Hanham, that is devoid of political ideology and principle, was an exaggeration of the aristocracy's political influence, and an overly simplistic interpretation of the practice of politics.[2] The strategy of dissent, the public life of William Smith, MP, and the movement of 'social and civic equality' for dissenters, was all evidence of that.[3] Richard noted at the outset of his book that Smith was not a dominant figure, but a man who preferred to work behind the scenes, politically astute and possessing a 'remarkable grasp' of what was politically possible. His public life began when he entered parliament in 1784 as MP for Sudbury, and promised his constituents that he would do his best to preserve England's constitution and the rights and privileges of all Englishmen and, particularly, those who elected him. That quickly brought Smith into reform politics as MP for Norwich, associating with the Society for Constitutional Information and the leaders of the dissenting community into the campaign to repeal the Test and Corporation Acts. Smith quickly learned that extra-parliamentary popular movements aroused fear and a condemnation for that cause. He opted for a safer and quieter approach – negotiation. And negotiate he did, for the remainder of his career. Smith worked with Lord Sidmouth, broadening the Toleration Act of 1812. He negotiated for the unitarians to be recognized as a distinct movement within dissent, negotiated with the United Committee (deputations representing the whole dissenting community), the Canningites and the Catholic Association. He talked with Lord John Russell and Robert Peel. And in 1828, he saw the fruit of his strategy in the repeal of the Test and Corporation Acts.

Smith's legacy was, according to Richard, to open the door to parliamentary reform through an expanded electorate. His hopes for the Reform Act of 1832 were enormous and the whig interpretation of its triumph would have delighted him. But, as Richard noted, there is often a difference between how some envision the public good and others interpret and implement it. In his second book, *Political Change and Continuity, 1760–1885: A Buckinghamshire Study* (1972), Davis carefully examined the county of Buckingham, testing the sweeping conclusions made by whig historians that the Reform Act of 1832 gave the middle classes a new voice in politics, and thus ended the aristocratic domination of politics, allowing for a process of democratisation to take place, one reform measure at a time. He also tested the theory, put forth by D.C. Moore,

---

[2] Norman Gash, *Politics in the Age of Peel* (1953); Gash, *Reaction and Reconstruction in English Politics, 1832–52* (Oxford, 1865); H.J. Hanham, *Elections and Party Management in the Time of Disraeli and Gladstone* (1959).

[3] Richard W. Davis, *Dissent in Politics, 1780–1830: The Political Life of William Smith, MP* (1971), p. iii.

that this was not the case, and from 1832 on, the aristocracy were, in fact, in 'control
. . . in the majority of remaining small boroughs, and . . . English country divisions'.[4] In
turning to local history, Richard sought to look closely at the county and six borough
elections (reduced to four after 1832) to end the persistent belief that these constituencies were completely under the control of the landed classes without 'independence of
mind and action of many drawn from other classes in village and small-town society'.[5]

His conclusions and the influence he had on other historians' research were profound.
Examining the electoral behaviour in the county and borough elections, Richard
concluded that principles mattered and rejected prevailing arguments about political, and
particularly, electoral practice in England made by Gash, Hanham and Moore. Dissenting
communities played a role in shaping voter behaviour, and church rates were critical in
the late 1840s. Landlord influence existed, but was inconsistent. A working class vote
proved indifferent in elections, failing to plump for reform leaguers, while the influence
of the Russells required the money and support of the Rothschilds and *vice versa*. Farmers
were still deferential, but, by mid century, few Buckinghamshire landlords forced
tenant farmers to vote against strongly held opinions and preferences. In the end,
Richard contended that from the 18th century to the eve of the Third Reform Bill,
Buckinghamshire politics had political continuity that was 'more apparent than real', but
had also undergone change that was 'profound'.[6]

The importance of *Political Change and Continuity* cannot be underestimated. First, it
resulted in years of heated discussions between Richard and D.C. Moore, whose *Politics
of Deference* provided the theoretical foundation for the Namierite view. The two had
heated exchanges in journal pieces, reflected by Richard's 'The Whigs and the Idea
of Electoral Deference: Some Further Thoughts on the Great Reform Act' (*Durham
University Journal*, 1974) and 'Deference and Aristocracy in the Time of the Great Reform
Act' (*American Historical Review*, 1976).[7] Richard has reminisced about their showdowns
at conferences where they evidently drew large audiences.

Second, Richard's call to rid our minds of the obviously false, but remarkably
tenacious notion that there was a monolithic 'middle class' opposing a monolithic 'landed
interest' controlling post-Reform Bill politics in England, inspired more historians to do
the work needed to do so beyond Buckinghamshire and the politics of deference.[8] Soon
after Richard's Buckinghamshire study, Frank O'Gorman and John Phillips started
publishing on the issues of party, electoral behaviour, and the influence of local issues,
religion and principle in national politics. O'Gorman's *The Rise of Party in England*
(1975) and later, *Voters, Patrons and Parties* (1989), and Phillips's *Electoral Behavior in
Unreformed England: Plumpers, Spitters and Straights* (1982) and *The Great Reform Bill in the
Boroughs* (1992), further contributed to the argument that the aristocratic elite were
not in control of national politics. Not only did Phillips further the argument that
Richard has made, namely that religion – specifically the role played by dissent – could

---

[4] D.C. Moore, 'The Other Face of Reform', *Victorian Studies*, v (1961–2), 33–4.

[5] Richard W. Davis, *Political Change and Continuity, 1760–1885: A Buckinghamshire Study* (1972), 10.

[6] Davis, *Political Change and Continuity*, 227.

[7] The exchange actually began with these pieces well before their celebrated monographic attacks on each
other's scholarship, specifically in Davis's *Political Change and Continuity*, and Moore's *The Politics of Deference*
(1976).

[8] Davis, *Political Change and Continuity*, 225.

explain the correlation between electors and political parties, he showed that in several towns, boroughs with active dissenting interests boasted more contested elections than those more uniformly anglican. He affirmed Richard's argument that religion, rather than socio-economic class, could explain the role of the electorate and the rise of political party loyalties.[9] Phillips's work at the Laboratory for Historical Research at UC-Riverside enabled him to further the attack on D.C. Moore's deference theory, which pleased Richard no end, but also showed that 1832 did matter, though in different ways to different boroughs.

In particular, Richard's professional and personal relationship to Phillips was of great importance to him. Phillips took the job at UC-Riverside that Richard had held years earlier, and while their styles of electoral research differed (I cannot imagine Richard 'QUASSHing', but maybe it's just me), their work did much to foster our understanding of what mattered to electors, before and after the Great Reform Act, and move Britain 'from an era of partisan politics and from there to one of factional politics – little guided by principle, at least at the national level – to one in which parties once more not only appealed to a broader public, but also began to deliver the reforms they promised and the public demanded'.[10]

The Buckinghamshire study led to an interest in the Rothschilds and Anglo-jewish history. In 1976, Richard wrote a biography of Disraeli for Little Brown, primarily, he claims, because Gladstone had already been taken. Yet anyone reading the book is sure to sense Richard's affection for the man. He gave credit to Disraeli for his courage to do the unpopular and advocate that it was Britain's duty to intervene against social evils throughout the world. He recognized the man's arrogance, realism, sensibility and elitism, all with equal measure, as well as his ability to exploit the tools of social reform and religious passion to his own political advantage. Still he could be, Richard tells us, 'to those who loved him, or at least did not get in his way . . . a most loveable character'.[11]

His interest in the problem of jewish-political power in 19th-century Britain, an offshoot of his general interest, was sparked by his work on Disraeli. He then began research which resulted in the first scholarly examination of the important political and economic dynasty which supported that prime minister and many other leaders. *The English Rothschilds* was published in 1983 and traced the rise of the family and its political influence. Still, the reward for political service, a peerage, was quite difficult for Victoria to embrace. But, as Richard argued, the family continued to serve British governments financially and was rewarded by policies in the empire that were financially beneficial to the family business. Even as Lord Rothschild influenced the legacy left by Cecil Rhodes to allow scholars to study at Oxford and embrace English culture to the fullest, Richard points out that continental anti-semitism was a growing problem and that 'Natty', for all his Englishness, was still seen by others – and himself – as a jew. But, as Richard wrote: 'The Rothschilds acted to stem the tide of prejudice not only as individuals, but as

---

[9] John Phillips, *Electoral Behaviour in Unreformed England: Plumpers, Splitters and Straights* (Princeton, NJ, 1982), 308–11.

[10] Richard W. Davis, 'Introduction', in *Partisan Politics, Principle and Reform in Parliament and the Constituencies, 1689–1880: Essays in Memory of John A. Phillips*, ed. Clyve Jones, Philip Salmon and Richard W. Davis (Edinburgh, 2005), 1.

[11] Richard W. Davis, *Disraeli* (Boston and Toronto, 1976), 222.

bankers. The Jewish question is the greatest exception to the rule that they never attempted to use their financial power to dictate policy to potential customers.'[12]

But Richard had had enough dabbling in social and economic history. He knew it was time to get back to his true interest – political history and its relationship to religion as a factor in party and policy. He published 'The Politics of the Confessional State, 1760–1832' (1990), and 'The Whigs and Religious Issues, 1830–35' appeared two years later in the *festschrift* he co-edited in honour of Bob Webb's retirement, *Religion and Irreligion in Victorian Society* (1992). 'Whigs in the Age of Fox and Grey' (1993), immediately followed.

But by this point in his research, Richard had shifted his focus almost exclusively to the political role still enjoyed by the upper house of parliament, in part, he has confessed, as a response to political correctness that dismissed such research as elitist. He published the edited collection, *Leaders in the Lords: Government Management and Party Organization in the Upper Chamber, 1865–1902*, published as a special edition of *Parliamentary History* in 2002. He also edited a volume for Stanford University Press entitled *Lords of Parliament: Studies, 1714–1914* (1995), in which appeared his own article, 'The Duke of Wellington and the Resurgence of the House of Lords'. That research interest continued in 'Wellington and the "Open Question": The Issue of Catholic Emancipation, 1821–1829' (1997) and 'The Duke of Wellington and the Ultra Peers' (1999). His presentation, 'Wellington, Peel and the Politics of 1830s and 1840s', was the 14th Wellington Lecture given at Southampton University in 2002, part of which appeared in an article in a *festschrift* he co-edited in memory of his dear friend, John Phillips (2005).

Richard's latest manuscript is *The History of the House of Lords from 1811 to 1846*. In it, he reminds scholars that 'parliament' was more than the house of commons, electoral results and parliamentary parties. The Lords, he argues, had a far more central role in setting the political agenda for the nation. Whig opposition to tory governments in the first two decades of the 19th century, he argues, was stronger than previously believed. They played to a more politically-sophisticated public, and this is why the tories really feared the whigs. The duke of Wellington, far from being the displaced soldier, is revealed to be a skilful politician and a figure who shaped the direction of political supporters and opponents. Grenville, Grey, Brougham, Holland and Stanley, he argues, were all far more significant players in shaping the political future for the nation than historians have previously shown.

Growing out of that work, Richard's latest research is now on *The Grenvilles: A Great Political Family*. He wants to examine their acquisition of great electoral and parliamentary power in the late 18th century, as well as how they lost it by 1848.

Throughout his career, Richard has mentored nearly two dozen graduate students to PhDs in modern British history, introducing many to the basics of primary source research, the subtleties of analysis, and arguing matters of interpretation, and he has conducted countless research seminars and independent studies. To everyone's amazement, he willingly edited and proofread literally hundreds of student papers – judiciously, thoroughly and encouragingly. He advised everyone and anyone who asked about research, job prospects and strategies for getting through graduate studies. He and

---

[12] Richard W. Davis, *The English Rothschilds* (1983), 229.

Elisabeth included students at their home for the traditional 'white' Thanksgiving (all the food was a shade of white or beige. This was Richard's mother's tradition and while it meant mashing potatoes and turnips for Elisabeth, she performed this ritual every year. Richard's tradition was to continually pour the champagne). The Davises created a sense of family for so many who were separated from their own and feeling the isolation of graduate study, including students from Britain and China. Bob Webb should know how grateful we all are that he showed Richard kindness as a graduate student with a dinner invitation. Richard kept up the practice from which we have all benefited.

And he has made us laugh. We laughed at his anecdotes (the Columbia orals story was always a tension-reliever), we laughed at the enormity of the work we faced, and we laughed at ourselves. Those students lucky enough to be at Washington University during the Center of the History of Freedom years, got to laugh with Elisabeth, who was the administrator of the centre, laughing at Richard. And this is perhaps the thing that rings so true for each and every student of Richard's – his enormous humanity and his gentle indulgence in treating each and every student as though he or she were the most important one. The turmoil of trying to find employment, get the first article published, meet grant deadlines, all of our anxieties paled in comparison to the absurd number of non-academic trials that Richard faced from his students. Personal and health crises occurred, that, upon reflection, seem unbelievable for their frequency and severity. One of his young students suffered a stroke, another was diagnosed with brain cancer. There was the sudden and tragic death of one advisee's spouse. Throughout it all, Richard and Elisabeth cared for, both physically and emotionally, his students and their families. To a person, to this day, when we speak about Richard, we openly marvel at how lucky we were to have found an advisor who would teach us about Britain, guide us through the research process, advise us on career choices, instruct us in the art of chairing and commenting on conference papers, and so forth. Not the least of his services to us has been his untiring writing of reference letters and recommendations. We were then, and still are, aware of how different Richard was from so many other graduate advisors and how blessed we were to have been both guided by him as students and embraced by him and his wife as extended family.

He was equally generous with others' graduate students, whether they needed a family for Thanksgiving or needed academic or career advice. Many students of other historians and advisors think of him as their own mentor. Philip Salmon from the History of Parliament was greatly influenced by Richard's 'careful demolition of D.C. Moore's "deference voters" ', and was very pleased to get the chance to work with him on the *festschrift* they co-edited in honour of John Phillips. William Anthony Hay met Richard in 1995 after asking a question at a North American Conference on British Studies (NACBS) panel. Richard approached him at the end of the session, complimenting him on the question and admitting to him his own interest in Lord Brougham. Richard became a mentor and helped Hay gain access to the Lansdowne papers which the latter had believed were unavailable to researchers. Later, Richard reviewed Hay's book manuscript on Brougham and an article he intended to submit. Hay put it simply: Richard W. Davis 'has always been very engaged in the field as a whole beyond his own graduate students and scholarship'.

In Richard's 'Confession', he has bemoaned the scholarly fixation with being 'on the cutting edge'. This is not to imply that Richard ignores the importance of intellectual trends or underestimates the way these 'position' one's work. He believes that the pursuit of academic fashion tends to deaden us to the enduring value of what we find in the past. Richard is a very English kind of empiricist who believes that thorough knowledge of the raw material of history is essential to the historian's craft, and that archival and contemporary sources must command our attention whatever our theoretical engagements. As a teacher, Richard was never unduly impressed with our dogmatic pronouncements about Namier, Block, E.P. Thompson, Foucault, or whatever other guru we had seized upon. Theory was useful so long as it allowed us to make sense of sources and to fashion plausible arguments about them. It is characteristic of Richard also that he regards obsession with intellectual fashion to be, when taken to great lengths, uncollegial and needlessly divisive. 'If people try too hard and too fast to be in the vanguard they are likely to come to grief, and given the swinish tendency of our profession . . . they are likely to take many others tumbling over the cliff with them.'[13]

I hope that Richard will be pleased with this volume of studies that treats political history as the study of individuals and the political work they did which demonstrated, 'the play of power and influence and how they are mobilized to get things done'. It reflects Richard's style of archival research and interpretation of politics and religious (or other intellectual) movements working hand in hand to shape opinion, lead political opinion and shape change. It is the 'traditional' historical work that Richard enjoyed to read, write, teach and comment on. We hope he enjoys it and reflects well on how much he is responsible for the work many of us have chosen to undertake. Still, if there was anyone with whom we would wish to 'tumble over the cliff', academically speaking, of course, we are certain that, to a person, we would want that person to be Richard Davis.

[13] Davis, 'Confession of a Political Historian', 13–14.

Introduction

NANCY LOPATIN-LUMMIS

Richard Davis's body of scholarship consistently demonstrated the philosophy espoused by the man whose political biography launched his publishing career. William Smith, dissenter and MP, said: 'if the wisdom of man did not actively employ itself in correcting what was bad, and fortifying what was good, no form of society or of national policy could go on, as Providence intended it should, in a progression of improvement'.[1] *Public Life and Public Lives* is a collection of essays that reflects the work of individuals seeking improvement in the representation of political beliefs within Britain and its larger empire between the late 18th century and the early 20th century. It looks at a number of disparate political and religious leaders in modern Britain who, like Smith, tried to correct society and national policy for the better. The essays address such themes as the interconnection between spiritual beliefs and political policy, electoral politics, voter registration, and reform agendas in local and national elections, as well as British national interests competing with the free practice of religious and cultural practices in Africa and India, while in the larger empire. They look at the nature of political action from the perspective of politicians, both elected and non-elected, and political outsiders seeking the vote through extra-parliamentary action and popular pressure. They examine the philosophies and cultures that shaped political views and political objectives – particularly at the important intersection between faith and politics – at home and throughout the empire.

In the first half of the volume, the essays focus on some of the political practices that constituted public life, and discussions as to how a national character or identity developed in modern Britain. Important contributions in the areas of historical research, education and religious organisation, all played roles in creating a national character in modern Britain. This, in turn, helped to create the sense of what contributed to the public good and whose life and work was thus devoted. Edwin Jaggard looks at the matter of party electoral organisation in the 1850s. Voter registration, the selection of potential candidates and new and invigorated agents helped, Jaggard argues, turn around the Conservative Party's prospects in the south-west of England. Following the disastrous 1857 election, Sir John Yarde Buller started to work as a Conservative Party electoral agent, using influence, patronage and common sense in selecting candidates, securing electors and shaping upcoming elections. As a mid-level electoral manager, Buller could only do so much to secure Conservative electoral victories, but agents with social and political status such as he could greatly influence local political matters. They, in turn, could affect national candidacies and elections. The Conservative Party, Jaggard argues

---

[1] Richard W. Davis, *Dissent in Politics, 1780–1830: The Political Life of William Smith, MP* (1971), 146.

was invigorated and by 1859, rebounded in Devon, Cornwall, Somerset and Dorset, thanks to the attention to detail of a breed of new electoral agents, serving the public through their party.

Public life often took place in private places, through private conversations. Such was the case whenever spies were utilised in the acquisition of political information that served the public good. Padraic Kennedy's essay looks at the reliability of E. Trelawney's efforts, as a spy in the service of Benjamin Disraeli, to prove a secret combination between Liberal leader, William Gladstone, and the Vatican. What Trelawney found, through a series of interviews with bishops, was that catholic 'clerical support of religious, land, and education reforms, and of Irish constitutional nationalism more generally', existed in the mid 19th century. He chose to connect them, without any evidence, to the papacy. Kennedy argues that Disraeli so fully expected to find something incriminating against Gladstone, that the spying – that began as a tool in fighting the 1868 election – continued after the Liberals' victory. Conspiracy and conspiracy theories always have had their place in politics and public life, but Kennedy's demonstration that Disraeli was so invested in their potential success, he allowed wishful thinking to cloud his better judgment in the creation of political strategies and election platforms on the Irish Question which might have truly benefited his party at the next general election.

In a different interpretation of public life, Richard A. Cosgrove turns to the influence of the 19th-century historian in shaping British national identity. He examines the works of three 19th-century historians and how their interpretations each shaped and reshaped the narrative of British history to suit different political purposes. James Anthony Froude emphasized the religious character of England. Edward Freeman attacked Froude's scholarship and emphasized the institutional continuity in politics that existed from the Anglo-Saxons on, as the critical characteristic of the British nation. John Horace Round then attacked Freeman, arguing that the Normans and their introduction of practices and law grounded more in inheritance rather than an elected or representative presence, produced a 'seismic change in English history'. National identity was tied to a conservative, knightly and landed tradition, rather than the liberal identification with a parliament and constitution. Historians, Cosgrove shows, contributed to the public perception that the British nation grew out of a particular political tradition and, therefore, assisted those in public life to persuade the general pubic in maintaining that national identity through the electoral support of a particular political platform.

Denys P. Leighton continues looking at national character in late 19th-century England through the work of T.H. Green and his idea of a democratic localism. Though seemingly at odds with a national framework for understanding politics, Green, Leighton argues, clearly articulated a form of patriotism and an English national consciousness that was rooted in religious dissent and the political and social policies that grew from it. They were conducive to a collective state and, inevitably, the British welfare state, and, therefore, inextricably linked with definitions of public life and public good. Green, though an anglican his whole life, found the 'evangelical conscience' of protestant groups completely compatible with both the divine and creating a commonwealth from which toleration and the 'liberation of human consciousness' could shape a state of law, community and democratic administration.

Timothy Parsons examines the interconnection between the empire, specifically South Africa, and British popular culture in the late 19th and early 20th centuries. Robert

Baden-Powell, the creator of the Boy Scouts, utilised Zulu tribal elements into the national programme of scouting in order to serve a public good, specifically to promote national fitness. While a firm believer in British superiority in all ways, Baden Powell recognized that the skills and toughness of African warriors was to be appreciated and could be adopted by the British, to serve their own public good in furthering the interests of racial segregation and colonial domination. Public interest in Africa made scouting popular and, therefore, sending that message all the easier for Edwardian politicians, clergymen, military leaders and social commentators. The nation's youth could, through Zulu traditions as taught and practised in the Boy Scout movement of the early 20th century, be prepared for the physical and moral challenges that awaited them in the empire, or in conflict with European rivals. It needed only an English antiseptic wash to purify it for public use at home.

That arrogance was also displayed by the British government, according to Andrew Muldoon, in dealing with Indian nationalism in the 1930s. Muldoon argues that British officials believed that the Raj could be maintained in India by the deliberate exploitation of religious and regional differences. Provincial elections leading up to the 1935 Government of India Act, Muldoon argues, reinforced this view and justified, so the British thought, continued involvement in Indian governance at all levels. The British happily accepted the belief that 'Indian immaturity' would lead to the end of the Congress and greater reliance on British rule. The 1937 elections, Muldoon argues, opened the eyes of the British. Regional elections failed to return Justice Party members in the numbers the British anticipated. Their policy and legislation, based on British arrogance and incorrect assumptions about Indian religious beliefs and practices, religious divisions, and internal squabbles underestimated the greater universal desire that Indians had to elect members of the National Congress and seek independence from British imperial rule. The British, with their miscalculation, began their own political decline through the very regional elections they anticipated would bolster the Raj for years to come.

The second half of the volume provides closer examination of some half dozen political lives, all of whom greatly contributed to changes in British political perception and participation in the same time frame. Susan Mitchell Sommers looks at the role of Sir John Coxe Hippisley, an ambitious politician who became MP for the contested and heavily dissenting Suffolk borough of Sudbury, and, in turn, the chief advocate for catholic emancipation, and the British government's liaison with Rome in the early 19th century. A quixotic figure, Sommers contends, Hippisley spent decades cultivating the trust of influential catholics, colleagues and even the grudging support of constituents, only to wilt under political pressure when the 1801 Act of Union placed catholic disabilities squarely in the crosshairs of the problem of Ireland. Hoping to convince the British politicians and public alike that Rome's influence in Ireland was exaggerated and that catholicism could be entirely compatible with the English constitution, Hippisley antagonised, rather than assuaged, public fears with his speeches and pamphlets. Urged to change course, or at least his tactics, so as to allow for anti-catholic sentiment, particularly in his own borough, to subside and not endanger emerging political sentiment and proposed legislation to reduce disabilities to catholics, Hippisley could not manage to do so. His diligence, stubbornness and sense of righteousness all shaped his successes and failures as a public man.

Joseph Parkes was never an MP. He was a Birmingham solicitor and an electoral manager whose work in manipulating public opinion, shaping parliamentary legislation and turning out whig voters, revealed the consummate public figure who was satisfied with working for the larger good behind the scenes. As I argue in my essay on Parkes, his political work was fundamentally shaped by his identification with the political realities of his birthplace, Warwick. Parliamentary and legal reform and the systematic return of men to the house of commons committed to that cause, was Parkes's all-consuming objective. He meticulously analysed the canvassing and finances required in turning out the vote in parliamentary borough after borough and used the press as a tool to shape public support for reform. Though disappointed with the extent of reform and the men who promised him their support, Parkes never entered electoral politics himself. He always remained a political figure who preferred the shadows. It was here that both his (sometimes) unscrupulous methods and frequent disillusionment with political allies, could be hidden from public view.

In sharp contrast, Michael A. Rutz's essay looks at the work of a man quite willing to act out openly on behalf of his beliefs. James Read was a controversial figure from the London Missionary Society (LMS) based in southern Africa. His support for the Khoi in Grahamstown and the Kat River Settlement pitted him against the established leadership within the LMS. The Khoi wanted to appoint Nicholas Smit, their former schoolmaster, to lead the Kat River Settlement mission, rather than the Rev. John Locke, whom they believed to be solely interested in the needs of English settlers. The conflict over the pastoral priorities of the missionaries – English souls versus African ones – was at the heart of Read's concerns and the focus of his detractors. Read supported the Khoi's argument that they were invoking the traditional congregationalist right to appoint their own minister. Opponents of the Khoi (and Read), Rutz argues, rejected the 'theological and ideological influences that accorded Africans a fundamental humanity and equality' in earlier missionary thinking. Those influences were, he contends, 'losing ground to the advance of new and more racist attitudes within British society'.

The public life of another humanitarian evangelical is the subject of Richard R. Follett's essay. Follett explores the controversies and actions pursued by the quaker anti-slavery MP, Thomas Fowell Buxton, and his evolving campaign to end all disabilities against aboriginal peoples in Africa. Confronting enormous evidence of slaving and cruel treatment of Africans at the hands of British subjects, Buxton urged a solution that would involve the abolition of slavery in any region where the British had trade. Treaties with natives, private enterprise and active missionaries would replace existing means of attaining such resources as gold, iron, copper and, especially, sugar cane and cotton. The Niger Expedition, an experiment in humanitarian colonial policy, was largely due to his influence. Buxton, Follett shows, was a leader in the shifting of the evangelical movement in Britain. As a group, these men could not agree on poor relief, Irish tithes and education reform, but Buxton convinced many that their role as christians seeking the public good, was to change popular views and political policy concerning British colonial rule and the ill-treatment of those aboriginals under its authority.

R.K. Webb's well-known work on the political role of unitarians continues in this volume with an essay on Henry W. Crosskey. Webb looks at the complicated nature of political activism and religious belief in mid 19th-century England. The unitarian's human, not divine, Jesus, was at the core of sectarian intolerance towards it as a recognized religious denomination. Crosskey, leading the New Meeting in Birmingham, was active in forming the National Education League and the formation of a secular national school scheme. He emphasized the potential of government to improve the lives of citizens, particularly by offering them the means for continued self-improvement. For him, public life meant implementing his religious beliefs in ways that would create 'civic betterment'. He was a new kind of unitarian in the 19th century, working on public service and pragmatic reforms, as well as the ending of doctrinal differences that had divided the unitarian movement earlier in the century. Public work, for this unitarian minister, was for the good of all British citizens.

There was a different interpretation of the public work of Randall Davidson, arch-bishop of Canterbury, as parliament discussed constitutional reform in the early part of the 20th century. Derek Blakeley argues that Davidson saw the political role of the anglican episcopacy as having national implications and, therefore, advised the crown as to the proposed political limitations on the upper House with a perspective that considered far more than the protection of the Church of England. His work with Lord Curzon and others clearly emphasized his role as politician. But as the leader of a church, he was aware that there could be a cost for his followers if the public believed it blocked a reform measure for its own protection. Davidson's concern that public backlash against the church, should the bishops vote against reform, played its role alongside party politics in Davidson's decision to vote with the government for the 1911 Parliament Act.

Arthur Bryant, journalist, historian and polemicist, did not worry about a correspond-ing backlash against any particular institution while writing for the *Illustrated London News* (*ILN*) in the early 20th century. Reba Soffer's examination of the man and his work, contends that Bryant sought to sell to as many people as possible that Conserva-tism, as a party affiliation and ideology, was the future of Britain and the empire. His 'Our Note Book' column in the *ILN* enabled him to promote realistic and Conservative solutions to public questions of national and international concern, create national identity through the war, emphasize a paternalistic elite, romanticise rural interests and agricultural labour, and monarchy. He ridiculed the intelligentsia and the political 'left', claiming they were a threat to tradition, liberty and property. But Bryant also attacked Hitler's racism and aggression, shaping the public acceptance of war and public policies that would separate Britain from the rest of fascist Europe. A man with specific views, Bryant is lauded as a principled man, but a pragmatic one too, concerned with presenting a populist message and aware of the power that a public man had to shape a nation's future.

Bryant's world could not be more different from those of the missionaries, historians, politicians and clergyman examined in these essays. But all served the public good as they individually understood it. They all believed they were morally responsible for improv-ing the state of things for all British citizens and those living under British rule, just as William Smith articulated some 200 years ago. They also knew that while intentions were laudable, results mattered more. After all, what made them public figures was the recognition and support of the public. They would have, for all their principles, appre-ciated Joseph Parkes's self-deprecating (and self-promoting) comment to Lord Durham as he worked tirelessly towards corporation reform in the 1830s: 'A public man must keep a large account with the public. You can't reasonably expect constant recollection of retrospective acts.'[2] Historians can, however, recall public acts and remind students what public responsibility and public action meant in modern Britain, and how individuals changed the direction of a nation and history. Richard W. Davis did just that for generations of historians. We hope we have continued his work.

<hr />

[2] Durham Papers (Lord Lambton, Lambton Castle, Co. Durham): Joseph Parkes to Lord Durham, 21 July 1835.

Managers and Agents: Conservative Party Organisation in the 1850s*

EDWIN JAGGARD

During the 1850s in the wake of the calamitous Peelite split, Britain's Conservative Party struggled to rebuild its numbers in the house of commons. The structure of the party's electoral organisation is well known-parliamentary leaders, election managers such as Sir William Jolliffe and Philip Rose, plus local constituency based agents. Jolliffe's and Rose's 1859 election notebooks help understand this, but they also reveal serious gaps in the Conservatives' information networks. This article delineates the electoral activities of Sir John Yarde Buller (first Baron Churston) and his ally Samuel Triscott, who supplemented the spasmodic flow of information from small boroughs in at least two counties. Mid-level or second-tier managers, to whom no attention has previously been given, assisted the Conservatives in their gradual electoral recovery. Their roles also suggest that the party's organization may have been more complex than previously believed.

Keywords: Conservative Party; 19th century; organisation; agents; managers; elections; parliamentary

Early in 1855, it seemed likely that there would be a vacant seat in the house of commons for the small Devon town of Totnes. The duke of Somerset's health was failing, therefore the current member, his heir Lord Seymour, would move to the house of lords. Wishing to retain this long-held seat, the Conservative Party's agent moved quickly to seek advice from Sir William Jolliffe, the chief whip:

> There is no doubt I believe that Totnes will be vacant in the course of a few days. We have the name of Sir J.Y. Buller against the place as the party to be referred to. Will you open a communication with him and ascertain the extent of his connection with the borough and get what information and advice you can from him?
>
> We have no agent there to whom we can refer direct.[1]

In the context of the Conservative Party's electoral organisation, this letter is significant for several reasons. Firstly, as might be expected, Jolliffe and Philip Rose, the party's principal election agent, were alert to any opportunity for by-election victories, especially in a town which had previously elected Conservatives – from 1839 to 1852. Secondly, with fewer than 350 voters, Totnes was a small borough and therefore one of

* I am grateful to Colin Harris of the Bodleian Library, and the staff of the Somerset Record Office for their assistance with the research on which this article is based.

[1] Somerset RO, Hylton MSS, HY/15/26: Philip Rose to Sir William Jolliffe, 15 Jan. 1855.

a category of constituencies of particular interest to the Conservatives, for whom success in such towns, and counties, was the key to prospective election victories. Indeed Rose acknowledged this two months later, observing that the party had to direct its attention to small boroughs 'where numbers will count', adding, 'this has long been the policy of our opponents and it has attended with success'.[2] Thirdly, the reference to 'no agent there' indicates that the party did have a network of agents (even if incomplete) in some English constituencies, men who could supply Jolliffe and/or Rose with 'information and advice'. Their 1859 election notebooks provide the details for more than 100 constituencies, including Totnes which by then had an agent, Theodore Bryant.[3] Finally, there is the role of Sir John Yarde Buller, obviously not a constituency agent nor a member of the Conservative Party's elections management group headed by Jolliffe and Rose. So why was he asked for advice? Was it because he was the long-serving Conservative member for South Devon, his seat was close to Totnes and therefore he was likely to have some knowledge of the borough? Or was there another reason, arising from the party's organisational structure during the 1850s?

Robert Stewart referred to the Conservative Party outside parliament at this time as 'The party under Jolliffe', who became chief whip in 1853.[4] As Stewart says, he [Jolliffe] was 'a landed gentleman of no ministerial ambition, well connected with the network of Conservative families and therefore able to exercise powerful influence over the back-benchers and move easily in the complex tangle of local influences' which characterised constituency politics.[5] Jolliffe had overall responsibility for electoral management, so it was expected that he would carry on an extensive correspondence with party agents and supporters in various constituencies. He was assisted in his organisational responsibilities by Philip Rose, Disraeli's solicitor and a partner in the London-based firm of Baxter, Rose, Norton and Co., who had day-to-day oversight of electoral affairs including voter registration lists, possible candidates, and correspondence with 'our friends' in the various boroughs. Markham Spofforth helped with this, as well as visiting many boroughs where he had contact with the local agent or agents. The intelligence he collected was at Rose's disposal; he, in turn, supplied much of it to Jolliffe. The party's leaders, Benjamin Disraeli and, to a lesser extent, Lord Derby, expected to be kept informed by the chief whip and Rose of the more important electoral details.[6]

At the other end of the organisation were 'the men on the ground', the agents who made up the network of informants in specific constituencies. Their dominant concern was the registration of voters between elections, but they showed widely varying interest in this crucial activity. Many of them were listed in the 1859 election notebooks, for example, Thomas Commins (Bodmin), George Caunter (Ashburton), 'Mr Patch' (Tiverton), and Thomas Hawker and John Beer (Devonport), each of them solicitors. Alderman Mennie was the Plymouth agent, while his Helston equivalent was John Rogers of Penrose, a wealthy member of the Cornish gentry who shared his duties with a local

[2] Caroline Harvey, 'The British General Elections of 1857 and 1859', University of Oxford PhD, 1980, p. 36.

[3] Bodl., MS Eng. hist. e343, Sir Philip Rose's Election Notebook, 1859, entry for Totnes.

[4] Robert Stewart, *The Foundation of the Conservative Party 1830–1867* (1978), 324–39.

[5] Stewart, *Conservative Party*, 279.

[6] Stewart, *Conservative Party*, 326–9, for a discussion of the roles of Jolliffe, Rose and Spofforth. See also Harvey, 'Elections of 1857 and 1859', 34–5.

firm of solicitors.[7] So the agents were a mixed bag in terms of social status. There were also sub-agents: at Bridport in Dorset: 'Sub agent. Very useful. Thom Legg. But dangerous.'[8] Usually these agents communicated directly with Joliffe, or Rose's assistant, Markham Spofforth – when they chose to write.

Together, managers and agents guided the Conservatives' electoral fortunes. However, an analysis of three election notebooks, plus Sir John Yarde Buller's role in the party's organisation, suggests that in south-west England – and maybe elsewhere – there was a second-tier management level. The notebooks expose the limitations on the party's knowledge of constituencies and the electorate, gaps occurring because there were no agents, or agents who were purely nominal. Therefore the level of information was overcome by the use of men such as Buller, whose parliamentary duties in London allowed him to have regular contact with Jolliffe and Rose. At other times, when resident in Devon he could monitor local developments in his home county and Cornwall. Assisting him in this was Samuel Triscott, an unreliable informant whose correspondence with Jolliffe reveals how he and Buller worked to help the Conservative Party win vital seats. What their correspondence suggests is that the previously accepted dichotomy between managers and agents may need to be reconsidered. However before examining this, what was the organisational context in which these developments took place?

1

Like the 1847 general election before it, but for different reasons, that of 1852 was a disappointment to the Conservatives. When it finally concluded in July, the party found itself in a minority of 74 seats, meaning office remained a distant dream. According to Stewart: 'At the end of 1852 the Conservative Party was not simply discredited and demoralised. It was also, at least by comparison with the days of Fremantle and Bonham [the 1830s and 1840s], decrepit.'[9] Under the control of the chief whip, William Beresford, electoral organisation was shambolic, so the need for change was urgent. These were the circumstances culminating in the 1853 appointments of Jolliffe, Rose and Spofforth who were faced with an enormous task, compounded by their lack of organisational experience.[10] Beginning with the party's network and local contacts, the organisation needed to be rebuilt from the bottom upwards.

Progress was painfully slow. The election notebooks compiled for Rose and Jolliffe help us to understand this. In the 1850s, there were 203 English and Welsh boroughs; the notebooks contain details on 134 or 66%, omitting numerous small towns which Rose acknowledged would play a crucial part in any Conservative resurgence.[11] In fact, of the 69 boroughs for which there were no entries, 36 had fewer than 1,000 voters and therefore could be classified as small. Some of these, for example, Eye, Horsham,

---

[7] Bodl., Rose Election Notebook, 1859.

[8] Bodl., Rose Election Notebook, 1859, entry for Bridport.

[9] Stewart, *Conservative Party*, 268.

[10] Stewart, *Conservative Party*, 279–80. Unlike F.R. Bonham, the Conservative Party's first full-time agent in the 1830s, neither Rose nor Spofforth had been members of parliament.

[11] Bodl., Rose Election Notebook, 1859; Somerset RO, Hylton MSS, HY/24/23, Sir William Jolliffe's Election Notebook, 1859.

Midhurst and Launceston, were longstanding Conservative strongholds, while others, such as Chichester, Evesham and Winchester, had a history of shared representation which the Conservatives wisely avoided challenging. In both instances, where the *status quo* was accepted, there was no point wasting ink or effort.

The notebooks also reveal a lack of additional information which could be regarded as essential for efficient organisation. For example, the names of the sitting members are recorded for 134 boroughs; only 20 of the 134 (15%) included references to visits by Spofforth in 1855, 1856 or 1857 – to evaluate local prospects.[12] Registration information, i.e., whether a supporter or agent was attending to the register, appeared in only 12 instances (9%). Far more encompassing were summaries of correspondence with agents or other influential figures; these were available for 70 of the boroughs (54%). However, the compiler(s) of the notebooks – and Jolliffe's is the same as the Rose version, apart from additional summaries of correspondence in March and April 1859 – provided the most detailed information (visits, registrations, etc.) for only those boroughs beginning with A or B, whereas correspondence summaries ranged from Abingdon to Weymouth. On this evidence, between 1853 and 1859 the rebuilding of the party's organisation was far from complete. There were agents in 134 boroughs but it appears that in only 73 was there an effort to maintain contact with the managers.[13]

In south-west England, where there was a high proportion of small boroughs compared to elsewhere (Wales being an obvious exception), the amount of information was greater. Twenty-four of the 26 boroughs in the counties of Somerset, Devon, Cornwall and Dorset had fewer than 1,000 voters; and Jolliffe *et al.* corresponded with 18 (70%), sometimes at great length. The south-west also illustrates the party's fluctuating fortunes in small boroughs at the three general elections in the 1850s, when nationally the Conservative minorities were 74 (1852), 142 (1857), and 42 (1859) respectively.

Borough election results

	1852		1857		1859	
	Cons	Libs	Cons	Libs	Cons	Libs
Dorset	4	7	2	9	5	6
Devon	4	10	3	11	5	9
Cornwall	7	3	2	8	5	5
Somerset	3	4	2	5	3	4
Totals	18	24	9	33	18	24
England	117	206	97	226	117	206

These totals illustrate the extent of the Conservatives' losses in 1857, despite four years of organisational effort. One reading of this might be that nothing had been achieved, but this can be countered by arguing that the turnaround two years later proves that the foundations of the party's electoral organisation were in place, otherwise it could not

[12] Bodl., Rose Election Notebook, 1859.

[13] Bodl., Rose election notebook, 1859; Somerset RO, Hylton MSS, HY/24/23, Joliffe Election Notebook, 1859.

have responded so positively in the small boroughs in particular. Admittedly principles, local issues, Palmerston's policies and parliamentary reform played a part in the 1857 and 1859 general elections. In addition, the Conservatives were in government in 1859 and had been for more than a year, so, potentially, the 'loaves and fishes' of patronage were available to supporters. Nevertheless, a party's electoral organisation was an important measure of its potential fortunes, as the Conservatives' recovery in the 1830s had shown.

If the 1857 general election was a disaster for the Conservatives, a wake-up call that much more needed to be done, 1859 may be seen as the climax to the initial rebuilding phase. A list of prospective candidates had been compiled, funds were available for selected contested elections, and in 1859 the losses of 1857 were regained, giving the party a stepping-stone towards the next phase – defeating the Liberals at a general election. But what is missing in this analysis of the revival organised by the party's managers, and reliant on the assiduity of local agents, is the contribution made by those who may be termed second-tier managers, Sir John Yarde Buller, first Baron Churston, being an example.

2

Sir John Yarde Buller (1799–1871) was a wealthy country gentleman of the kind who were the backbone of the Conservative Party, and whose opinions carried weight among their fellows. Member for South Devon from 1837 until he was raised to the peerage in 1858, Buller succeeded to the baronetcy in 1853. He was a descendant of one of the oldest and most influential families in Devon and Cornwall, many of whose members intermarried with the Cornish gentry in particular. Owner of more than 10,000 acres, Buller was the patron of two livings, a lieutenant-colonel in the South Devon militia, and deputy warden of the Stannaries, the quasi-governmental body which once administered tin mining in the south-west.[14]

Perhaps the most notable feature of Buller's parliamentary career, apart from moving a no-confidence motion in the tottering Melbourne government in January 1840, was his support for Benjamin Disraeli. Despite Moneypenny's confusing version of what happened, Buller was foremost among those who, in January 1852, agreed that the time had come to appoint Disraeli as the party's leader in the house of commons.[15] Also, early in 1858, when Derby and Disraeli were constructing a cabinet for their short-lived government, Buller was mentioned as a possible replacement for two potential ministers who were being petty and demanding. Obviously the party, and Disraeli in particular, held him in high esteem, so it was unsurprising that later in the year the government successfully recommended his elevation to the peerage as Baron Churston.

Buller, however, had a behind-the-scenes career too, in a party which, in the 1850s, seemed to be in decline. For example, after the 1857 general election, Jolliffe was advised that electoral failure (whether in the south-west or nationally is not clear) lay in 'the

[14] The biographical information on the first Baron Churston has been obtained from various sources including: Michael Stenton, *Who's Who of British Members of Parliament* (4 vols, Hassocks, 1976–81), ii, 55; John Bateman, *Great Landowners of Great Britain and Ireland* (Leicester, 1971), 90.

[15] Sources for this paragraph include: W.F. Monypenny and G.E. Buckle, *The Life of Benjamin Disraeli, Earl of Beaconsfield* (6 vols, 1910–20), iii, 141, 315; iv, 118; Robert Blake, *Disraeli* (New York, 1966), 253, 298.

want of energy, unity and harmony amongst the Conservatives themselves'. The party was described as 'dispirited and careless', registrations were neglected, and there was little discipline.[16] This was the electoral organisation overseen by the managers – Jolliffe, Rose and Spofforth – and to a lesser degree by Buller in his extra-parliamentary mode. What then was his management role?

There are clues to this before Rose's 1855 Totnes letter. Two years earlier, Jolliffe informed Disraeli: 'I wrote to Sir J.Y. Buller hearing that [Sir Ralph] Lopes was likely to resign in South Devon, and that exertion would be necessary to keep out a supporter of the Govmt.'[17] Then in 1854, Buller himself discussed with Jolliffe various electoral matters in Barnstaple, Devonport, and Penryn and Falmouth.[18] Whether Buller was in frequent contact with Jolliffe's predecessor, William Beresford, is unknown; what is clear is that from 1853 until 1864 he forwarded political information from various Devon and Cornwall constituencies to the party's electoral managers, particularly the chief whip. Consequently, Jolliffe's knowledge of particular constituencies came from several sources: his spasmodic personal correspondence with local agents, Rose, Spofforth and men such as Buller. In 1853, when Lopes's resignation seemed imminent, Buller reassured Jolliffe that the county member would consult 'his friends' before acting.[19] After Lopes died there was no opposition to his Conservative replacement, Lawrence Palk.

At various times between 1853 and 1856, Buller kept Jolliffe informed of developments in Ashburton, Barnstaple, South Devon, Penryn and Falmouth, Devonport, Totnes, Westbury and Dartmouth. The last named was of particular concern to him in March 1856: 'There is a suspicion that money sent to Dartmouth to keep up the registration has been misapplied, and some of our best friends are most anxious to have this matter cleared up, and I have received a letter from them.'[20] Instead of the Dartmouth agent, (if there was one) raising this, presumably he and other supporters asked Buller to do so on their behalf.

During the same years 1853 to 1856, while providing details on specific constituencies Buller also paid attention to other issues, one being a self-appointed party manager who wished to usurp his position. In 1855, William Snell, an East Cornwall farmer who had been vocal at rural protectionist meetings several years earlier, caused Buller some anxiety. 'Mr Snell of Callington . . . is meddling with certain Boro's in this county [Devon] Cornwall and Dorset and will I am afraid make much mischief by dividing the Conservative Interests.'[21] Buller told Jolliffe that Snell had done this previously at Totnes. Now he was proposing that he and Samuel Triscott should become allies, ignoring Buller. According to Philip Rose, Snell was an 'adventurer' and a poseur who claimed he was employed by the party, a potentially damaging pretence quickly exposed by Buller.[22] Little more was heard of Snell.

[16] Somerset RO, Hylton MSS, HY/24/11/42: memorandum from Triscott to Jolliffe, 5 Apr. 1857.

[17] Bodl., Hughenden MSS, B/XX/J/3: Jolliffe to Benjamin Disraeli, 15 Oct. 1853.

[18] E.g., see Somerset RO, Hylton MSS, HY/24/7/13: Buller to Jolliffe, 9 Mar. 1854.

[19] Bodl., Hughenden MSS, B/XX/J/3: Jolliffe to Disraeli, 15 Oct. 1853.

[20] Somerset RO, Hylton MSS, HY/24/10/5: Buller to Jolliffe, 10 Mar. 1856.

[21] Somerset RO, Hylton MSS, HY/24/9/10: Buller to Jolliffe, 26 Nov. 1855.

[22] Somerset RO, Hylton MSS, HY/24/18/23: Rose to Jolliffe, 29 Nov. 1855. In 1852 and 1858, Snell attempted to interfere in Helston politics.

Buller's involvement in electoral matters seemed to intensify after the party's defeat in 1857, and especially when the Conservatives took office in February 1858. For the next twelve months, among his many concerns was winning at least one Devonport seat at the next election. This required Dockyard vacancies to be filled with Conservative rather than Liberal supporters, something difficult to do when the Liberals had been entrenched in government for more than a decade. An exasperated Thomas Hawker, one of the party's Devonport agents, explained the problems to Jolliffe. The master ship-wright in the yard was a Liberal, Mr Edge, who 'always selects his own partisans' for vacancies, and even after the Conservatives took office he was still forwarding recommendations which were approved by the board of the admiralty.[23] This continued for several months, to the dismay of the Devonport Conservatives: 'Our friends here in the yard, and out of it', Hawker told Jolliffe, 'are disheartened, and disgusted at a lack or want of feeling for them, as has been shown by those who now have the power to have given them their fair rights.'[24]

Buller's part in reversing this began by meeting Hawker and his fellow agent, John Beer, who explained to him: 'what is required to be done and Sir John will see the Sec'ts of the Admiralty upon it'.[25] Buller was supplied with a list of names of local Conservatives which could be used to circumvent Mr Edge. This list was duly presented to the board, and representation made by Buller to by-pass Edge, but progress was slow, so slow that there seemed to be credence to the rumour that Sir John Pakington, the first lord of the admiralty, was in league with the whigs.[26] Buller continued to work to alter the situation, so much so that on 17 January 1859 Samuel Triscott explained to Jolliffe that ideally Churston (the now ennobled Buller) should replace Pakington at the admiralty because this would make a difference of six seats in Cornwall, 'without even looking across the Tamar'.[27] He mentioned Buller's political weight, moral influence, his knowledge of patronage, and the widespread respect for his opinions.

Triscott was certain Buller's likely influence would not be confined to Cornwall. If he was first lord of the admiralty he could return one member for Plymouth (two Liberals had been elected in 1857) and another for Totnes, while 'Dartmouth and Ashburton would succumb to his position and power: the scales in both have been pretty nearly balanced, but the distribution of the loaves and fishes have turned the balance'.[28] Triscott's sweeping statements were typical of his judgment in electoral matters; he placed great faith in the potential influence of men such as Buller, or other individuals who impressed him.

Prior to the 1857 and 1859 elections, Buller was also a leading participant in meetings of leading Cornwall and Devon Conservatives: 'Sir John Buller, Lord Vallefort, Coryton

[23] Somerset RO, Hylton MSS, HY/24/18/80, 83: letters from T.H. Hawker to Jolliffe, 22 Mar. and 8 May 1858. Additional correspondence from Hawker on this topic, from Apr. to Oct. 1858, may be found in HY/18/6.

[24] Somerset RO, Hylton MSS, HY/24/18/83: Hawker to Jolliffe, 8 May 1858. He wrote that 'This week there has been an entry of upwards of 200 men, and Mr Edge as usual, has entd all his own followers – our party had not a chance – in fact, we knew nothing of it, until too late.'

[25] Somerset RO, Hylton MSS, HY/18/6/80: Hawker to Jolliffe, 22 Mar. 1858.

[26] Somerset RO, Hylton MSS, HY/18/6/92: Hawker to Jolliffe, 12 Oct. 1858.

[27] Somerset RO, Hylton MSS, HY/24/17/13: Triscott to Jolliffe, 17 Jan. 1859.

[28] Somerset RO, Hylton MSS, HY/24/17/13: Triscott to Jolliffe, 17 Jan. 1859.

of Pentillie and about 12 more of our Conservative friends dined with me [Triscott] last week. All in very good spirits . . . I have had a long conversation with him [Buller] and he agrees with me that our prospects are gradually brightening in this neighbourhood.'[29] Moreover, Buller was closely involved in the machinations following the death in June 1858 of the West Cornwall Liberal MP, Michael Williams. According to Triscott, Williams's sons (and brother William) were ready to support the Conservatives with their considerable wealth and their over-rated (by Triscott) electoral influence. Buller was less sanguine than Triscott about this outcome, and ultimately his judgment was confirmed.[30]

An 1864 sequel to this episode revealed that Buller was still taking an interest in West Cornwall electoral politics, for he wrote to Sir Richard Vyvyan, the one-time ultra-tory and later MP for Helston, about electoral prospects 'in the West'. In particular he wanted an opinion on William Williams's son, Frederick, as a likely Conservative candidate, and whether or not Vyvyan and 'the Gentlemen of Influence in the Western Division of Cornwall' would offer support.[31] Buller thought Williams would be 'as good a Candidate as we are likely to find', but in two long letters in reply, Vyvyan dashed this optimism, pointing out that the register had been neglected for many years, Frederick Williams was virtually unknown in the division, he was also said to lack energy, and there was a better known candidate likely to stand.[32] From other sources, Buller had gained a different opinion: 'But no doubt your [Vyvyan's] information and knowledge of the District is far better than any that reaches me from other quarters.'[33] This implies that Buller continued to play a similar role in Conservative Party organisation to that which he had in the 1850s – gathering information and representing viewpoints to the party's managers. Moreover, with his estates in Devon, for Buller to be involved in Cornish affairs makes it highly probable that he continued to do so in Devon.

3

The correspondence of Samuel Triscott with Jolliffe in particular, sheds further light on both the Conservatives' organisation in the southwest, and Buller's activities. In the 1850s, Triscott was employed in the victualling yard of the Devonport dockyard, while also regularly writing to Jolliffe and Buller. Unfortunately though, 'poor old Triscott' as the chief whip referred to him, was not a particularly reliable source.[34] Buller mentioned this to Jolliffe in the context of a discussion about prospects at Devonport in an 1854 by-election. Triscott, he believed, was too sanguine. 'But I will see some others of our

[29] Somerset RO, Hylton MSS, HY/24/10/65: Triscott to Jolliffe, 25 Nov. 1856. See also, e.g., another letter to Jolliffe on the same topic, 2 June 1858: 'On Saturday last Sir J. Buller met the leaders of our party at my house.'

[30] For a detailed description of the episode see Edwin Jaggard, *Cornwall Politics in the Age of Reform 1790–1885* (Woodbridge, 1999), ch. 7. Triscott's long letter on this to Jolliffe on 23 June 1858 may be found at Somerset RO, Hylton MSS, HY/24/17/40: 'I am just returned from the obsequies of Mr M Williams as also those of the Conservative interest in West Cornwall: the first died a natural death, the latter by suicide.'

[31] Cornwall RO, Vyvyan MSS, V, 60/46/18: Lord Churston to Sir Richard Vyvyan, 4 Jan. 1864.

[32] Cornwall RO, Vyvyan MSS, V, 60/46/18: Vyvyan to Churston, 6 and 7 Jan. 1864.

[33] Cornwall RO, Vyvyan MSS, V, 60/46/18: Churston to Vyvyan, 12 Jan. 1864.

[34] Bodl., Hughenden MSS, B/XX/J/58: Jolliffe to [?Disraeli], 8 Oct. 1858.

party who, I think, have more judgement and knowledge of the matter than Mr T.'[35]
Several years later a more damming indictment of Triscott's involvement came from
Thomas Hawker, described as 'a great [Devonport] Dockyard Conservative'. He asked
Jolliffe to advise Disraeli, Derby and others to be cautious if they wrote to Triscott: 'some
men are unable to retain what is communicated to them, they must always know more
than their neighbours – and their vanity prompts them to let the world know that they
are on intimate terms and in confidential communication with the eminent leaders of
a party'.[36] Triscott's tendency to self-aggrandisement is very evident in much of his
correspondence with Jolliffe.

What then, was his position in the party? He seems to have been Buller's assistant,
overseeing electoral affairs in Devonport, Plymouth, and almost all of the Cornish
boroughs apart from St Ives and Launceston, both Conservative strongholds. His stream
of letters to the chief whip was constant and often self-serving: 'I am desirous of the
honor of a little conversation with you [Jolliffe] on some matters relating to the West.
I have this morning a letter from Mr Disraeli, which warrants my addressing you';[37] in
the political tug-of-war between Liberals and Conservatives to win the political allegiance of the Williams family when there was a vacancy in June 1858 in West Cornwall,
Jolliffe was confident that Buller 'will take care that any satisfactory movement will have
his encouragement'.[38] Triscott's response to this was blunt: 'Sir John has been deceived.
Now hear the truth.'[39] In fact, events later proved that it was Triscott who had been
misled – the late Michael Williams's wealthy eldest son, John, eventually gave his support
to the Liberals.

His surviving letters portray Triscott as an indefatigable supplier of information on
everything from the national political scene to the Conservative Party's election results. He
worked closely with Buller; many letters are sprinkled with such phrases as: 'It appears from
what Sir John Buller says . . .', and 'Sir John thinks', and, 'I had a long conversation with
him [Buller].'[40] Yet while he deferred to Buller on almost all matters, and displayed great
respect for him as both a politician and a person, this did not prevent him from acting
independently as he did in the case of the Williams family, Cornish mining and banking
magnates, but also epitomising 'new wealth' which was very slowly assimilated into the
county's ruling class. From early 1858, Triscott worked assiduously to persuade this prolific
family – Michael Williams, Liberal MP, and his brother, William, had nine sons between
them – to support the Conservatives.[41] It would be true to say that he was besotted by the
family's wealth and apparent influence, even persuading Buller of their likely electoral

[35] Somerset RO, Hylton MSS, HY/24/7/13: Buller to Jolliffe, 9 Mar. 1854.

[36] Somerset RO, Hylton MSS, HY/24/17/14: T.H. Hawker to Jolliffe, Jan. 1859. It was Jolliffe who
described Hawker to Disraeli as 'a great Dockyard Conservative'. See Bodl., Hughenden MSS, B/XX/J/63:
Jolliffe to Disraeli, nd.

[37] Somerset RO, Hylton MSS, HY/24//9/120: Triscott to Jolliffe, 1855, nd.

[38] Somerset RO, Hylton MSS, HY/24/17/40: Triscott to Jolliffe, 23 June 1858.

[39] Somerset RO, Hylton MSS, HY/24/17/40: Triscott to Jolliffe, 23 June 1858.

[40] See, e.g., Somerset RO, Hylton MSS, HY/24/17/4–60: Triscott's letters to Jolliffe between June 1858 and
Jan. 1859.

[41] Somerset RO, Hylton MSS, HY/24/17/36,47,48: letters from Triscott to [?Jolliffe], June 1858, and 1 Oct.,
which reveal how efforts were made to get the late Michael Williams's eldest son, JM (who allegedly inherited
one million pounds from his father), to meet Churston and also Lord Valletort.

value. Ultimately almost nothing eventuated. Only one of the nine sons entered the house of commons as a Conservative, the rest remaining political onlookers. So much for the seven or eight Cornish seats which Triscott believed could be won in 1859, if the family could be persuaded to throw their weight behind the Conservatives.[42] Three seats were gained, none attributable to the Williams family's involvement.

Accompanying these delusional summaries was a persistent effort by Triscott to secure a better position for himself from the shortlived Derby government. Early in 1858, he had high hopes, which were quickly dashed.[43] Later, writing to Jolliffe, he bemoaned the fact that his eight years' service to the party (he soon changed this to 20!) was being ignored, and he was being treated with neglect and contempt.[44] Then his spirits lifted when he believed efforts *were* being made on his behalf, by Buller and others, to be appointed as treasurer to the county courts of Devon and Cornwall. Unfortunately for Triscott, behind the scenes his prospects were being condemned. In a letter to Jolliffe, Thomas Hawker wrote: 'Now, altho' I shd be very glad to see Mr Triscott appointed to some more lucrative office in his *own Department* – yet, take my word for it, if such an office as . . . be conferred on him, it will damage the Government and party in the 2 counties of Devon and Cornwall beyond recall.'[45] Hawker believed that the government's patronage should not be diverted from its proper channels.[46] Even worse for Triscott, Jolliffe told Disraeli that he agreed with Hawker, adding in a later letter that 'the Admiralty should have provided for him ["old Triscott"], but he has never been wise, talking and writing far too much'; while also pointing out that Lord Churston (the former Sir John Yarde Buller) tried to work with him.[47] In fact, according to Triscott, Buller personally made representations to Disraeli on his behalf, and there were even references to the governorship of Bermuda becoming available, but nothing eventuated.

Although in October 1858 Jolliffe confessed to Disraeli that 'I continue to carry on a most awful correspondence with poor old Triscott, and I keep his grievances attended to as well as I am able', also complaining that over the years he had received enough letters 'for three volumes',[48] nevertheless Triscott did help as well as hinder. In March 1858 he sent Jolliffe 'a Handbook for the West. Of course as circumstances arise I will send you additional data to put in it.'[49] It is conceivable that the 'Handbook', with its details on Devonport, Truro, St Ives, Devon County, Plymouth, Liskeard, Helston, Falmouth, East Cornwall, West Cornwall, and Bodmin, was the forerunner to the notebooks eventually compiled for Rose and Jolliffe, although the style is very different.

[42] Jaggard, *Cornwall Politics*, 161–2.

[43] Somerset RO, Hylton MSS, HY/24/17/6: Triscott to Rose, 14 Mar. 1858, In this and other correspondence he refers to the governorship of Bermuda, which he preferred to other possibilities. Buller and others were enlisted to promote his claims.

[44] Somerset RO, Hylton MSS, HY/24/17/46: Triscott to Jolliffe, 12 Sept. 1858.

[45] Bodl., Hughenden MSS, B/XX/J/63C: Hawker to Jolliffe, 22 Dec. 1858.

[46] Bodl., Hughenden MSS, B/XX/J/63C: Hawker to Jolliffe, 22 Dec. 1858.

[47] Bodl., Hughenden MSS, B/XX/J/63C: Hawker to Jolliffe, 22 Dec. 1858.

[48] Bodl., Hughenden MSS, B/XX/J/58: Jolliffe to [?Disraeli], 8 Oct. 1858.

[49] Somerset RO, Hylton MSS, HY/24/17/20: Triscott to Jolliffe, 31 Mar. 1858. In this letter, Triscott referred to the importance he attached to converting the Williams family to the Conservative side, adding that he (Triscott) was the 'go-between' linking the family and Buller.

Whereas they were essentially summaries of information and contacts, Triscott's notebook entries were similar to his letters: wordy, reflecting his growing obsession with Michael Williams MP and his family, misplaced optimism, and personal opinions.[50] For example, on Truro, 'There is a strong Conservative party in the Borough, but, as usual, a stronger Conservative mismanagement. The deciding power is with Mr Williams of Trewince', i.e., the Liberal MP for West Cornwall. In fact his ability to unify the local Conservatives was negligible, especially as he sat as a Liberal! Again, according to Triscott he personally was responsible for a Conservative, C.J. Mare leading the Plymouth poll in 1852, 'which shows what may be done by hard work and good arrangement'. Mare was unseated on petition one year later. Triscott also claimed he could manage affairs in Bodmin, adding: 'Mr M Williams has influence here as in fact in all Cornish towns.' The electoral value of the author's flights of fancy may be gauged by the omission of almost all Triscott's observations from Rose and Jolliffe's notebooks.

Reviewing Triscott's position within the organisation, firstly, he worked for the party's interests in an idiosyncratic manner, perhaps inflating his self-importance because he lacked the status to be particularly influential among the gentry who spasmodically ran party affairs. Secondly, the proof of his position may be judged by his relationship with Sir John Yarde Buller. Although once or twice he claimed to have better knowledge of particular circumstances, he always deferred to the wealthy, landowning MP whose membership of the Commons, and access to the chief whip meant he was far better informed than Triscott. Thirdly, Triscott's activities, his discussions with prospective candidates, long conversations with Buller, meetings with the party's local gentry leaders, and encouragement of the Williams family's transferral of loyalty to the Conservatives underlines the conclusion about Buller too, that Rose and Jolliffe relied on second-tier managers for electoral information.

Mid-level managers such as Buller and Triscott could only do so much to affect the outcome of specific elections, although the latter apparently believed his importance was far greater than others judged it to be. In fact it was Buller, with his much more substantial social and political status who was more likely to change the course of events, but he, too, ultimately deferred to Jolliffe and Rose. Their information was less than perfect, they were sometimes slow to act, and they walked a fine line when making judgments about local matters, especially the wielders or potential wielders of influence. Hence, given the ramshackle state of the party's organisation in 1852 it is not surprising that the Conservative Party struggled to overcome the Liberals' supremacy in the 1850s.

4

This analysis has reviewed the Conservative Party's electoral organisation in the 1850s, and, in particular, the regional responsibilities of Sir John Yarde Buller and Samuel Triscott. Buller was the primary point of contact for Sir William Jolliffe and Philip Rose, his involvement seeming to commence early in the 1850s, whereas Triscott's began at least a decade or so beforehand. Throughout the 1850s both Buller and Triscott managed

---

[50] Somerset RO, Hylton MSS, HY/24/23, Part I, Triscott's Election Notebook. All quotations in the remainder of the paragraph are from this source.

the Conservative Party's interests in Devon and Cornwall, constantly attempting to energise supporters in the various constituencies, seek suitable candidates, and satisfy those whose political influence could be of most value to the party. Buller was the primary point of contact, and his views carried most weight. Triscott too, was at times a useful source, but he was always subservient to Buller, and as Jolliffe, Rose and Disraeli knew, his egotism often clouded his political judgment.

What the two election notebooks indicate, and this is reinforced by a survey of Rose and Jolliffe's correspondence, is the spasmodic flow of electoral information from most constituency-based agents. Once an election was called, many quickly took up their pens to appeal to the party managers for various forms of assistance, but between times nothing was heard from them. When they did communicate, naturally they reported on affairs in their own constituency, because they were in no position to have a wider perspective. The uneven flow of information could not be compensated for by Rose and Spofforth 'who both went about the country to assist local parties', as there was simply too much to do.[51] Consequently, the Conservative Party's organisation was neither, 'encompassing in its scope, or uniform in its agency'.[52] Buller and Triscott helped fill the information gap by familiarising themselves with the affairs of the party in Devon, Cornwall and occasionally elsewhere, then notifying Jolliffe in particular. This meant that in a number of small boroughs, the Conservatives were not caught unprepared when an election was imminent.

What did they achieve? Because south-western counties such as Devon, Cornwall, Somerset and Dorset had a disproportionately large number of small boroughs, this was a region of vital importance to the Conservatives. Defeating the Liberals depended on winning more seats in these towns, as well as in the counties which were their acknowledged stronghold. Using this yardstick, neither the party, nor Buller and Triscott could have been satisfied in 1857, when nine seats were lost in the region, six in Devon and Cornwall. Possibly it was this which prompted Triscott to compile his 'Handbook for the West' for Jolliffe. In turn this may have been the reason for the more detailed 1859 notebooks listing constituencies in England and Wales – perhaps a recognition by Rose and Jolliffe that there needed to be much greater attention to detail.

The way in which the party rebounded in 1859, regaining its 1857 losses in the south-west, confirms that plenty of productive organisational work had been done earlier in the decade. Otherwise, without this groundwork, the results in 1859 may well have continued the trend begun in 1857. Buller and Triscott worked tirelessly between 1857 and 1859, to improve the Conservative position, their correspondence with the chief whip illustrating this. Hence, in mid February 1859, the two of them spent three hours discussing the likely benefits of persuading almost all members of the prolific Williams family to support the Conservative Party; at least six seats would be the reward. Buller and his ally were vital links between the constituencies and those with final responsibility for electoral organisation. Ultimately, their assiduity helped stabilise the electoral fortunes of 'The Party under Jolliffe', although at the end of the 1850s, the hoped-for defeat of the Liberals was still 14 years away.

[51] Stewart, *Conservative Party*, 328.
[52] Stewart, *Conservative Party*, 326.

'Underhand Dealings with the Papal Authorities': Disraeli and the Liberal Conspiracy to Disestablish the Irish Church

PADRAIC C. KENNEDY

During the parliamentary election of 1868, Prime Minister Benjamin Disraeli sent a 'gentleman spy' to Ireland to seek evidence showing that William Gladstone had agreed to disestablish the Church of Ireland in return for the Vatican's promise of Irish catholic votes. Proof of this conspiracy, Disraeli hoped, would prompt an anti-catholic backlash and tip the election to the Conservatives. Disraeli's spy spent four weeks interviewing various Liberal politicians and Irish catholic prelates and claimed to have discovered not only a secret agreement between Gladstone and the bishops, but also a vast Vatican conspiracy to use Irish nationalist agitation to undermine the English constitution. Unfortunately, he never found written proof of any either scheme. The Liberals won the election by a large margin and soon passed an act disestablishing the Church of Ireland. Although out of office, Disraeli remained in contact with his secret agent, using him for further missions in England and on the continent. Despite its failure, the spy's mission offers fresh insight into Disraeli's character and policies. Disraeli combined opportunistic political scheming with a weakness for conspiracy theories. His agent's mission to Ireland was certainly an intrigue meant to turn the political tables on the Liberals but was based on Disraeli's belief that Rome actually had conspired with Gladstone. Recognition of Disraeli's faith in the existence of papal conspiracies helps to make his public statements about disestablishment more comprehensible and suggests a new explanation for his ongoing inflexibility in regard to Irish grievances and reforms.

Keywords: Disraeli; Gladstone; bishops; disestablishment; 1868 election; conspiracy; Vatican; Trelawney; Ireland; spy

In September 1868, two months before the parliamentary election, Prime Minister Benjamin Disraeli received a 'startling' offer of 'confidential services in connection with the elections . . . to the advantage of conservative interests'. The offer came from E. Trelawney, a self-proclaimed 'gentleman spy' who had worked for the home office's recently disbanded secret service department.[1] Trelawney claimed to know of secret

---

[1] Bodl., Hughenden Deposit [hereafter cited as HD] 127/3, ff. 52–3: Trelawney to Disraeli, 7 Sept. 1868; ff. 54–5: Trelawney to Feilding, 8 Sept. 1868; ff. 48–9: Feilding to Disraeli, 7 Sept. 1868. Trelawney never signs a first name. He first appears in the archives in Oct. 1865, when he offered his services to Home Secretary Sir George Grey and Lord John Russell, then foreign secretary in Palmerston's administration. Claiming to have inside information about Fenian activities in Europe and the United States, Trelawney was presumably trying to cash in on the Fenian conspiracy (which first gained wide recognition after arrests in Dublin in September 1865). TNA (PRO), FO 1335, 11 Oct. 1865. His letter to Russell was signed 'E. Brereton Trelawny', which suggests some sort of connection to Edward Trelawny, the Romantic poet and friend of Byron, or Harry Brereton Trelawny, Edward's brother. However, I found no reference to him in the Brereton or Trelawny family records.

negotiations between William Gladstone and the Vatican concerning the disestablishment of the Irish church and promised: 'I [should] soon furnish Mr. Disraeli with information the source of [which could] never be guessed at, [which would] be dangerous weapons in skillful hands and that particular chord in the British mind which of course the Prime Minister wants to strike could be struck to some purpose: denial would be useless or impossible and a conservative reaction would be greatly assisted.'[2]

Trelawney's former employer at the secret service department, Leutenant-Colonel William Feilding of the Coldstream Guards, had forwarded the spy's letter to Disraeli, noting: 'being a gentleman by education, birth and person [Trelawney would] have considerable power in the manner suggested by him, especially as he is a Roman Catholic and thoroughly unscrupulous as to means provided the end is attained'.[3] Feilding also offered a compelling description of Trelawney:

> In appearance he is insignificant, a sound English face, very fair hair and small stony blue eyes would make you believe that he was a little shop boy or an usher in a school, but he was born with half a dozen languages in his mouth, speaks French, German, and Italian without accent, and when turned loose into a foreign town without introductions is generally found to be on intimate terms with a cabinet minister or a cardinal within the week.

Disraeli enthusiastically approved of the plan, and arranged to fund it using home office secret service funds. He reasoned, 'even if the elections were to go against us, the elected House, acted on by national opinion might take a very different course from that originally intended'.[4] Two weeks later, on 7 October 1868, Trelawney began his mission. Feilding, who had agreed to act as liaison, verbally instructed him: 'to discover the connection which exists between the ultramontane party in Ireland, and the ultra-liberal party in England; and if possible to obtain such proofs of underhand dealing with the papal authorities through an Irish medium, as would, if exposed to the nation; cause the downfall from popularity of the ultra-liberal party'.

The colonel expected that the most likely evidence of conspiracy would be, 'promises which may have been made to [the priests], in return for their political support of liberal candidates, [especially] with regard to the re-division of the property of the Irish church'.[5] With letters of introduction provided by the catholic English peer, the earl of Denbigh (Feilding's elder brother), Trelawney, posing as a tourist, travelled around Ireland for more than a month. He visited various Irish churchmen and politicians, engaged them in conversation about the parliamentary election, and reported his findings in ten letters sent to Feilding and passed on to the prime minister.

Despite Trelawney's efforts, his mission produced no tangible evidence that suggested the existence of a secret combination between Gladstone and the Vatican. Even

---

[2] Bodl., HD 127/3, ff. 61–2: Trelawney to Feilding, 17 Sept. 1868.

[3] It is unclear whether his unscrupulousness derived from his gentlemanly ways or Roman catholic beliefs. Bodl., HD 127/3, ff. 48–9; HD 127/3, ff. 56–7: Mayo to Disraeli, 20 Sept. 1868.

[4] National Library of Ireland, Dublin [hereafter cited as NLI], 11164 (Mayo Papers): Disraeli to Mayo, 23 Sept. 1868.

[5] Bodl., HD 127/3, ff. 66–7: 'Memorandum of Instructions', 7 Oct. 1868 attached to ff. 64–5: Feilding to Disraeli, 7 Oct. 1868.

had he provided such proof, it might not have prevented the Liberal Party's over-whelming election victory in November, given the limited appeal of anti-catholicism outside Lancashire.[6] Disraeli resigned before parliament met again and would not climb back to the top of the greasy pole until 1874. The spy's failure and the Conservative defeat at the polls probably explains why this sidelight to the 1868 elections has passed largely unnoticed by the scores of biographers who have so eagerly and assiduously picked over the scraps of Disraeli's remarkable personal life and political career.[7] This morsel seems only to confirm what many of his political opponents and most of his biographers (unsympathetic or otherwise) have argued – that Disraeli was an opportunist with a talent for intrigue who would support practically any scheme that promised political advantage. Even J.P. Parry, the most recent scholar to try to revise this negative image, concedes Disraeli's opportunism and fascination with intrigue, although as the short-term means by which to implement his deeply-held Conservative principles.[8] Also, given the completeness of Gladstone's political coup, it is hardly surprising that Disraeli tried to find a sensational way to turn the tables. As Feilding noted in forwarding Trelawney's proposal, 'stirring times require stirring measures'.[9]

But focusing on Disraeli's lack of scruples obscures the more interesting and enlightening aspect of this episode – the conspiracy he expected Trelawney to discover. Here we gain fresh insight into an aspect of Disraeli's character often ignored or rationalised by modern biographers. What distinguished Disraeli from other politicians was not that he engaged in political plotting, or even his skill and success at it, but his belief that secret intrigues and conspiracies were key agents of political change. Disraeli's views are most obvious in his novels and other writings, but are also remarkably apparent in his political speeches and correspondence.[10] In the case of Irish disestablishment, the underlying intrigue is outlined in detail in the private correspondence regarding Trelawney's mission, but Disraeli had already referred to a version of this conspiracy when, in his Commons speech against Gladstone's motion, he announced that 'High Church Ritualists and the Irish followers of the Pope have been long in secret combination and are now in open confederacy',[11] to sever the con-

---

[6] Disraeli probably underestimated the popularity of Irish disestablishment as a campaign issue and over-estimated the strength of a protestant backlash against Roman catholics and ritualism. W.F. Monypenny and G.E. Buckle, *The Life of Benjamin Disraeli, Earl of Beaconsfield* (6 vols, 1910-20), v, 89; Robert Blake, *Disraeli* (New York, 1966), 513.

[7] Only Stanley Weintraub mentions the incident in passing, though mistakes the dates. Stanley Weintraub, *Disraeli: A Biography* (New York, 1993), 456. The mission is covered in more detail in Leon O'Broin, *Fenian Fever: An Anglo-American Dilemma* (1971), 240–2.

[8] J.P. Parry, 'Disraeli and England', *HJ*, xliii (2000), 703.

[9] Bodl., HD 127/3, f. 49.

[10] Usually expressed through the most worldly and exotic characters, such as in his political novel *Coningsby*, where he portrays the dashing jewish banker Sidonia as privy to secrets that 'would throw a curious light on those subterranean agencies of which the world in general knows so little, but which exercise so great an influence on public events'. Benjamin Disraeli, *Coningsby or the New Generation* (New York, 1962), 231. For the most extensive analysis of this aspect of the novels, see John Vincent, *Disraeli* (Oxford, 1990); Hansard, 3rd ser., cxliii, 773–4 (14 July 1856); ccxxxi, 213 (31 July 1876); cclviii, 1931 (1 Mar. 1881); J.M. Roberts, *The Mythology of the Secret Societies* (New York, 1972), 7n.

[11] Hansard, 3rd ser., cxci, 924.

22 *Padraic C. Kennedy*

nection between the state and the church. This assertion was met with laughter and derision from the opposition benches. Gladstone attributed it to 'the influence of a heated imagination', perhaps insinuating that Disraeli was drunk, a charge also levelled by an unsympathetic American reporter watching from the gallery.[12] Even Disraeli's ally, Home Secretary Gathorne Gathorne-Hardy, called the speech 'obscure, flippant, and imprudent'.[13] Nevertheless, Disraeli repeated his accusations in an open letter published in *The Times*, which identified an 'extreme faction' within the high church party whose 'fatal machinations' with the Romanists were aimed at a separation of church and state in England.[14]

Modern historians have generally interpreted Disraeli's occasional remarks about conspiracies lurking behind affairs of state as nothing more than flights of fancy from England's most self-consciously flamboyant and provocative personality. Monypenny and Buckle referred to his indulgence in intrigues 'as part of Disraeli's Oriental equipment'; Lord Blake remarked that the tory leader had 'a mind as romantic as it was subtle', an opinion shared by Paul Smith, who notes Disraeli's 'childlike thrill in knowing secrets and penetrating mysteries which led him to ascribe ludicrously much to backstairs intrigue and the secret societies'.[15] Nevertheless, biographers have generally maintained that these eccentricities, though sometimes regrettable, did not detract from Disraeli's political acumen, and often served as further proof of his political opportunism. His exaggerated public statements concerning disestablishment are a good example of this. Scholars have interpreted Disraeli's Commons speech as a desperate and unsuccessful attempt to stave off Gladstone's Irish gambit by raising the 'no-popery' cry to rally Conservatives around the English Church.[16] Or, as Disraeli simply venting his frustration and bitterness over what the tory leader saw as a betrayal by Cardinal Manning and the Irish bishops, with whom he had been negotiating the establishment of an Irish catholic university.[17] Allen Warren has offered a more subtle interpretation of Disraeli's position

[12] Hansard, 3rd ser., cxci, 924; Blake, *Disraeli*, 500; Weintraub, *Disraeli*, 465–6. Disraeli was known to fortify himself with brandy, though there is little to suggest it affected the content or delivery of his speeches. For example, he supposedly drank two bottles of clear brandy while delivering his famous speech at Manchester, Monypenny and Buckle, *Disraeli*, v, 187.

[13] Gathorne Gathorne-Hardy Cranbrook, *Gathorne Hardy, First Earl of Cranbrook: A Memoir with Extracts from His Diary and Correspondence* (1910), 273. P.M.H. Bell calls it a 'famous piece of rhodomontade' and notes that the *Saturday Review* opined that 'no one would take it seriously outside Bedlam'. P.M.H. Bell, *Disestablishment in Ireland and Wales* (1969), 89–90.

[14] *The Times*, 27 Mar. 1868, p. 9; 14 Apr. 1868, p. 7.

[15] Monypenny and Buckle, *Disraeli*, iv, 68; Blake, *Disraeli*, 404; Paul Smith, *Disraeli: A Brief Life* (Cambridge, 1996), 184. Not surprisingly, contemporaries attributed both his unscrupulousness and his romanticised vision of politics to his 'eastern', or jewish heritage, while historians argue that these traits were means by which he dealt with the handicap of anti-semitism. Vincent, *Disraeli*, 30; Parry, 'Disraeli and England', 702–3; Weintraub, *Disraeli*, 454–7; Christopher Hibbert, *Disraeli: The Victorian Dandy Who Became Prime Minister* (New York, 2006), 260, 364.

[16] Blake, *Disraeli*, 500; Monypenny and Buckle, *Disraeli*, iii, 427–9; Richard Shannon, *The Age of Disraeli, 1868–1881: The Rise of Tory Democracy* (1992), 41, 59; K. Theodore Hoppen, *The Mid-Victorian Generation, 1846–1886* (Oxford, 1998), 446; Richard W. Davis, *Disraeli* (Boston, 1976), 157–8. The exception is J.M. Roberts, who uses Disraeli as a prominent example of the widespread Victorian belief in secret societies, Roberts, *Secret Societies*, 3–7. A number of earlier biographers not only noted Disraeli's belief in conspiracies, but praised him for his insight. Walter Sichel, *Disraeli: A Study in Personality and Ideas* (1904), 253–4; D.C. Somervelle, *Disraeli and Gladstone, a Duo-Biographical Sketch* (New York, 1926), 288–9; Hesketh Pearson, *Dizzy: The Life and Personality of Benjamin Disraeli Earl of Beaconsfield* (New York, 1951), 147.

[17] Weintraub, *Disraeli*, 465.

against disestablishment, arguing that this overheated rhetoric reflected the tory leader's real concerns about the position of the Church of England, already weakened by divisions over ritualism, the threat of scientific rationalism, and the challenge of dissent.[18] All conclude that Disraeli cried 'conspiracy' in the heat of the moment or as a calculated political manoeuvre.

But what if Disraeli meant what he said? This article will contend that the details of Trelawney's mission, the confidence Disraeli expressed in the spy, and the fact that their relationship continued after the 1868 election suggests that the Conservative leader did believe in the existence of a conspiracy involving the Liberals and the catholic church. While his public statements and Trelawney's efforts were certainly desperate attempts to turn the political tables on the Liberals in the upcoming election, they were based on Disraeli's conviction that secret intrigues determined the important religious and political issues of the day.

Trelawney began his mission in Kilkenny where he secured an invitation to dine with the bishop of Kerry, David Moriarty. The spy's account of this meeting established one of the themes that he returned to in each report. Trelawney emphasized that Moriarty sympathised with the Conservative Party, portraying the bishop as an Anglophile who hated the 'republican' Liberals, but supported Gladstone entirely for the promise of disestablishment.[19] This report also established Trelawney's practice of sharing some of the subtleties of his craft with his employers, enabling him to vindicate his lack of progress while reminding them of his considerable skills. Trelawney admitted that the conversation with the bishop of Kerry had provided no proof of a conspiracy but explained that the bishop would serve as a 'stepping stone':

> Through Dr. Moriarty I shall come to know the 'extreme' members of the ultramontane party, though he does not belong to it himself. The liberals would never choose such a man as this bishop for the negociations which assuredly have been entered into with others. Though a man of exceptional ability and intelligence he has not the remotest flavour of the astute and [resolute] Jesuitism which really directs the actual 'situation here'.[20]

A few days later, Trelawney congratulated himself on the success of this strategy when Moriarty introduced him to Richard O'Brien, the dean of Limerick, 'an Irish Irishman' whose 'demonstrative' nature revealed him as one of 'these impulsive people [who] are so easily read and 'managed'. Unfortunately, since O'Brien was a guest of the bishop, Trelawney could not invite him to dinner alone, which, the spy explained, was 'the one

---

[18] Allen Warren, 'Disraeli, the Conservatives and the Government of Ireland: Part 2, 1868–1881', *Parliamentary History*, xviii (1999), 145–9; Allen Warren, 'Disraeli, Conservatives and the Church', *Parliamentary History*, xix (2000), 110–2; Allen Warren, 'Disraeli, Conservatives and the National Church, 1837–1881', *Parliamentary History*, xx (2001), 96–117.

[19] Bodl., HD 127/3, ff. 70–1: Trelawney to Feilding, 9 Oct. 1868.

[20] Bodl., HD 127/3, ff. 70–1: Trelawney to Feilding, 9 Oct. 1868. Ironically, Bishop Patrick Leahy feared that Moriarty was negotiating with Gladstone and Monsell to secure state endowment of the Irish catholic church using the proceeds of the disestablishment of the Church of Ireland. Leahy to O'Neill Daunt, 12 Sept. 1867, in Mark Tierney, 'Correspondence Concerning the Disestablishment of the Church of Ireland, 1862–1869', *Collectanea Hibernica,* xii (1969), 178–9.

single way of drawing men out . . . I must have the talkative old dean *tete a tete* and encourage his enthusiasm into a glow of confidence and this is my plan.'[21]

Forced to put aside his investigation of the dean of Limerick for the moment, Trelawney moved on to Cork where he had an introduction to Bishop William Delaney, who had 'just enough of the Irish warmth of temperament to be accessible to sympathetic personal impressions, and to speak freely under their influence'. According to the spy, Delaney, like Moriarty, professed a dislike of Gladstone and even a preference for Disraeli's 'genius' (to which Trelawney dedicates a full paragraph). Delaney also confided that he and the other bishops only supported Gladstone because of a 'palpable compact' – (quoting Delaney) 'we cannot get the disestablishment without him and he cannot get into power without us'.[22] Trelawney used this account of his interview with Bishop Delaney to introduce another recurring theme – that the churchmen were simply using Gladstone as part of a subtle master plan to disrupt the union between Ireland and Britain. The bishop supposedly asserted: 'We all know perfectly well that Gladstone is "desperate" for power: we know his impulsiveness and his ambition, we could not have a better instrument.'[23] Trelawney returned to this subject a few days later, in an obvious attempt to reassure his employers of his loyalty and motivation despite his lack of progress. His task required patience: 'live Deans are not ready to one's hand like Bishops and Knights on a chess table. I only wish they were – for I am a good chessplayer, and could then read the game that is being so astutely played by the great power we know of.'[24] Trelawney reminded his readers that, though a convert to catholicism, he was also an Englishman who, 'fervently desire[d] the integrity of my [government] to be maintained'. 'Knowing the power and craft of Rome, and that the inevitable results of their operation here must be a *separation of Ireland from Great Britain* . . . I side, *politically*, against . . . the worldly schemes of . . . my church.'[25]

Trelawney moved next to Limerick where he had arranged his private dinner with Dean O'Brien. In his report on the meeting, the spy credited his 'long habit of looking for people's weak places' for enabling him to identify and capitalise upon O'Brien's flaw, his vanity. Flattery evidently prompted O'Brien to divulge more details about the compact between Gladstone and the Roman catholic hierarchy. By Trelawney's account, O'Brien asserted that, 'Gladstone *did actually promise* that *certain important concessions* besides the entire disestablishment [should] positively be made to the Irish Catholics'. However, the details of this secret agreement remained obscure because (quoting O'Brien): '[William] Monsell [Liberal MP for Limerick] was allowed to tell me this, but we and the few who know the actual nature of those concessions, have *promised on no account* to mention what they are, and I only tell you so much as this because I see how earnest and how fair your views about Ireland are.'[26] Trelawney not only uncovered the conspiracy he was sent to find, but managed to do so in a way that highlighted his talents as a spy, suggested the possibility of further, more substantive, information, and, most

[21] Bodl., HD 127/3, ff. 72–6: Trelawney to Feilding, 12 Oct. 1868.

[22] Bodl., HD 127/3, ff. 78–80: Trelawney to Feilding, 17 Oct. 1868.

[23] Bodl., HD 127/3, ff. 78–80: Trelawney to Feilding, 17 Oct. 1868.

[24] Bodl., HD 127/3, ff. 87–92: Trelawney to Feilding, 22 Oct. 1868.

[25] Bodl., HD 127/3, ff. 87–92: Trelawney to Feilding, 22 Oct. 1868. For all quotations, emphasis in original.

[26] Bodl., HD 127/3, ff. 99–106: Trelawney to Feilding, 26 Oct. 1868.

importantly, ensured this revelation could never be used publicly. O'Brien did not admit that an agreement existed; only that Monsell had told him so.

Not surprisingly, Trelawney's subsequent discussion with Monsell in Dublin failed to confirm Gladstone's promises. The spy found the MP for Limerick too 'shrewd, cautious and energetic' to reveal any information under questioning. Nevertheless, Trelawney did meet a number of French priests at Monsell's table, one of whom so assiduously avoided political discussions that the spy suspected him of being an emissary sent from Rome to report on the progress of the scheme. Trelawney ended this letter by recapping his main themes:

> *En resume*, it may be accepted as absolutely certain that *there is* a confidential understanding – not the less definite because it is secret – between Gladstone and the Catholic leaders; and I must add it is equally sure that this impulsive statesman will find himself a mere tool in their hands to effect measures which will ultimately endanger in a manner and degree which I need not enter into the union of Great Britain and Ireland.[27]

Trelawney's final stop in Ireland was Dublin where he secured an invitation to meet Cardinal Paul Cullen, the head of the Irish catholic hierarchy. Although Trelawney seemed inappropriately impressed with the cardinal (whom he considered 'suave and affable beyond measure'), the spy's report had Cullen proclaiming that his 'sympathy with the liberals only went as far as the measures of Justice to Ireland to which they are pledged: and . . . *we will take care that they redeem their pledges!*'.[28]

The report on Cardinal Cullen apparently convinced Feilding that despite Trelawney's 'unusual tact and ability', 'I do not think that he will succeed in obtaining *proof* (written) of the contract made between the ultramontane and the Liberal parties'. Nevertheless, the colonel allowed Trelawney to visit Liverpool 'to discover from the Priesthood there, whether there be any agreement made between them and Mr. Gladstone personally'. Perhaps realizing that this represented the last chance to prolong his mission, Trelawney claimed to discover from his host, the archbishop's assistant, Dr Fisher, that 'apropos of a letter from Rome from which [Fisher] read me an extract and *which contained a lithographed slip of paper in Latin which he said he could not possibly allow any layman to read,* though I tried very hard to get a peep at it', English and Irish catholics were working in lockstep in the election campaign according to 'a definite plan' sent from the Vatican.[29] While the publication of papal instructions concerning the election might indeed have inflamed anti-catholic sentiments, Trelawney must have recognized that the existence of correspondence from Rome to an archbishop hardly comprised proof of a conspiracy. The end of his Irish mission in sight, Trelawney made one more bid to remain on the payroll, proposing that he work behind the scenes for a Conservative Party victory in the

---

[27] Bodl., HD 127/3, ff. 111–3: Trelawney to Feilding, 28 Oct. 1868.

[28] Bodl., HD 127/3, ff. 123–6: Trelawney to Feilding 2 Nov. 1868. In his cover letter to Disraeli, Feilding worried that Trelawney 'has been influenced by his contact with the RC priests'. Bodl., HD 127/3, ff. 107–8: Feilding to Disraeli, 31 Oct. 1868.

[29] Bodl., HD 127/3, ff. 127–8: Trelawney to Feilding, 9 Nov. 1868.

Lancashire election contests. Feilding rejected this offer, thanked the spy for his efforts, and paid the remainder of his expenses (£90) out of the home office secret service funds Disraeli had forwarded.[30]

Trelawney's distortions and fabrications seem painfully obvious. His assertion that the Irish bishops preferred the Conservatives was presumably aimed at edifying Disraeli, who had tried to convince Irish catholics that the tories were their natural allies. Other sources indicate, however, that other than Moriarty, few bishops favoured Conservatives. Indeed, despite Disraeli's overtures on the issue of an Irish catholic university and fears of radical designs against denominational education, most catholics still complained that the tory administration in Dublin Castle had a decidedly 'Orange' tint.[31] The notion that the Irish bishops were sufficiently united or obedient enough to quietly and efficiently carry out a secret papal plot would probably have struck Cardinal Cullen as a cruel joke. He had failed to rally wide support for the moderate constitutionalist political organisation, the National Association, and some bishops actively resisted his insistence that Irish disestablishment must not be accompanied by state endowment of the Irish catholic church. Indeed, disestablishment seemed to be the sole issue that could unite the Irish hierarchy.[32] Hence, Gladstone hardly needed prompting from Rome to recognize the importance of this grievance to the Irish, or to recognize the political support the measure would elicit from English nonconformists. Gladstone had also made it clear that disestablishment was simply his first Irish reform. He had already announced his intentions to offer a land bill and an education bill, effectively replicating the programme advanced by the Cullen's National Association. Given that Gladstone's and Cullen's stated goals corresponded to the public platform offered by the other, why would either man have any need for a secret agreement?[33]

Trelawney's assertion that disestablishment was only the first step in a papal plot to eventually separate Ireland from the Union, while not demonstrably false, seems ridiculously far-fetched, even in the age of the 'Da Vinci Code'. In essence, the spy attributed clerical support of Irish religious, land, and educational reforms, and of constitutional nationalism more generally, to a papal conspiracy. Leaving aside the Vatican's opposition to liberal and nationalist movements throughout Europe, not even the revelations in Trelawney's reports support the existence of this scheme beyond the supposed tendency

---

[30] Bodl., HD 127/3, ff. 135–6: Feilding to Disraeli, 15 Nov. 1868. Feilding thought that Trelawney had taken some liberties with his expenses, but thought 'it best not to haggle about £3 or 4 when so useful a man is to be settled with'. Although the use of secret service funds might sound unethical to modern readers, in general, both parties treated this money as belonging to the administration and party rather than to the state. Both Liberals and Conservatives used Irish secret service money to cover party election expenses in Ireland. K. Theodore Hoppen, *Elections, Politics and Society in Ireland, 1832–1885* (Oxford, 1984), 301. Eunan O'Halpin, 'The Secret Service Vote and Ireland 1868–1922', *Irish Historical Studies*, xxiii (1983), 92.

[31] Mayo, the chief secretary, offered scant patronage to Irish catholic job-seekers, and the prime minister, the earl of Derby, made his anti-catholic sentiments abundantly clear during a Lords debate on the Catholic Oaths Bill in 1865, when he characterised the church as 'a most vicious animal, and nothing prevents him pulling you and me to pieces except the muzzle which is put around his nose'. Hoppen, *Elections*, 303–4, 315n; Emmett Larkin, *The Consolidation of the Roman Catholic Church in Ireland, 1860–70* (Chapel Hill, 1987), 586; R.V. Comerford, *Fenians in Context* (Dublin, 1985), 150–1; Oliver Rafferty, *The Church, the State, and the Fenian Threat 1861–75* (1999), 108–11.

[32] Hoppen, *Elections*, esp. 186–95.

[33] Larkin, *Roman Catholic Church*, 340–93, 590. Also see articles cited in n. 18 above; Bell, *Disestablishment*, 77–84.

of the bishops to dismiss Gladstone as a dupe. Of course, evidence of any plot this grand and subtle would be very difficult to find. The search for proof might keep a diligent spy employed for years.[34]

Despite Trelawney's dubious revelations and his obvious attempt to secure longer-term employment, neither Feilding nor Disraeli seemed to doubt their spy's integrity or ability. Even when the investigation seemed stalled and Trelawney felt it necessary to reassure his employers, Feilding wrote immediately to reaffirm his trust in the agent.[35] At the conclusion of the mission, Feilding 'complimented [Trelawney] on the tact and ability he has displayed', and pleaded with Disraeli to find a permanent position for the spy. Feilding thought Trelawney's 'zeal and tact' and talent for languages would make him a good vice-consular officer or private secretary. Placing the spy in such a position offered the added benefit that it 'would enable you to lay your hand on him for any special mission, at any time'.[36]

Although he did not find a position for Trelawney and discouraged the spy from taking a position under the incoming Liberal administration, Disraeli also expressed his good opinion. The prime minister wrote to Feilding: 'Tell our friend that I am well pleased with his labours, [and] that I think his views were perfectly well-founded. When he returns to England, I shall be happy at a convenient time to make his acquaintance.'[37]

Disraeli's apparent gullibility probably stemmed both from his fascination with intrigue and from his lack of experience in actually uncovering its existence. Great Britain had no institutionalised intelligence bureau outside of Dublin Castle, and though confidential information reached the foreign office through its consular officers and the home office from the few constabulary forces that had effective detective police, most ministers had little expertise in dealing with intelligence or with the mechanics of espionage. 'Secret messages, code names and all the paraphernalia of melodrama ever appealed to the author of Vivian Grey',[38] and he received rumours and information from a number of personal correspondents, but Disraeli had no familiarity with professional spies and seemed to lack the healthy scepticism necessary in handling them.[39]

Disraeli had hoped to remedy the government's (and his own) shortcomings in intelligence by helping to establish a secret service department in London in late 1867. Fenian outrages in England convinced the cabinet of the necessity of such a force, but Disraeli championed the new department as means of protecting the country from the danger of European secret societies. The tory leader perceived a grander and more dangerous conspiracy behind the relatively unthreatening and inconsequential Irish-American plotters – a view shared by the head of the secret service department, Colonel

---

[34] Trelawney's ongoing effort to obtain continuing employment illustrates how difficult it was for a young man without money to sustain his claim to be a gentleman. Later in his relationship with Disraeli, Trelawney unctuously explains that he would not consider taking a position from anyone other than Disraeli: 'I am well content to await the time when, if it is your pleasure, you can give me such advantage of your patronage as you may think I deserve. Mine is not only a party spirit but also a personal devotion and it surely need be no effort to you to believe in such a feeling and in my profession of it.' Bodl., HD 145/2, ff. 81–2: Trelawney to Disraeli, 8 June 1869.

[35] Bodl., HD 127/3, ff. 87–8: Feilding to Disraeli, 23 Oct. 1868.

[36] Bodl., HD 127/3, ff. 135–6: Feilding to Disraeli, 15 Nov. 1868.

[37] Warwick RO, Feilding Papers, CR2017/W2: Disraeli to Feilding, 20 Nov. 1868.

[38] Blake, Disraeli, 364.

[39] Bernard Porter, Plots and Paranoia: A History of Political Espionage in Britain 1790–1988 (1989), 65–100.

Feilding.[40] Trelawney's frequent asides about correct methods of espionage and his hints about the hidden forces that lurked behind public figures suggest that he recognized and tried to gratify his employers' beliefs and interests.

In January 1869, two months after the election, Disraeli granted Trelawney a private audience, which marked a new phase in a relationship that lasted for nearly two more years. Given the absence of any further letters from the Conservative leader, it is more difficult to use Trelawney's ongoing correspondence as a gauge of Disraeli's continued credulity. However, Trelawney's letters indicate that the two men met privately a number of times and that he carried out one, and possibly more, secret assignments on Disraeli's behalf. In early 1869, the spy reported from London on Gladstone's legislative plans, apparently based on interviews with a 'Lady L' and Irish Liberal MP, William Monsell. Trelawney then left for Paris and sent back a précis of his conversation with the prefect of police about secret societies.[41] The spy regularly wrote to pass on (apparently un-solicited) intelligence and to offer his services for various proposals, but the difficulty of funding the missions while the Conservatives were out of government seemed to rule out any sustained employment.[42] The relationship ended in September 1870, when Trelawney wrote to beg Disraeli for £100 to help cover legal expenses. Trelawney had been arrested for indecently soliciting a young boy and was too deeply in debt to pay his counsel. A magistrate later threw out the charges, but because Disraeli never replied, Trelawney painfully concluded, 'I have lost the favour of your personal recognition.'[43] The awkwardness of the incident perhaps reminded the tory leader of his father's warning, given nearly 40 years before: 'Beware, my dear, of secret agents.'[44]

Although he seemed finally to have soured on Trelawney, Disraeli's 1870 novel *Lothair* gave fictional life and breath to the conspiracies the spy had been hired to uncover. In the story, Lothair, a wealthy young English nobleman, becomes entangled in the 'mighty struggle' between the secret societies and the Roman catholic church, 'the only two strong things in Europe'.[45] The secret societies aim to bring, 'the civil governments of the world, and mostly the governments who disbelieve in their existence, to the brink of a precipice, over which monarchies, and law, and civil order, will ultimately fall and perish together'. The church is portrayed as unscrupulous and tyrannical, with the influential Cardinal Grandison, and the 'inexhaustible intriguer', Monsignore Berwick using 'Roman audacity and stratagem' to thwart the secret societies and undermine English protestantism.[46] Through a series of implausible plot twists involving a saintly female

---

[40] Bodl., HD 90/3, ff. 22–3: Mayo to Disraeli, 12, 18 Aug. 1868; Padraic Kennedy 'The Secret Service Department: A British Intelligence Bureau in Mid-Victorian London, Sept. 1867 to April 1868', *Intelligence and National Security,* xviii (2003), 100–27.

[41] Bodl., HD 145/2, ff. 59–62: Trelawney to Disraeli, 30, 31 Jan. 1869. Based on a reference to 'Lady L's' son, Lewis Strange, she might have been Lady Powerscourt, the wife of the Irish Viscount Powerscourt.

[42] On one occasion, Feilding, again acting as liaison, mentioned the funding difficulty in a letter to Disraeli. Bodl., HD 127/3, ff. 26–7: Feilding to Disraeli, 4 May 1869. Trelawney's letters to Disraeli are preserved in Bodl., HD 145/2, ff. 49–124.

[43] Bodl., HD 145/2, ff. 119–20: Trelawney to Disraeli, 17 Oct. 1870. Trelawney drops from view after his correspondence with Disraeli ends, although I have not made a thorough search of foreign office or home office registers after 1869 to see whether he continued to offer his services to others.

[44] Monypenny and Buckle, *Disraeli,* i, 210.

[45] Benjamin Disraeli, *Lothair* (1870), 218, 211.

[46] Disraeli, *Lothair,* 347, 211, 243.

revolutionary, Lothair finds himself fighting for the secret societies in Italy. After he is wounded and captured by papal forces, he narrowly escapes an insidious – and even more ridiculous – plot to convert him to Roman catholicism. In the novel's happy ending, he remains true to his protestant faith and country. At least in fiction, Disraeli triumphed over the forces of darkness.[47]

No-one familiar with Disraeli's political reputation would be surprised to discover that he had indulged in a dubious scheme in the hopes of boosting his party's chances in the 1868 election. Nor would readers of his novels be surprised that he believed conspiracies and intrigues were the secret means of personal and political success. However, it is worth considering what impact his conspiratorial view of politics had on his policies. We might dismiss Trelawney as a charlatan, and his conspiracy theories as a mixture of paranoia and place-hunting; yet, Disraeli seemed to trust both the man and his reports. In this light, the Conservatives' failure to offer a compromise or counter-measure to negate the popular appeal of Irish disestablishment reflected Disraeli's conviction that malevolent forces, rather than a shrewd calculation of public sentiment, were behind Gladstone's motion. A belief in conspiracies might offer a reassuring means of explaining away political disappointment, but it could not produce electoral success. More significantly, if Disraeli believed Trelawney's assertion that dismantling the Irish church was only the first of a series of demands ultimately intended to disrupt the Union, then he might see land reform, educational reform, and even home rule as extensions of the same Roman scheme. Alternatively, we have seen that Disraeli believed continental revolutionaries had conjured up Fenianism for their own sinister ends, offering another conspiratorial explanation for any demands for Irish reform or political autonomy. If Irish troubles did not derive from indigenous concerns, but were stirred up by sinister foreign powers, then palliative measures such as those proposed by Gladstone would have little positive effect. Might Disraeli's belief in powerful conspiracies help explain why his Irish policies after 1868 featured so few initiatives to address Irish grievances?[48]

At the very least, the fact that Disraeli took Trelawney's reports so seriously suggests how willing he was to ignore or deny the growing strength of Irish nationalism and its influence on Irish parliamentary politics in 1868. Gladstone had identified and proposed redress for Irish grievances, harnessing, briefly, Irish nationalists to the Liberal team. By indulging in conspiracy theories that precluded a clear grasp of the situation in Ireland, Disraeli only complicated efforts to oppose Gladstone's policies or to devise constructive measures of his own.

---

[47] In more ways than one, given his profits from book sales. Blake, *Disraeli,* 519–20.
[48] See Warren, 'Disraeli, Conservatives and Ireland, Part II', 151–67.

A Usable Past: History and the Politics of National Identity in Late Victorian England

RICHARD A. COSGROVE

For the past two decades, issues of English national identity have provided a fertile field for historical investigation. In the late Victorian era, the development of professional standards of scholarship within the academy gave a new dimension to historical debates. The bitter quarrels about appropriate research techniques from the 1860s to the 1890s, among James Anthony Froude, Edward Freeman and John Horace Round, acted as a proxy for the vision of national identity that each historian espoused. After 1870, the development of a national narrative focused on constitutional history as its primary vehicle. The battle over historical reconstruction represented a surrogate for divergent views about political values and national identity. What sometimes seemed frivolous scholarly skirmishes, therefore, had a much greater political importance. As a result, the long feud had greater importance than the eccentric personalities of the participants appeared to indicate. For Froude, the Tudor age of discovery and religious reformation represented the best of English character. For Freeman, a strong Gladstonian Liberal, consensus and continuity over many centuries defined English history best. John Horace Round, a Conservative stalwart, thought that Freeman had slanted his historical conclusions to validate his Liberal politics and reinterpreted the Norman conquest to express his own political beliefs. Thus the quibbles about shield walls and other issues provided a terrain for the real cause of antagonism: different views of national identity that history furnished. Each historian constructed a usable past in order to justify contemporary discussions of national identity.

Keywords: J.A. Froude; E.A. Freeman; J.H. Round; national identity; constitutional history; professional history; Norman conquest; Anglo-Saxonism; archival history

That scholars and politicians have used and misused national history for political advantage comes as no surprise, for every society manipulates its past for a variety of purposes. In Victorian England, especially after 1870, the period when academic historians adopted professional standards, the development of a national narrative focused on constitutional history as its primary vehicle. The triumph of the whig interpretation of history, however defined, supplied a political agenda all of its own by emphasizing such consensus values as continuity and progress in retelling the national story.[1] A number of specific events illuminated the manner by which history acted as a political instrument. In 1967, for example, Olive Anderson explained how the Crimean War was turned into a critique of aristocratic privilege and a plea for the endorsement of middle class values

---

[1] Richard A. Cosgrove, 'Reflections on the Whig Interpretation of History', *Journal of Early Modern History*, iv (2000), 147–67.

that stressed merit, not birth.[2] Another example emerged from the discussion of early Anglo-Saxon village communities and the alleged existence of communal property. Arcane debate about 17th-century social structure became a surrogate for late Victorian arguments about whether private property or property held in common represented a natural state, with its implications for the contemporary debate about the merits of capitalism and socialism.[3] Such instances provided concrete examples of how the ostensible examination of the past disguised political debate.

For the past two decades, within the British Studies community the issue of national identity has turned into a growth industry. National identity has also become a political issue as well, incorporating such topics as the potential dissolution of the United Kingdom to who qualifies as British nationals for compensation as a result of incarceration by the Japanese during the Second World War. Many subjects, from sport to imperial sentiment, expressed identity and have required changing approaches to the past. Recent attempts to fashion a national narrative have reflected more sophisticated attempts to interpret the past in cultural terms.[4] Writing the history of England provided one opportunity to offer beliefs about the present and future as well as an often idealised past. In the late Victorian period the appearance of new criteria for interpretation and emphasis on archival research presented the chance to restate the English past, especially the skill of the English people in self-government demonstrated by its unbroken constitutional evolution.[5] Pride in traditions of liberty and governance as quintessential aspects of national identity made historical research an excellent medium to explain how the past reflected different elements of national identity.

Perhaps the most famous instance of this type of argument came in the triangular feud that pitted James Anthony Froude against Edward Freeman and then Freeman against John Horace Round, and lasted from the 1850s until the 1890s. Long familiar to scholars for the length and bitterness of these personal vendettas, the relationships among these pillars of Victorian scholarship rested on the differing visions of national identity that each possessed. Explanations of this interminable drama have usually fixed on either evolving scholarly criticism or personal hatreds. Upon further review, however, while not discounting the previous emphases, these three scholars used the polemics they launched against each other to advance political causes that had little to do with their quarrels about the past. In the end the three historians, whatever similarities or dissimilarities they shared, turned their work into depictions of national identity. Whether concerned with the Norman conquest or the Tudors, critiques of historical detail masked underlying differences about perceptions of the national past and future. As the standards for

[2] Olive Anderson, 'The Political Uses of History in Mid-Nineteenth-Century England', *Past and Present*, No. 36 (1967), 87–105.

[3] John W. Burrow, '"The Village Community" and the Uses of History in Late Nineteenth-Century England', in *Historical Perspectives: Studies in English Thought and Society in Honour of J. H. Plumb*, ed. Neil McKendrick (1974), 255–84, esp. 268–9, where Burrow pointed out how other historians, such as Edward Freeman, appropriated the issue for political designs. For a broader perspective, see Paul Readman, 'The Place of the Past in English Culture c. 1890–1914', *Past and Present*, No. 186 (2005), 147–99.

[4] For a review of the national identity issue in its many manifestations and complexities, see Krishan Kumar, *The Making of English National Identity* (Cambridge, 2003).

[5] Reba N. Soffer, *Discipline and Power: The University, History, and the Making of an English Elite, 1870–1930* (Stanford, 1994).

historical scholarship altered, this circumstance created the perfect context to camouflage political arguments within the new criteria for accuracy.

James Anthony Froude (1818–94) had first attracted public notice by his participation in the theological controversies that convulsed Oxford in the 1840s. At first sympathetic to the theology of John Henry Newman, Froude ultimately could not follow his friend on the road back to Rome. He took deacon's orders in 1845 but soon recognized that he possessed no clerical vocation. In 1849, Froude's religious ambiguities were expressed in *The Nemesis of Faith*, in part an account of his own theological wanderings and in part a protest against religious conformity. The book caused a scandal in Oxford, whereupon Froude resigned the fellowship that he had held since 1842. Without private means he turned to historical writing in the 1850s to support his family. Froude chose the English reformation as his preferred area, in part because the liberation from Rome expressed his admiration for the original protestantism that had eroded by the 19th century. This commitment resulted in his epic work on the heart of the Tudor century, the 12 volumes that covered from 1529 to 1588.[6] Not only did the Tudor period suit his religious preferences, it conveyed a sense of English achievement needing explanation because he believed 'that the English educational system failed to inculcate any sense of national identity in its students'.[7] Froude placed the core of English greatness in religious temperament, not constitutional accomplishment: 'It was not only that he took no interest in constitutional questions, there was positive distaste.'[8] Froude wrote his history for an educated public which appreciated sound judgment and literary flair.

As is the case with most great Victorian historians, Froude is now more consulted than read thoroughly. The *History*, however, retains a majesty that superseded the errors of fact and interpretation that otherwise mar the narrative. Critics such as Freeman pounced upon these faults during the 1860s and 1870s in the name of the professional history now synonymous with the nascent academic discipline. Freeman's criticism of Froude broke new ground in its virulence, for Freeman found in the 16th century as described by Froude a repugnant theory of politics and ultimately an embrace of national identity he rejected.

With respect to issues of methodology, even Froude's most fervent admirers conceded that numerous problems plagued his work, for 'Froude proved an exceptionally careless copyist who compounded his errors by failing to make clear where he substituted paraphrases within quotations or excerpted without ellipsis marks.'[9] The issue of research habits turned, in the judgment of Freeman, into a consistent pattern of scholarly misdeeds that had no excuse. Individual mistakes by scholars of the highest reputation occurred all the time, but Froude was charged with persistent misconduct to the point where other historians thought him 'constitutionally inaccurate'.[10] To his contemporary, Goldwin Smith, Froude's aim 'is and always has been sensation. He is simply the most

[6] James A. Froude, *History of England from the Fall of Wolsey to the Defeat of the Spanish Armada* (12 vols, 1856–70).

[7] Jeffrey Von Arx, *Progress and Pessimism: Religion, Politics, and History in Late Nineteenth Century Britain* (Cambridge, MA, 1985), 193.

[8] John W. Burrow, *A Liberal Descent: Victorian Historians and the English Past* (Cambridge, 1981), 237.

[9] Rosemary Jann, *The Art and Science of Victorian History* (Columbus, 1985), 135.

[10] Herbert A.L. Fisher, 'Modern Historians and Their Methods', *Fortnightly Review*, lxii (1894), 804.

unveracious writer who ever profaned the calling of a historian.'[11] Scholarly sins alone, however, did not account for the torrent of abuse with which Froude had to cope. Foremost among those who scorned Froude's work was Edward Freeman (1823–92), who proved the most relentless of adversaries. The bitter rivalry between these two intellectuals began in 1864 when Freeman, anonymously, launched a series of critical articles in the *Saturday Review* that called Froude's scholarly integrity into question. One part of the animosity stemmed from Freeman's antipathy toward Froude's religious unorthodoxy. Freeman reflected the attitude of his friend and historian, William Stubbs, who doubted whether it was possible for a dissenter to write the history of England;[12] only a steadfast anglican could undertake that task. The robust protestantism of the English reformation that sundered the church from Rome, as championed by Froude, offended Freeman's faith in a moral unity that defined the history of christianity.

In addition, Freeman asserted famously that history was past politics and the unity of history made the politics of one era equivalent to those of another. As a result, Freeman emphasized an institutional continuity that encompassed the centuries from the Anglo-Saxons to modernity. Wedded absolutely to the Germanic origins of English society as the salient foundation of all English history, Freeman regarded Froude's emphasis on the 16th century as a tear in the seamless fabric of continuity that was at the heart of English history. No single epoch could stand out, as Froude suggested, for this would destroy the neat pattern of historical development that Freeman professed to find in English history.

Finally, no doubt Freeman envied Froude's financial achievement as well: 'Freeman resented the overwhelming popular success of a writer who ignored what he considered professional standards.'[13] Freeman determined to have his accomplishments both ways; he desired the monetary rewards available to amateur historians, yet he thought of himself as in the front line of adopting professional criteria for historical research.[14] He struggled to keep his audience in focus: the general reading public or the new academic historians at the ancient universities. The sales of his books paled in comparison to those of Froude, and to those of his friend and erstwhile protégé, John Richard Green, despite the fervid passages in which Freeman specialised and the set pieces (such as battle scenes) in which he took great pride. He once complained that:

> one thing which puzzles me is the seeming belief that Froude can tell a story and that I can't. I believe that I can tell a story much better. Could he have done my battle stories in Vol. III [of the *Norman Conquest*]? Besides that he would fight Senlac on a plain in Northumberland on a Monday in April, & set the English on horseback & armed the Normans with axes.[15]

Freeman indulged in much hatred, including an unpleasant racism and a complete disdain for the French and their accomplishments, and Froude had the misfortune to join

[11] Cornell University, Carl A. Kroch Library, Goldwin Smith MSS: Goldwin Smith to James Bryce, 5 June 1874.
[12] Bodl., William Stubbs MSS, MS.Eng.Misc.e.148: William Stubbs to Edward Freeman, 3 Nov. 1859.
[13] Jann, *Art and Science of Victorian History*, 136.
[14] Leslie Howsam, 'Academic Discipline or Literary Genre? The Establishment of Boundaries in Historical Writing', *Victorian Literature and Culture*, xxxii (2004), 535.
[15] Bodl., James Bryce MS 7: Freeman to James Bryce, 10 Apr. 1881.

this list. These attitudes contributed to the quarrel, but in the end the two men portrayed the past in ways that taught different political lessons.

Froude had taken the 16th century and made it a symbol of England on the brink of modernity and establishing a heritage of liberty in deliverance from Rome. The Tudor era also witnessed the embrace of a seafaring tradition that helped inaugurate an imperial destiny. Froude, who had entertained radical religious ideas as a youth, was nonetheless an individual of otherwise conservative instincts. The liberation from the papacy transformed England by unleashing hitherto suppressed energies; the 16th century, therefore, accounted for the modern version of national identity. The medieval period was consigned by Froude to the distant past, not joined to the present as asserted by Freeman. He demanded similarities with the past, whereas Froude emphasized their differences. The new clericalism of the 19th century, of which Froude had personal experience, threatened the English future much as the medieval clergy had done prior to 1529. Froude wished to conserve the spirit of the Tudor epoch but he expressed considerable doubt whether this outcome would prevail. Pessimism about the future led Froude to embrace a conservative temper that Freeman abhorred.

For nearly two decades, Freeman stalked Froude with critical reviews intended to crush the latter's reputation. From the work of Thomas Arnold he had drawn a philosophy of history that stressed its moral unity. Englishmen of the ninth century were the same as those in the 19th century. The national narrative, therefore, must emphasize the continuous record of moral progress and constitutional achievement. Freeman's version of the whig interpretation featured cultural identity within a racial framework based on Germanic origins.[16] His views on race led him to an unseemly denigration of Africans and an anti-semitism marked by his visceral hatred of Benjamin Disraeli, usually referred to as 'the dirty Jew'.[17] Such comparisons across temporal boundaries provided Freeman 'the means of ordering the new knowledge about the antiquity of man into a coherent pattern of development, while retaining belief in cultural and racial hierarchy'.[18] Freeman translated this synthesis into strong support for Liberal politics.

For Freeman, English history originated in the remote forests of ancient Germany where free villagers formed self-governing communities and became the progenitors of subsequent free institutions. The proto-democratic life of Anglo-Saxon England anticipated the generation of liberal attitudes. Convinced that the Liberal Party represented the embodiment of original Anglo-Saxon virtues and the engine for continued political progress, Freeman could not tolerate the privileged status accorded to the 16th century by Froude. At stake here were alternative conceptions of national identity that lurked beneath the surface of domestic and imperial fortunes in the latter half of the 19th century. Applause for the Tudor era made no sense to Freeman, for it represented a century when the constitution veered toward royal authoritarianism rather than liberal individualism. Froude admired the strong leadership of Henry VIII even when oppression resulted; Tudor despotism violated Freeman's faith in steady liberal improvement since

[16] Hugh A. MacDougall, *Racial Myth in English History: Trojans, Teutons, and Anglo-Saxons* (Hanover, 1982), 100–1.

[17] John Rylands University Library Manchester, Edward Freeman MS: Freeman to John Richard Green, 27 June 1875.

[18] Doris Goldstein, 'Confronting Time: The Oxford School of History and the Non-Darwinian Revolution', *Storia della Storiografia*, xlv (2004), 15.

the seventh century. Were ordinary English individuals capable of controlling personal destiny or had they relied on royal direction? When Freeman began his campaign against Froude, the stakes about national identity were high.

Freeman charged Froude with an indifference to the standards of the professional history that appeared in the 1860s, especially the emphasis upon investigation of archival sources. On this issue, Freeman, for all his rhetoric in support of this ideal, was on the wrong side. Froude had examined manuscripts in many archives at home and abroad in preparation for his work; in contrast, Freeman utilised only his private library of printed materials. He never made use of archives, had little knowledge of paleography, and rarely visited research libraries: 'I tremble at the notion of going to the Vatican library, I, who never in my life had any dealings with any library at all, save very slight once with our Bodleian.'[19] When Freeman ultimately faced retribution for his work methods, he had little argument with which to protect his own reputation.

In what would prove a damaging model to the popularity of academic history, Freeman employed the unfortunate tactic of focusing not on Froude's overall interpretation of the English story in the 16th century (where Freeman lacked expertise). Instead he cited minor factual errors that Freeman blew all out of proportion to their seriousness in order to destroy Froude's credibility. When James Bryce made this point to him, Freeman replied: 'So you think that I was hard on Froude. Most men say I let him off too easily.'[20] Freeman's penchant for nitpicking became so notorious that he felt compelled to deny the practice: 'But I don't think that *in my writings published with my name* I am open to the charge of constantly challenging on small points etc.'[21] In Freeman's mind, anonymity condoned such criticisms and legitimised the ferocious critique of Froude on petty matters.

When at last Froude responded to Freeman in 1879, in a dignified and remarkably reasonable tone given Freeman's many provocations, he accused his antagonist of personal vindictiveness as the source of the long vendetta. Froude certainly seemed on safe ground, although Freeman replied rather disingenuously that 'such a feeling, in any strictly personal sense, is impossible on my part'.[22] Freeman stressed that Froude's unfairness to catholicism spurred his antipathy, although this line of criticism had never figured prominently in his attacks. In the end, for the general public at least, Freeman's campaign to discredit Froude by quibbling about minor matters, did not harm the Tudor historian, because literary skills more than compensated for occasional errors. In response to charges that Freeman had misled his audience about the nature and extent of Froude's defects, Freeman wrote defensively: 'One does feel a sense of injustice when one is treated in this way; I am conscious that I have never *misrepresented* Froude.'[23] Freeman apparently never understood the irony of this situation.

---

[19] Bodl., Bryce MS 7: Freeman to Bryce, 27 Mar. 1881; see also Freeman's recollection: 'I have never tried the British Museum, I never use Bodleian oftener than I can help . . . I must have my materials in my house or other place that acts as such for the time: a room in an inn or a friend's house will do.' Quoted in John P. Kenyon, *The History Men: The Historical Profession in England since the Renaissance* (1983), 154–5.

[20] Bodl., Bryce MS 5: Freeman to Bryce, 6 Mar. 1870.

[21] Bodl., Bryce MS 6: Freeman to Bryce, 20 Apr. 1873.

[22] Edward Freeman, 'Last Words on Mr. Froude', *Contemporary Review*, xxxv (1879), 217.

[23] Bodl., Bryce MS 7: Freeman to Bryce, 23 Dec. 1883.

Freeman's attempt to offer an alternative view of national identity through an epic history came in his *History of the Norman Conquest*, ostensibly a political narrative but in many places a plea for his perception of the Victorian nation. A Gladstonian to the core, and obsessed with a belief in the Germanic nature of English identity, Freeman used this as a proxy for contemporary political debate. The *Norman Conquest*, like Froude's *History*, is now sampled more than read in its entirety; its organisation, judgments, and style strike the modern reader as well over the top. The interpretations are frequently uncritical and injudicious, the evidence is remorselessly detailed, and it is written in a prose that adored long, languid sentences. Despite its many flaws, however, the narrative possessed a dramatic rhythm that unfortunately led to an unceasing flow of information. Too many sections of the work came adorned in bright purple hues, a habit that frequently hid his insights in endless pages of numbing detail. Volume 1, for example, did not even reach 1066 before its close. Finally, in contradiction to his own stated goals of objectivity, Freeman made the work a polemic that expressed his political ideas.

At the heart of Freeman's liberalism lay a sense of national identity expressed best in the constitutional arrangements of Anglo-Saxon England and their resonance in the Victorian period. He conceded that this succession was not precise, but insisted that the historian could discover 'the germs alike of the monarchic, the aristocratic, and the democratic branches of our constitution'.[24] The putative democratic elements of the pre-1066 constitution existed primarily in the relationship between the witan and the king, whereby the witan elected the monarch and he could do little without the witan's express consent. This highly romantic interpretation of a democratic Anglo-Saxon polity in anticipation of the Victorian constitution made the political points Freeman desired. Founded on Freeman's faith in historical continuity, the governing genius of the national character survived still in the ideals of Gladstonian democracy.

No matter how fraught with error, Freeman's depiction of the Norman conquest played a role in reversing the conquest, making the Anglo-Saxons the model of national identity.[25] The Normans had indeed triumphed in 1066 but only temporarily; the Anglo-Saxon spirit of liberty survived and ultimately conquered the Normans.[26] The constitution of the English nation in the tenth century under Edgar the Peaceable (959–75) remained the same under the government of Duke William; as Freeman wrote: 'I cannot too often repeat, for the saying is the very summing up of the whole history, that the Norman conquest was not the wiping out of the constitution, the laws, the language, the national life of Englishmen.'[27] Even in defeat, the Anglo-Saxons had triumphed by incorporating their conquerors into their institutional life. The connection between Anglo-Saxon past and Norman present fulfilled the need for historical continuity.

Freeman, by his emphasis on linking racial solidarity to constitutional development, placed constitutional history at the centre of national identity issues. His success in uniting Anglo-Saxon superiority with constitutional destiny reassured his readers that the

---

[24] Edward Freeman, *The History of the Norman Conquest: Its Causes and Its Results* (5 vols, Oxford, 1867–79), i, 1.

[25] Clare A. Simmons, *Reversing the Conquest: History and Myth in Nineteenth-Century Literature* (New Brunswick, 1990).

[26] Peter J. Bowler, *The Invention of Progress: The Victorians and the Past* (Oxford, 1989), 61.

[27] Freeman, *History of the Norman Conquest*, i, 71.

future of England was secure, in spite of the unsettling challenges of the 1870s and 1880s: 'This was the importance of the Victorians' sense of belonging to an Anglo-Saxon race.'[28] By giving to the late Victorians an identity rooted in ninth-century liberty and institutions, Freeman fixed national identity firmly in constitutional history. Teutonic antecedents, particularly their survival after 1066, were crucial to who the English people had become.[29] In its Gladstonian guise, as portrayed by Freeman, the English constitution truly symbolised English national exceptionalism.

The greatest triumph for Freeman came in 1884, after the resignation of Stubbs as regius professor to pursue his episcopal career, when he succeeded his friend to the professorship at Oxford. Freeman, having vanquished Froude in the academic arena, now stood at the height of his reputation. Almost immediately, however, Freeman became a target for criticism in much the same manner that he had scrutinised Froude's scholarship. His nemesis was John Horace Round (1854–1928), ironically a student of Stubbs at Balliol during the 1870s. No sooner had Freeman accepted the academic honour than Round began to pursue Freeman systematically. Freeman first acknowledged Round's existence when he complained of the latter's criticism in 1885 'on the smallest point', the date of Colchester castle.[30]

For his part, Round is now remembered as much for his scholarly combativeness as for his undoubted contributions to medieval English historiography. Lord Annan, for example, wrote of the 'horrible Horace Round, who in controversy had the manners of a ferret'.[31] His reputation for ferocity repelled most other scholars and not until 2001 did a comprehensive biography appear.[32] Round never held an academic appointment, but he did embrace the evolving standards of historical research with a vengeance, holding others to account with a tenacity that frightened many other scholars. From Stubbs he had acquired a passion for the discovery of sources, and much of his early work was aimed at teasing out the implications of his mentor's scholarship. Round soon found bigger game to hunt in Freeman, the new regius professor.

Round maintained that he simply wished to apply to Freeman the scholarly rigour that the latter had used in his campaign against Froude. Round employed his passion for accuracy and original documents to great advantage and he became the primary contributor to the erosion of Freeman's reputation. The tools that Round utilised included an eye for detail and a constant hunt for manuscripts; in 1896, for example, he wrote to H. Maxwell Lyte, deputy keeper at the Public Record Office: 'I am happy to say that I am on the track of a fine series of nearly 30 charters of a French Abbey.'[33] Round was happiest when in pursuit of archival materials unknown to other scholars. The search for such documents made a sharp contrast to Freeman, who rarely undertook such quests. Round called this spirit the 'modern ardour for discovery',[34] an

---

[28] Christopher J.W. Parker, 'The Failure of Racial Liberalism: The Racial Ideas of E. A. Freeman', *HJ*, xxiv (1981), 827.

[29] M. Edwin Brachtel, *Edward Augustus Freeman and the Victorian Interpretation of the Norman Conquest* (Ilfracombe, 1969), 15.

[30] Bodl., Bryce MSS, 7: Freeman to Bryce, 22 July 1885.

[31] Lord Annan, *The Dons: Mentors, Eccentrics and Geniuses* (Chicago, 1999), 91.

[32] W. Raymond Powell, *John Horace Round: Historian and Gentleman of Essex* (Chelmsford, 2001).

[33] TNA (PRO), H. Maxwell Lyte MSS, 1/158: John H. Round to H. Maxwell Lyte, 15 Apr. 1896.

[34] John H. Round, 'Historical Research', *The Nineteenth Century*, xliv (1898), 1007.

eagerness for archival exploration that dominated his work. So intense was the concentration on sources that most, but not all, of his publications consisted of short articles (no more than six pages) or research notes; as he once recorded: 'I am very glad that you like the critical study of records in my last book. It is, I think, its strongest point.'[35] The culture of archival discovery, and Round's place in promoting it, became so successful that Reginald Lane Poole, editor of the *English Historical Review*, wrote: 'I hope you realise that the articles are normally the least important things in the Review. They are mostly, or largely, derelicts abandoned by other periodicals. The really good feature is the section on Notes and Documents, and it is this feature I am endeavouring to extend.'[36] The emphasis on detail and context placed Round in a good position to criticize Freeman, who paid little attention to such accuracy in his own work.

Round possessed a unique gift for going after the scholarly jugular, a trait that endeared him to few. In the felicitous phrase of John Kenyon, Round was a 'destructive miniaturist'.[37] In his many articles and reviews, Round usually concentrated on a single point and subjected it to withering analysis. Round dissected the work of others (a mistaken date or the erroneous translation of a word or line) and exaggerated the significance to impugn the totality of the author's conclusions. His lack of perspective led him to take a single error and then harp on it to invalidate the findings of a lengthy work. In return Round never forgot a scholarly slight; he attacked opponents decades after they had possessed the temerity to criticize his own publications.

In his zeal for manuscript discovery, Round made himself a parody of archival research, for the documents became the end goal, not the means of advancing knowledge. His excursions into narrative exposition were relatively few. His attitude was well exemplified when Round declined the invitation of Lord Acton to contribute to the *Cambridge Medieval History* on the ground that the projected volume 'is somewhat alien from that of my minute researches'.[38] In the end, this concentration steered Round into a parochial view of the expanding nature of historical scholarship.

Round gloried in the style that he had perfected, for it afforded him the opportunity to sustain his career through periodic scholarly quarrels. The professional isolation he endured was self-inflicted, for other historians advised Round to moderate the tone of his criticisms; in 1894, Samuel Rawson Gardiner warned him about his 'unparliamentary' language in dealing with other scholars.[39] The best example of how Round grafted his analytic skills on to his refusal to abandon past disputes occurred in 1914, when he submitted a brief article to the *English Historical Review* that ostensibly corrected a statement by Stubbs. Reginald Lane Poole advised Round that the critique was valid but Round had also used the occasion to launch a bitter attack on Hubert Hall, then assistant keeper at the Public Record Office, for conclusions that had appeared nearly 20 years earlier. In 1897, Round had believed that he had made an unassailable case against Hall:

[35] Yale University, Sterling Library, George Burton Adams MSS, box 6, folder 30: Round to George Burton Adams, 3 Mar. 1900.

[36] John Rylands University Library Manchester, Thomas F. Tout MSS, 1/953/3: Reginald Lane Poole to Thomas F. Tout, Easter eve 1905.

[37] Kenyon, *The History Men*, 283.

[38] Cambridge University Library, Lord Acton MSS, Add. MS 6443: Round to Lord Acton, 23 Jan. 1897.

[39] London University Library, John Horace Round MS 663: Samuel Rawson Gardiner to Round, 5 Feb. 1894.

'Mr. Hall *has not rebutted a single one of the charges* of error that I brought against him in my paper.'[40] Poole explained: 'What I expected was an explanation of the manner in which Stubbs was misled into altering for the worse; but I did not expect an elaborate criticism of a forgotten book which Mr. Hall published.'[41] This thirst for scholarly vengeance was the more remarkable in this case because Hall and Round had once enjoyed a firm friendship.[42]

When Round targeted Freeman for comprehensive criticism, it was as if he recognized a mirror image of himself in prejudices and allegiance to partisan politics. Round shared Freeman's anti-semitism, with sentiments such as: 'I noted lately a fearful result of miscegenation observing in an illustrated paper a young Jew with strongly marked Hebraic features addressing the house, I looked to see if it were a Simon or a Samuel . . . It had the same effect on me as the Mongol-European half caste in Burma.'[43] Round, too, turned this bias into political capital. About the Marconi scandal in 1912–3, Round observed: 'Our friends the Jews seem to be on "Queer Street" at last. I wonder what you, ever quickest to scent scandal, would have said of this Isaacs Marconi business now being investigated or of this Samuel "Montagu" India Office deal – if they had been Conservatives.'[44] Even by the standards of the day, Round conflated racial and political prejudices to a notable degree. Conservative in politics and conservative in temperament, Round had no sympathy for Liberal nonsense.

Round, who had stood unsuccessfully for parliament in the Conservative interest, recognized that a national story stressing Liberal ideals of national identity should not go unchallenged. In order to counter Freeman's tale of the Anglo-Saxons as Gladstonian Liberals, Round pounced on Freeman where the latter's fame was greatest, his account of the Norman conquest. Unfortunately for Round's subsequent reputation, the most thorough attack, long in preparation, appeared just after Freeman's sudden death early in 1892.[45] The article appeared anonymously, so Round seemed doubly unethical: a secret disparagement of an individual who could no longer defend himself. In the process of criticizing Freeman's account of 1066, Round initiated a second battle of Hastings that exposed how historical argument substituted for opposed visions of national identity.

In the *Norman Conquest* Freeman had minimised the impact of 1066, because he accentuated the continuity of Anglo-Saxon institutions as the cardinal principle of English history. The *Conquest* interpreted the Norman victors as a group which was quickly acculturated and so did not affect the fundamental unity of the English past. Freeman loathed the French, so they could not play a central role in defining England. Freeman never hid his anti-French opinions: 'They disturbed the peace of Europe, they were Catholics, and unlike the Teutons, they were dishonest.'[46] Round cast substantial doubt upon this version of the island story and, in the process, tarnished Freeman's reputation to a point from which it has never recovered.

[40] TNA (PRO), Lyte MSS, 1/158: Round to Lyte, 15 Apr. 1896.
[41] London University Library, John Horace Round MS 663: Poole to Round, 17 Oct. 1914.
[42] Centre for Kentish Studies, Hubert Hall MSS, U890, F5/1: Round to Hubert Hall, 14 Nov. 1886.
[43] West Sussex RO, Oswald Barron MSS, Add. MS 732: Round to Oswald Barron, 26 May 1910.
[44] West Sussex RO, Oswald Barron MSS, Add. MS 732: Round to Barron, 14 Nov. 1912.
[45] John H. Round, 'Professor Freeman', *Quarterly Review*, clxxv (1892), 1–37.
[46] Simmons, *Reversing the Conquest*, 195.

As far as the historical evidence was concerned, Freeman's race-based explanation of English historical continuity was already disappearing under the scrutiny of professional history. A genetic interpretation of history ceased to provide a suitable intellectual framework for the complexities of 1066 and afterwards. Round's utilisation of academic norms made Freeman's scholarship an inviting target. Neatly invoking Freeman's own standards against himself, Round wrote: 'We have weighed it in the balance in which he weighed the work of others, and we have found it wanting.'[47] Freeman's failure to consult manuscripts and his desire for a general audience made him subject to imaginative flights that could not withstand detailed examination. Round exposed Freeman's 'account of the battle of "Senlac", his league of the western cities and a whole series of lesser magnitude errors; and traced them with precision to their ultimate origin in the misinterpretation of an original source'.[48] Freeman's death precluded any attempt to salvage his stature, as Round discovered from Gardiner: 'I think I ought to tell you that the last time or nearly the last time I saw Freeman, he told me of your articles on knight service, and said that he meant to read them together that he might see what they proved.'[49] An apocalyptic confrontation between Freeman and Round never materialised and the latter won the historical arguments in convincing manner.

Freeman had coaxed from Round the most important piece of scholarship he had ever produced, the three-part article in 1891–2 on the Norman conquest and the introduction of knight service.[50] Round had spent much time in preparing this project, for he called it the 'fruit of long original research'.[51] In the aftermath of the, then, innovative argument that the Normans had introduced knight service into England, Round basked in the praise of his fellow scholars. He did not note the incongruity that this important landmark in the historiography of the Norman conquest came in 59 pages, not the five- or six-page pieces that he preferred. Round argued that the feudal obligation of military service for the Anglo-Norman tenant-in-chief in no way derived from the Anglo-Saxons. This refuted previous interpretations, especially Freeman's, which claimed the basic survival of Anglo-Saxon society and the relatively lesser impact on England by the Norman conquerors. Round supplied significant evidence to those who asserted a revolutionary change in English history in consequence of the Norman victory.

Round's reasoning that the conquest initiated a seismic change in English history gained immediate acceptance from his peers and this conclusion prevailed for several decades. Poole had assured Round in advance of publication that 'I do not hesitate to say I think you have made out your point.'[52] One later historian has noted, however, that Round, the champion of history based on documents, founded his claim on the evidence of one writ and the words of three chronicles.[53] Nonetheless Round played a major role in reinterpreting the conquest, putting to rest the racial theories that Freeman had

---

[47] Round, 'Professor Freeman', 37.

[48] H.A. Cronne, 'Edward Augustus Freeman, 1823–1892', *History*, xxviii (1943), 91–2.

[49] London University Library, John Horace Round MS 638: Gardiner to Round, 25 May 1893.

[50] John H. Round, 'The Introduction of Knight Service into England', *EHR*, vi (1891), 417–43, 625–45; vii (1892), 11–24.

[51] TNA (PRO), Lyte MSS, 1/158: Round to Lyte, 7 July 1891.

[52] London University Library, John Horace Round MS 663: Poole to Round, 29 Jan. 1891.

[53] John Gillingham, 'The Introduction of Knight Service into England', *Proceedings of the Battle Conference in Anglo-Norman Studies*, iv (1981), 53–4.

espoused. The influence that Round exerted may be gauged from the comment of legendary Oxford history tutor A.L. Smith in his notes for undergraduates: 'Hence also N. C. becomes the centre & starting point of E. const. hist.'[54] If Round had so completely triumphed, why did the dispute with Freeman continue to escalate?

The controversy gained wider publicity when admirers of the deceased Freeman, especially Kate Norgate and Thomas Archer, took up his cause and attempted to vindicate his scholarship. Norgate in particular denounced Round for hiding so long behind a dastardly anonymity and charged that he 'had not the courage of his opinions'.[55] Such an accusation drew Round's fury and Norgate remained a special target for his venom ever after. Indeed, Round hounded Norgate so relentlessly that his behaviour occasioned a final breach even with the usually placid Frederic Maitland.[56] Round responded to Norgate that he had tracked Freeman's scholarship since 1884 and that Norgate's imputation of cowardice was an insult 'so reckless, so offensive, and so capable of instant disproof could only have been made by the advocate of a desperate and routed cause'. Where his reputation was concerned, Round produced a 50-page article with no difficulty. The caustic debate Round attributed not to his own conduct but to the fact 'not merely that I have ventured to assail Mr. Freeman's sacrosanct authority, but that I have been successful'.[57] Even beyond these points, however, Freeman and Round had engaged in an early version of historical interpretation as a culture war: was England fundamentally a liberal or conservative nation?

What transformed Round into such a tenacious critic was his hatred of Freeman's Liberal politics: 'dangerous nonsense incarnate'.[58] Round denounced Freeman as 'a democrat first, an historian afterwards; history was for him unhappily, ever "past" politics'.[59] The unity of history, according to Freeman, justified the commingling of past and present. Freeman's attempts to depict the Norman conquest were 'fantasies of a brain viewing plain facts through a mist of moots and witan, we have what can only be termed history in masquerade'. Round turned the conquest into a Conservative admonition by portraying the end of Anglo-Saxon England as a lesson in the absence of firm tory government. Anglo-Saxon society had suffered from 'the want of a strong rule'. The quasi-democratic susceptibilities of the Anglo-Saxons, 'an almost anarchical excess of liberty', had been no match for the discipline of Norman power. The Normans had brought to England an appropriate blend of individual duty and central government.

Round hated the new Liberalism of government growth even more than the limited power of the old Liberalism: 'It always strikes me as odd that the Radical-Socialist gang will not understand that apart from politics and the merits of this or that act, Englishmen

---

[54] Balliol College, Oxford, A.L. Smith MSS, box 8, IA 4/3.

[55] T.A. Archer and Kate Norgate, 'Controversy Regarding the Account of the Battle of Hastings', *EHR*, ix (1894), 1–76.

[56] Frederic Maitland, review of Round's *The Commune of London*, in *Selected Historical Essays of F.W. Maitland*, ed. Helen Cam (Cambridge, 1957), 259–65.

[57] This and the preceding quotation are from John H. Round, 'Mr. Freeman and the Battle of Hastings', *EHR*, ix (1894), 259.

[58] Piet B.M. Blaas, *Continuity and Anachronism: Parliamentary and Constitutional Development in Whig Historiography and in the Anti-Whig Reaction between 1890 and 1930* (The Hague, 1978), 54.

[59] This and the following quotations are from John H. Round, *Feudal England: Historical Studies in the Eleventh and Twelfth Centuries* (1895), 303, 405, 303, 302.

have a stubborn hatred of being *dragooned*.'[60] Round substituted his version of Conservative principles to define national identity as a sense of liberty tempered by a habit of authority to legitimate government. In this fashion, 11th-century English society did make a revealing backdrop to late Victorian politics. In conclusion, therefore, the scholarly contests among these three historians started with bickering over historical details that hid political differences. Beyond this, each scholar produced an authentic picture of national identity. Froude found English destiny in emancipation from catholicism and the beginnings of empire; Freeman argued that national identity reposed in a romanticised Anglo-Saxon past replete with the constitutional foundations that made the English a governing race; and Round offered a contradictory amalgam that gloried in efficient Norman rule joined to a fear of government expansion. Reading the trio's work in this fashion demonstrated the greater significance of the historian's task, because each used the past to articulate his version of an ideal national identity.

[60] West Sussex RO, Oswald Barron MSS, Add. MS 732: Round to Barron, 17 May 1913.

T.H. Green and the Dissidence of Dissent: On Religion and National Character in Nineteenth-Century England

Thomas Hill Green (1836–82) has been widely recognized for his contributions to Liberal political-social theory and for his Liberal partisanship. Historians and political theorists continue to emphasize his advocacy of limited state interference and democratic localism, as well as his anti-imperialist statements. Recent scholars of English nationalism, national identity and patriotism, including Peter Mandler, Julia Stapleton, Krishan Kumar, H.S. Jones, Roberto Romani and Georgios Varouxakis, acknowledge Green as an acolyte of Giuseppe Mazzini, a Cobdenite and a Little Englander. While they place Green's ideas within a continuum of Victorian Liberal nationalist ideas (blending into Conservatism and socialism during the 20th century), their investigations foster the view that Green placed little value in the nation as a focus of individual and collective identification. In their readings of Green, the abstract 'community', free of national peculiarities, was to him the antidote to both individual and national narrowness. However, examination of Green's statements about community, the moral ideal and religion reveals that his theorising was informed by a view of national character different from that of most contemporary liberal intellectuals. Green rejected the 'Liberal anglican' view that a national church or clerisy was necessary to guide the development of the English nation. He identified ideas and practices of protestant dissenters as progressive forces in English history and endorsed them as means of national development. Religious pluralism and forms of ecclesiastical organisation promoting democratic localism were to Green among the essential characteristics of Englishness.

Keywords: T.H. Green; Thomas Arnold; F.D. Maurice; Matthew Arnold; Liberal anglicanism; puritanism; dissent; Liberalism; nationalism; Liberal Party

Almost all his [T.H. Green's] definite opinions might be endorsed by Bright or Cobden . . . He argues for the most utilitarian of political schools, on idealist principles, and, attaching the greatest importance to national life, constantly expresses a contempt for so-called 'national' honour and imperial greatness which might perhaps offend the patriotism even of Mr. Cobden.[1]

As far as he had been an observer of English life, he should say Congregationalism was an essential element in what he might call the higher life, especially of English towns.

---

[1] A.V. Dicey, journal entry, summer 1862, in *Memorials of Albert Venn Dicey*, ed. R.S. Rait (1925), 37–8. The journal covers the long Oxford vacations of 1862 and 1863, when Dicey visited Germany and Switzerland with Green, James Bryce and other young Oxbridge men, subsequently described by Matthew Arnold as 'the Lights of Liberalism'. See Christopher Harvie, *The Lights of Liberalism: University Liberals and the Challenge of Democracy, 1860–86* (1976). I am grateful to Peter Nicholson for his comments on a draft of this essay.

He always felt sure, when coming among Congregationalists, that he should meet men who appreciated the true nature of political freedom.[2]

1. *Introduction*

The past 20 years have witnessed a proliferation of writing by political theorists and intellectual historians about the Oxford idealist philosopher and Liberal partisan, Thomas Hill Green (1836–82), while historians of Victorian thought and politics have recently begun to devote attention to connections between Liberalism and British (or English) 'national identity'.[3] What has most interested historians and political theorists is Green's idea of community based on democratic citizenship and service to society, an idea transformed into an ideal by generations of social reformers, politicians and officials, beginning in the 1870s.[4] Green has been lauded and criticized as a pioneering theorist of the welfare state, although some scholars maintain that his paramount concern for 'self-realisation' in community context, coupled with his horror of class politics and his activities in the service of Liberal causes mitigate claims that he was

[2] 'Congregationalism': 27 May 1880 speech of T.H. Green as reported in *Oxford Chronicle and Berkshire and Buckinghamshire Gazette*, 29 May 1880, p. 8, reprinted in *Collected Works of T.H. Green*, ed. Peter Nicholson (5 vols, Bristol, 1997), v, 368. Although other recent compilations of Green's writings have included unpublished notes, letters and reported speeches/addresses, Nicholson's edition in five volumes is comprehensive.

[3] Even the recent literature on Green, philosophical idealism and Liberalism is too vast to list here. Newer monographs include: Bernard Wempe, *Beyond Equality: A Study of T.H. Green's Theory of Positive Freedom* (Delft, 1986); Geoffrey Thomas, *The Moral Philosophy of T.H. Green* (Oxford, 1987); Peter Nicholson, *The Political Philosophy of the British Idealists* (Cambridge, 1990); Colin Tyler, *Thomas Hill Green and the Philosophical Foundations of Politics: An Internal Critique* (Lampeter, 1997); Maria Dimova-Cookson, *T.H. Green's Moral and Political Philosophy: A Phenomenological Approach* (Basingstoke, 2001); Matt Carter, *T.H. Green and the Development of Ethical Socialism* (Exeter, 2003); Denys P. Leighton, *The Greenian Moment: T.H. Green, Religion and Political Argument in Victorian Britain* (Exeter, 2004); Alberto De Sanctis, *The 'Puritan' Democracy of Thomas Hill Green* (Exeter, 2005). On 'Liberalism' and nationalism in Britain, see especially, John R. Gibbins, 'Liberalism, Nationalism and the English Idealists', *History of European Ideas*, xv (1992), 491–7; Peter Mandler, ' "Race" and "Nation" in mid-Victorian Thought', in *History, Religion, and Culture: British Intellectual History 1750–1950*, ed. Stefan Collini *et al.* (Cambridge, 2000), 224–44; Julia Stapleton, 'Political Thought and National Identity in Britain, 1850–1950', in *History, Religion, and Culture*, ed. Collini, 245–69; Eugenio Biagini, 'Neo-Roman Liberalism: "Republican" Values and British Liberalism, ca. 1860–1875', *History of European Ideas*, xxix (2003), 55–72; Roberto Romani, *National Character and Public Spirit in Britain and France, 1750–1914* (Cambridge, 2002); Krishan Kumar, *The Making of English National Identity* (Cambridge, 2003); H.S. Jones, 'The Idea of the National in Victorian Political Thought', *European Journal of Political Theory*, v (2006), 12–21; Peter Mandler, 'What is "National Identity"? Definitions and Applications in Modern British Historiography', *Modern Intellectual History*, iii (2006), 271–97; Georgios Varouxakis, ' "Patriotism", "Cosmopolitanism" and "Humanity" in Victorian Political Thought', *European Journal of Political Theory*, v (2006), 100–18.

[4] E.g., Andrew Vincent and Raymond Plant, *Philosophy, Politics and Citizenship: The Life and Thought of the British Idealists* (Oxford, 1984), chs 1–2, 7; Avital Simhony, 'Beyond Negative and Positive Freedom: T.H. Green's View of Freedom', *Political Theory*, xxi (1993), 28–54; Avital Simhony, 'T.H. Green's Complex Good', in *The New Liberalism: Reconciling Liberty and Community*, ed. A. Simhony and D. Weinstein (Cambridge, 2001). On Green and social reform: H.M. Lynd, *England in the Eighteen-Eighties: Toward a Social Basis for Freedom* (1945); Standish Meacham, *Toynbee Hall and Social Reform, 1880–1914* (New Haven, 1987), chs 1–2; Gertrude Himmelfarb, *Poverty and Compassion: The Moral Imagination of the Late Victorians* (New York, 1992); Mark Bevir, 'Welfarism, Socialism and Religion: On T.H. Green and Others', *Review of Politics*, lv (1993), 639–61; Sandra den Otter, *British Idealism and Social Explanation: A Study in Late Victorian Thought* (Oxford, 1996).

a proto-socialist.[5] A few historians have drawn attention to Green's *localism*, that is, to his staunch advocacy of the local state as the sphere in which citizens and subjects were most readily able to identify their interests, needs, duties and rights, and where issues of sovereignty and allegiance were somewhat less abstract than in the national state.[6] Green believed that localism was, or could be, a natural extension or development of practices of voluntary association that were characteristic of English life. Julia Stapleton points out that Green was not alone in this: his friend Albert Dicey made a distinction between English associational life arising from the spirit of self-help and 'French' *droit administratif*.[7] But Stapleton goes further, to remark that Green, Bernard Bosanquet, L.T. Hobhouse and James Bryce, 'held at best very weak ideas of English national character as embracing certain preferences and practices (for example, for liberty and self-government, defiance of foreign tyrants and suspicion of officials)'.[8]

Stapleton and Roberto Romani (whose view she endorses) suggest that Green's liberal associationism, like that of some contemporaries, left no room for nationalism. The first of the quotations heading the present essay, from the young Albert Dicey, would seem to confirm the impression of Green's hostility towards patriotism and his apathy about British national identity, which was, yet, not irreconcilable with a romantic, 'Mazzinian' stance towards issues of national self-determination.[9] Green's evident internationalism and cosmopolitanism, seen again in his appreciation of Giuseppe Mazzini, in his criticisms of Palmerstonian 'meddlesome truculence' in international affairs, and in his subsequent (post 1874) lambasting of Conservative foreign policy, have long been taken for granted and adduced as evidence of his Liberal partisanship of a distinctly mid Victorian kind.[10] Green has long been acknowledged for his role in shaping a distinctive

---

[5] The British idealist, D.G. Ritchie, and the American, John Dewey, maintained that Green was, in fact, the first British political philosopher since Locke to have a viable theory of the state. D.G. Ritchie, *The Principles of State Interference: Four Essays on the Political Philosophy of Spencer, Mill and Green* (1891), 130–1; John Dewey, *Lectures on Psychological and Political Ethics: 1898*, ed. D.F. Koch (New York, 1976), 234. Among the studies disassociating Green from any genuine form of socialism are M.A. Lawless, 'Liberty and Class Conflict in the Nineteenth-Century British Liberal State', University of London PhD, 1976, and I.M. Greengarten, *Thomas Hill Green and the Development of Liberal-Democratic Thought* (Toronto, 1981).

[6] W.H. Greenleaf, *The British Political Tradition. Volume Two: The Ideological Heritage* (1983), ch. 4; Peter Nicholson, 'T.H. Green and State Action: Liquor Legislation', *History of Political Thought*, vi (1985), 517–50; John Prest, *Liberty and Locality: Parliament, Permissive Legislation, and Ratepayers' Democracies in the Nineteenth Century* (Oxford, 1990), 197–8; Leighton, *Greenian Moment*, 79–80, 210–47.

[7] Albert Dicey, *Lectures on the Relations between Law and Public Opinion in England During the Nineteenth Century* (1905), pp. lxxi, lxxviii, cited in Julia Stapleton, 'National Character in French and British Political Thought since 1750 [review essay]', *European Journal of Political Theory*, ii (2003), 354–5.

[8] Stapleton, 'National Character', 354.

[9] Harvie, *Lights of Liberalism*, ch. 5. Harvie contends that Green, Bryce, Dicey, A.C. Swinburne and other university Liberals of the 1850s and 1860s – many of whom came from evangelical backgrounds – were attracted to the Mazzinian conception of politics because it 'demanded a devotion to the ideal of *democratic nationalism* which was *religious* rather than calculating', and it was 'moral' rather than 'functional' (pp. 103–4, emphasis added).

[10] The phrase 'meddlesome truculence' is not Green's but rather Richard Shannon's characterisation of the oppositional stance taken by radicals, Gladstone and some moderate Conservatives during the 1850s and early 1860s. It well captures the sentiment of Green and many of his university friends at the time. Richard Shannon, *The Crisis of Imperialism 1865–1915* (1976), 40. Green contributed to debates in the Oxford Union. On 4 Feb. 1861 he made a Union speech vindicating Mazzini and a federal solution to Italian unification. Dicey remarks on this and other of Green's Union speeches (*Memorials of Albert Venn Dicey*, 38).

British idealist school of international relations in which claims of 'humanity' are taken as seriously as – perhaps more seriously than – those of nation-states.[11]

It comes as little surprise, then, that Green, as an advocate of limited state interference and of democratic localism, moreover, as an acknowledged Cobdenite and Little Englander, has received little attention from the new scholars of English nationalism, national identity and patriotism, including Peter Mandler, Julia Stapleton, Krishan Kumar, H.S. Jones, Roberto Romani and Georgios Varouxakis.[12] Or rather, while they have attempted to place Green within a continuum of Victorian liberal nationalist ideas (blending into Conservatism and socialism during the 20th century), their investigations, nevertheless, foster the view that Green placed little value in the nation as a repository of collective feeling and focus of identification. In their readings of Green, the abstract 'community', free of national peculiarities, was to him the antidote to both individual and national narrowness. This view gains credence from the fact that Greenians c.1880–1940 – who could be found among adherents of the Liberal, Conservative, and later the Labour and Independent Labour Parties – were rather less successful than orthodox Conservatives and Unionists in fitting Green's admittedly strong theory of community within a nationalist framework. Paradoxically, while it is not possible to identify an *imperial* idea in Green's teachings, there is evidence that Oxbridge men in the 40 years before the First World War took his invocation of social duty to apply to the uplifting (or control) of subject peoples, and some scholars have shown how ideas of Green (and of fellow idealists such as Bosanquet) influenced doctrines of imperial stewardship and colonial policy.[13]

The second quotation, from a speech Green delivered upon the opening of a dissenting chapel and school in Oxford, at least hints – in the phrase 'English life' – at his consciousness of English national character or characteristics, albeit one of a slightly unorthodox kind. The main purpose of this essay is to indicate how Green articulated a form of patriotism or nationalism rooted in protestant dissent – or, more precisely, in a conception of dissent's role in the formation of English national character and modern social and political institutions. Close reading of Green's statements about identity and collective purpose in connection with religion, reveals that he held a distinctive theory of English national character, that this theory contrasted in important respects with the nationalism of 'liberal Anglicans' (such as F.D. Maurice, Thomas Arnold and J.R. Seeley) close to, or at least on the margins of, the political establishment, and that Green's view of religion and national character accorded with that of mid and late Victorian dissenters who rallied to the party of Gladstone and were its shock troops down to 1914.

[11] See, among recent works commenting on Green and international relations, David Boucher, 'British Idealism, the State, and International Relations', *Journal of the History of Ideas*, lv (1994), 671–94; Jeanne Morefield, *Covenants Without Swords: Idealist Liberalism and the Spirit of Empire* (Princeton, 2005); Duncan Bell and Casper Sylvester, 'International Society in Victorian Political Thought: T.H. Green, Herbert Spencer, and Henry Sidgwick', *Modern Intellectual History*, iii (2006), 207–38.

[12] See n. 3 above. Green's widow, writing to James Bryce at the time of the latter's publication of *Studies in Contemporary Biography* (including a revised version of an 1882 essay on Green), observed of her husband: 'I always feel he would be now what is called a Little Englander'. Bodl., MS Bryce 73, ff. 4–5: Charlotte B. Green to James Bryce, 26 Apr. 1903, quoted in Leighton, *Greenian Moment*, 286.

[13] R. Symonds, *Oxford and Empire: The Last Lost Cause?* (1986); M.P. Cowen and R.W. Shenton, 'British Neo-Hegelianism and Official Colonial Practice in Africa: The Oluwa Land Case of 1921', *Journal of Imperial and Commonwealth History*, xxii (1994), 217–50; Morefield, *Covenants Without Swords*.

Those progressive liberals and radicals who, among other things, advocated church disestablishment and religious pluralism, as well as the cultural conservatives who played important roles in British intellectual life into the 20th century, appreciated Green not for the 'German' character of his ideas, but because of their Englishness.[14] One of the historians who has tried to recapture the sense of nation in Victorian thought, Peter Mandler, points out confusions and inconsistencies in recent historical writing about 'national identity' and warns that the term is now perhaps over-determining or over-whelming our understanding of other forms of collective identification.[15] While I am appreciative of Mandler's observations, I nevertheless argue that Green's pronouncements revealed a clear picture of the English national character and that his national idea prescribed specific social and political practices as conducive to collective development as well as self-realization.

2. *Liberal Ideas of the Nation in Green's Time*

There can be no doubt that nationalism and ideas of national identity had great social purchase in Victorian Britain. 'National feeling' and patriotism were expressed, for instance, in agitations and campaigns for *regional* cultural and political autonomy (in Wales, Scotland and Ireland), and it seems clear that British (and even English) nation-hood was never a closed issue. Most notably, Linda Colley has argued that a sense of Britishness *as English* national belonging and allegiance to the Hanoverian dynasty and its collateral lines was well established throughout Britain by the close of George III's reign.[16] But this neither explains away nor minimises the significance of the persis-tence of other collective allegiances that can properly be described as national. More-over, Krishan Kumar argues that English national identity was not well established until the close of the 19th century and that consciousness of Englishness as Britishness owed a great deal to British (protestant) missionary activities around the world.[17] Ernest Renan's famous pronouncement that a nation is a continuous plebiscite requir-ing a tacit 'desire to live together' applies as well to 19th-century Britain as to France.[18]

To a great extent, senses of 'national' separateness *and* belonging were mediated in Britain through religious sentiments, and articulated through claims about the status of religious institutions. The relationship between the Church of England and dissenting protestantism, as is well known, was not only a perennial issue of English politics down to the First World War, but also assumed significance in the Welsh, Scottish and 'Ulster'

[14] On the Conservatives, see Julia Stapleton, 'Cultural Conservatism and the Public Intellectual in Britain, 1930–70', *The European Legacy*, v (2000), 795–813.

[15] Mandler, 'What is "National Identity"?', 271–3.

[16] Linda Colley, *Britons. Forging the Nation 1707–1837* (New Haven, 1992). On the relationship between Englishness and Britishness, see esp. Kumar, *Making of English National Identity*.

[17] Kumar, *Making of English National Identity*.

[18] Ernest Renan, 'Qu'est-ce qu'une Nation?' [1882], *Oeuvres Complètes*, ed. H. Psichari (10 vols, Paris, 1947–61), i, 887–906.

national experiences.[19] Clyde Binfield observes, for instance, that nonconformists in Wales were always in a majority and 'what was most vital about them was expressed in the Welsh language, and therefore a different culture'.[20] The sense of cultural difference based in part, if not entirely, on different forms of christian observance and religious polity was an important aspect of local, regional and national political partisanship. G.M. Trevelyan remarked that 'the continuity of the two parties in English politics [until 1914] was largely due to the two-party system in religious observance, popularly known as Church and Chapel'.[21] Ernest Barker observed that 'the general relations, the general balance, and the general interaction of Anglicanism and Nonconformity have been a cardinal factor in English life and development for over three centuries'.[22] Many more recent observers have remarked on Gladstonian Liberalism as both a projection of the dissenting experience and a regional-cum-national phenomenon: between 1860 and 1914 the party scored some of its greatest electoral successes in the north and west of England (where old dissent and methodism were strongly represented) and on the 'Celtic fringe' of Wales and Scotland – once again, areas where the church was most hard pressed.[23]

Given the relationship between confessional identity and British national politics, in what sense can religious identity and thought be said to have shaped the 'national ideas' of 19th-century English intellectuals, and in what ways were their religious ideals informed by a sense of nationality? Peter Mandler and H.S. Jones have drawn our attention to national ideas in liberal anglicanism, a tradition by which T.H. Green was greatly influenced through Benjamin Jowett, F.D. Maurice and D.J. Vaughan (1825–1905, vicar of St Martin's, Leicester, Green's 'Uncle David'), and to which he contributed as a theologian and social reformer.[24] Without engaging in a thorough examination of liberal anglicanism and comparison of liberal anglican ideas to Green's, a few observations about these ideas, and particularly their continuity and influence, can convey sense of both the innovation and historical rooted-ness of Green's national idea.

[19] Keith Robbins, *Nineteenth-Century Britain. England, Scotland, and Wales: The Making of a Nation* (Oxford, 1988), chs 1–3; Christopher Harvie, 'Gladstonianism, the Provinces, and Popular Culture, 1860–1906', in *Victorian Liberalism: Nineteenth-Century Political Thought and Practice*, ed. R. Bellamy (1990); David Hempton, *Religion and Political Culture in Britain and Ireland: From the Glorious Revolution to the Decline of Empire* (Cambridge, 1996), chs 3–5.

[20] Clyde Binfield, *So Down to Prayers: Studies in English Nonconformity, 1780–1920* (1977), p. xi.

[21] G.M. Trevelyan, *An Autobiography* (1949), quoted in Donald Davie, *A Gathered Church: The Literature of the English Dissenting Interest 1700–1930* (Oxford, 1978), 2.

[22] Ernest Barker, *Britain and the British People* (1942), quoted in Davie, *A Gathered Church*, 2. For claims about Trevelyan's and Barker's sense of the importance of the nation, see esp. J. Stapleton, *Englishness and the Study of Politics: The Social and Political Thought of Ernest Barker* (Cambridge, 1994) and Stapleton, 'Revisiting the Center at the Extremes: "English" Liberalism in the Political Thought of Interwar Britain', *British Journal of Politics and International Relations*, i (1999), 270–92.

[23] John Vincent, *The Formation of the British Liberal Party, 1857–68* (2nd edn, Hassocks, 1976), pp. xxxviii–xlvi; Stephen Koss, *Nonconformity in Modern British Politics* (Hamden, 1975); Eugenio F. Biagini, *Liberty, Retrenchment, and Reform: Popular Liberalism in the Age of Gladstone, 1860–1880* (Cambridge, 1992), 16.

[24] Mandler, ' "Race" and "Nation" in Mid-Victorian Thought'; Jones, 'The Idea of the National'. Vaughan was associated with Maurice as well as with the christian socialists, F.B. Westcott (1825–1901) and J. Llewelyn Davies (1826–1916). To my knowledge, there exists no full-length study of Vaughan, but see A.J. Allaway, 'David James Vaughan: Liberal Churchman and Educationist', *Transactions of the Leicestershire Historical and Archeological Society*, xxxiii (1957), 45–58; Boyd Hilton, *The Age of Atonement: The Influence of Evangelicalism on Social and Economic Thought, 1785–1865* (Oxford, 1988), 286–8, 329–36; Leighton, *Greenian Moment*, 144–50.

Thomas Arnold, christian socialist, historian and the most famous of 19th-century public school headmasters, had asserted in echo of S.T. Coleridge's *On the Constitution of the Church and State* (1830) as well as the tractarians (including J.H. Newman and E.B. Pusey) that a national church must give shape to the development of society and state – or, in H.S. Jones's paraphrase, 'nationhood and religion must be coterminous'.[25] According to at least some of the mid century christian socialists, including Thomas Hughes, Charles Kingsley and John Ludlow, Arnold's brand of common-sensical, undogmatic christianity was sufficient to constitute a common bond among diverse English individuals, particularly if the teachings of the national church were preached by a cultured and broadminded 'clerisy'.[26] 'Christianity', proclaimed Arnold, 'gives us that bond perfectly, which race in the ancient world gave illiberally and narrowly.'[27] Arnold's broad church conception of nationality, of course, did not comprehend unitarians or jews (who in his opinion should be denied admission to the 'national' universities and other privileges of anglicans), but it was at least consonant with the religious profile of England. (Non-anglicans were already gaining access in large numbers to the franchise in national and local elections after 1828.) Arnold's view of national inclusiveness was innovative, and since it did not look backward or depend on historical precedents, it cannot even be counted an invented tradition. As Mandler has noted, Thomas Arnold's national vision was at least reasonably non-exclusive in social terms, and it was non-ethnic (unlike the German variant of nationalism which, Mandler claims, should not be used as the yardstick for other 19th-century nationalisms); and as H.S. Jones observes, Arnold's national theory bears comparison with the views of the French historians he admired, Jules Michelet and François Guizot, who were both of the opinion that national developments revealed the progress (or regress) of civilizations in the march of history.[28]

In Frederick Denison Maurice, some of the new historians of English nationalism have found the most profound religious nationalist (if not national religionist) of the Victorian era. Jones indicates that Maurice did not see mere aggregates of individuals under God but – like Mazzini – believed in the sacredness of nations that gave shape and meaning to individuals' activities.[29] In this respect, like so many others in the liberal anglican and christian socialist traditions, Maurice faulted the Benthamites for treating 'as mere accident all *national* distinctness'.[30] Jones observes that Maurice located the Old Testament as the place where 'the principles of national society [were developed,] while the New Testament developed the principle of universal society'. But Hebrew narrowness was not to be condemned outright. 'Nationhood', in Maurice's view, was to 'be understood positively because it was not a secular but a sacred thing: a sacramental sign of a universal fraternity'.[31] As Maurice's friend Thomas Arnold put it: 'The nation is holy

---

[25] Jones, 'The Idea of the National', 15.

[26] Ben Knights, *The Idea of the Clerisy in the Nineteenth Century* (Cambridge, 1978); E.R. Norman, *The Victorian Christian Socialists* (Cambridge, 1987).

[27] Arthur P. Stanley, *Life and Correspondence of Thomas Arnold, D.D.* (nd), 221, as quoted in Jones, 'The Idea of the National', 15.

[28] Mandler, ' "Race" and "Nation" in Mid-Victorian Thought', 226–8; Jones, 'The Idea of the National', 15.

[29] Jones, 'The Idea of the National', 16–17.

[30] Frederick D. Maurice, *The Kingdom of Christ* (2 vols, 1883), i, 221, as quoted in Jones, 'The Idea of the National', 16.

[31] Jones, 'The Idea of the National', 16.

as well as the Church', and Jones correctly identifies the resonances here with Fichte and other German romantics.[32] Maurice expressed greater appreciation of Fichte and Friedrich Heinrich Jacobi than of Hegel, and this may well be because these theologian-philosophers retained a sense of the church as coterminous with the nation in states of western Europe since the Reformation, whereas Hegel tended to *submerge* the church within the state – or to regard the modern state as the proxy for the church in the establishment and protection of *Sittlichkeit*, or national morality.[33]

Both H.S. Jones and Georgios Varouxakis regard Matthew Arnold, and in particular his polemical *Culture and Anarchy* (1867–9), as representing a culmination of liberal anglican thought with respect to nationalism and religion. Arnold's condemnation of 'hole-and-corner' religion – i.e., dissent and voluntary religious association – is not accompanied by invocations of orthodox religiosity, as is seen in the statements of the older christian socialists, but it nevertheless signals an aggressive assertion of English nationalism as rooted in religion. Jones observes that to Arnold the 'antonym of "national" was not "foreign", but, perhaps, "private", "sectional", "sectarian" or "narrow" '.[34] In an account of Arnold's nationalism, Varouxakis acknowledges that although dissenters were rattled by Arnold's invective and invocations of culture and broad-mindedness, in *Culture and Anarchy* and elsewhere, Victorian dissent was by no means the sole target of his critique.[35] Matthew Arnold developed a particular notion of nationalism that valorised the cosmopolitan outlook and suggested that Englishmen should be concerned about their reputation among foreigners; but in *Culture and Anarchy* he also expressed distaste for foreign imports, such as American ideas about religious liberty and democracy. Varouxakis observes that both James Fitzjames Stephen and Herbert Spencer were drawn to comment on Arnold's writings, certainly not out of sympathy for dissent, but because they found his condemnation of English boasting and denigration of foreigners to be beside the point; Arnold's critique, in their view, did not capture the *essence* of nationalism and patriotism as precisely those cohesive forces that could counteract narrowness of mind.

What Varouxakis and Jones do not emphasize is that Matthew Arnold's attack on 'Hebraic narrowness' (referring to protestant dissent, but not exclusively) marked a full circle from Maurice's pointed invocation of the virtues of judaism and the values of Old Testament patriotism, and Maurice's claim that the latter supplied, or might supply, the sense of civic purpose and co-operativeness that liberal anglicans and christian socialists claimed was so sorely lacking in their society. When Arnold recommended 'culture as the great help out of our present [national] difficulties' and defined culture as 'a pursuit of our total perfection by means of getting to know, on all the matters which most concern us, the best which has been thought and said in the world', he

[32] Jones, 'The Idea of the National', 16.

[33] For Maurice's appreciation of the nationalism of the German romantics, see the concluding sections of *Moral and Metaphysical Philosophy* (2 vols, 1873), ii. The submergence of the church in the state in Hegel's thought is widely recognized. See, for its implications for religion and nationality, John E. Toews, *Hegelianism: The Path Towards Dialectical Humanism, 1805–1841* (Cambridge, 1980); Laurence Dickey, *Hegel. Religion, Economics, and the Politics of the Spirit, 1770–1807* (Cambridge, 1987).

[34] Jones, 'The Idea of the National', 17.

[35] Varouxakis, ' "Patriotism", "Cosmopolitanism" and "Humanity" ', 103–4. But see Fred G. Walcott, *The Origins of 'Culture and Anarchy': Matthew Arnold and Popular Education in England* (Toronto, 1970).

named various contemporary dissenters as representative of the opinion of the entire English middle class, which was crippled by a narrow and materialistic patriotism: 'Nine Englishmen out of ten at the present day believe that our [national] greatness and welfare are proved by our being so very rich.'[36] He used 'Mialism' as a synonym for Hebraism and narrowness of mind, Edward Miall (1809–81) being the editor of the newspaper *Nonconformist* whose motto (an idiotic one, in Arnold's view) was 'The Dissidence of Dissent and the Protestantism of the Protestant religion.'[37] Miall's neo-puritanism was of a piece with 'the check given to the Renascence by Puritanism'. But whereas 'primitive Christianity' or Hebraism 'was legitimately and truly the ascendant force in the world' of the second century AD, 'Puritanism [in the 16th and 17th centuries] was no longer the central current of the world's progress, it was a side stream crossing the central current and checking it.'[38]

To F.D. Maurice, again, judaism had carried with it into primitive christianity a vision of humanity as a community divided into elect and ungodly nations, and such religiously defined 'nationalism' helped mediate individuals' sense of godliness and the immanence of divine providence; to Matthew Arnold, the need for such mediation was a sign of spiritual *and national* immaturity. Continuing in the tradition of Coleridge and Thomas Arnold, but essentially against Maurice, Matthew Arnold argued that only the properly cultivated members of a national church could keep Englishmen in tune with the central currents of human thought and creativity. To put dissent on a par with the establishment, to 'free' English national religion in the manner advocated by John Bright and other Liberals, to allow 'Mr. [Thomas] Binney' (congregational preacher, 1798–1874) to be 'afternoon-reader at Lincoln's Inn or the Temple', would ensure that England remained in a backwater of the wider currents of humanity.[39]

Not only Matthew Arnold's valorisation of culture but also his dissentophobia was widely shared by his own and later generations of English cultural critics, and by social reformers who believed that cultural uplift was essential to the moral health and greatness of the English nation. The tendency can be traced in men like J.R. Seeley, J.R. Green and Arnold Toynbee, all of whom believed in some role for a reconstituted or liberalised national church, as well as among later Victorian christian socialists like Charles Gore and Henry Scott Holland.[40] Significantly, Holland, canon of St Paul's and editor of *Commonwealth*, identified the 'Nonconformist capitalist' as the great enemy of the workingman and of Liberalism.[41] Toynbee's hostility to hole-and-corner religion was more muted, but he carried through the liberal anglican tradition in holding that neither utilitarian self-interest nor an interventionist state but only religion could meld isolated individuals into 'a loving interdependent whole'.[42] One who departed from the dissen-tophobic tendency in liberal anglicanism, T.H. Green, was teacher to both Toynbee and

[36] Arnold, *Culture and Anarchy*, ed. (with an introduction) by Samuel Lipman (New Haven, 1994), 5, 18.

[37] Arnold, *Culture and Anarchy*, 22–7.

[38] Arnold, *Culture and Anarchy*, 96.

[39] Arnold, *Culture and Anarchy*, 12–18 (quotation at 18).

[40] Jones, 'The Idea of the National', 18–19 (on Seeley and Toynbee).

[41] Carter, *T.H. Green and the Development of Ethical Socialism*, ch. 4.

[42] Arnold Toynbee, *Lectures on the Industrial Revolution in England* (1884), 237, quoted in Jones, 'The Idea of the National', 18.

Holland, and Green's view of the dissenting contribution (and the general interplay of religious forces) to English national identity merits greater attention.

3. *Green's National Idea and the Dissenters*

As many commentators have remarked, both admiringly and critically, Green's outlook was thoroughly religious. Some have also noted Green's preference for dissenting ideas and forms of worship and his friendly relations with leading dissenting clergy of the era (or, as Matthew Arnold would have it, philistines), such as R.W. Dale, James Martineau, and Hugh Price Hughes.[43] Melvin Richter has described Green's philosophy – with its theory of self-realization in community context and its invocations of civic duty – as a 'surrogate religion', representing a psychological adjustment to utilitarianism, evolutionism and a widespread crisis of religious faith.[44] Once again, it is widely supposed that Green's theory of social obligation and of freedom enjoyed in common was purely civic in character and was not motivated in any deep way by a vision of the English nation or of characteristically English associational forms. However, if we read Green's ideas about self-realization and associational life in connection with Maurice's teachings (such as those outlined above) and those of other christian socialists, we find indications that the nation and national character assumed some importance in his thought. Green had read Maurice's theological essays while at Rugby (which he entered in 1850, eight years after the death of Thomas Arnold), and he testified to his appreciation of Maurice's ideas. He also met Maurice at least once (in 1861), and we may suppose that Maurice was one of the inspirations for Green's participation in various efforts to educate and spiritualise English workingmen. One of these projects was the workingmen's 'college' established in Leicester by David Vaughan.[45]

Green remained to the end of his life an anglican, though he had advocated disestablishment during the 1860s and believed that Oxford and Cambridge universities did not do enough for the English nation in return for their endowments. He described himself as a poor churchman and many orthodox christians (both dissenters and anglicans) suspected him of infidelity. Green's approving view of puritanism as a force in English history and national development is well acknowledged; his 'Four Lectures on the English Revolution' (first published in the third volume of his collected works edited by his student Richard Lewis Nettleship) constitute an interesting analysis of what he saw to be the nonconformist contribution to English constitutional

---

[43] See Leighton, *Greenian Moment*, 133, 171–2, 222–6, 272–7. Hughes, social reformer and editor of *Methodist Times*, called Green 'the most splendid Christian that I ever met'. D.P. Hughes, *Life of Hugh Price Hughes* (1904), 134.

[44] See Melvin Richter, 'T.H. Green and His Audience: Liberalism as a Surrogate Faith', *Review of Politics*, xviii (1956), 444–72; Richter, 'Intellectual and Class Alienation: Oxford Idealist Diagnoses and Prescriptions', *European Journal of Sociology*, vii (1966), 1–26; Craig Jenks, 'T.H. Green, the Oxford Philosophy of Duty and the English Middle Class', *British Journal of Sociology*, xxviii (1977), 481–97.

[45] Green reported his reading of Maurice to his fellow Rugbeian, David Hanbury (1835–90): Balliol College, Oxford, T.H. Green Papers 1a: biographical material, Green to Hanbury, Sept. 1854. It was almost certainly with D.J. Vaughan's encouragement that Green read Maurice's writings, and it was through Vaughan that Green made Maurice's acquaintance. T.H. Green Papers 1d, box 1: 'Notes by Mrs. Green. THG 1850–70 copies'. On the college at Leicester, see Allaway, 'David James Vaughan'.

and political development.[46] First delivered in January 1867 to the Edinburgh Philosophical Institute under the title 'The English Commonwealth and the Protectorate', these lectures were accorded some respect by later historians of the Tudor-Stuart period, particularly C.H. Firth (regius professor of modern history at Oxford, 1904–25), who recommended their publication.[47] Green characterised the anglican (and presbyterian) 'spirit of ordinance' and its corresponding 'legal conscience' as Roman, popish and authoritarian, and he contrasted them to the 'evangelical conscience' of protestant sectaries, whose ecclesiastical polities and forms of worship ushered in 'the stage of [consciousness] in which the human spirit, perfectly conformed to Christ's death and resurrection . . . holds intercourse "high, intuitive and comprehensive" with the divine'.[48] The evangelical conscience, which Green located in Sir Henry Vane the Younger (1613–62, executed as a regicide) and Oliver Cromwell, as well as in the quietism of diggers and quakers, was subdued upon the Stuart restoration but nevertheless produced an enduring 'protest against the plausibilities of the world' and 'supplied [sic] a constant spring of unconventional beneficence to English life'.[49] As I have written elsewhere:

> Green's interpretation [in the 'Four Lectures'] of 'Puritanism' and 'Independency' clearly reflected evangelical principles: individual communion with God and the cultivation of the Spirit were the essence of the Puritan movement. He interpreted the Puritan episode in English history, culminating in the establishment of the Common-wealth, as a flawed experiment in government through the agency of what nineteenth-century evangelicals called the self that is Christed. Spiritual and social regeneration were to be achieved through the voluntary collaboration of individuals who felt the Christ rising within them.[50]

Green stated in his Oxford Whyte's professorship lectures 'On the Different Senses of "Freedom" ' as Applied to Will and the Moral Progress of Man' (1879) that 'modern Christendom' (i.e., that since the Reformation) was characterised by 'various forms of Christian fellowship' in which 'the moralising functions grow as those of the magistrate diminish, [and] the number of individuals in whom society awakens to interests in objects contributory to human perfection tends to increase'.[51] It was neither the national church of the liberal anglicans nor the state-mediated *Sittlichkeit* of Hegel that Green had in mind when he made this pronouncement. Whereas Matthew Arnold identified dissent with mental narrowness, refusal to enter the mainstream of national life and intolerance, Green located in dissent and puritanism, both past and present, arguments for toleration and the liberation of human consciousness from 'ordinance', legalism and conventional

---

[46] Melvin Richter, *The Politics of Conscience* (Lanham, 1983), 41; Leighton, *Greenian Moment*, ch. 3; De Sanctis, '*Puritan' Democracy of Thomas Hill Green*, 68–79, 121–31.

[47] See Nettleship's preface to *Collected Works of T.H. Green*, iii (1888). The four lectures occupy pages 277–364 of the same volume.

[48] *Collected Works of T.H. Green*, iii, 294–5.

[49] *Collected Works of T.H. Green*, iii, 341.

[50] Leighton, *Greenian Moment*, 173.

[51] T.H. Green, 'On the Different Senses of "Freedom" ', sec. 5, as reprinted in *T.H. Green: Lectures on the Principles of Political Obligation and Other Writings*, ed. P. Harris and J. Morrow (Cambridge, 1986), 232–3.

duty that corresponded with his conception of liberalism. John Coffey has argued that 'The gulf between puritanism and nineteenth-century nonconformity was not always as wide as some historians have suggested' and the 'radical tolerationist argument . . . pointed to many of the key elements of modern political liberalism'.[52]

The statements quoted above are drawn from Green's minor writings, but we might note that the lectures 'On the Different Senses of "Freedom" ' were incorporated into his better known *Prolegomena to Ethics* (1883). His English Revolution lectures, which might appear painfully idealistic to many present-day historians, take on somewhat wider meaning when we compare them to statements about political conditions of freedom in *Lectures on the Principles of Political Obligation*.[53] For present consideration, Green's statements, when taken as a whole, suggest a national idea that was not out of line with contemporary educated opinion. For example, while his favourable view of 'independency' was not one to which many liberal anglicans were sympathetic, the whig theory of English history certainly validated Green's unfavourable view of the Stuarts and the church establishment to which they were wedded. William Stubbs's *Constitutional History of England* (1873–8) represented the Stuart monarchy as an obstacle to growth of an organic principle of English freedom. Stubbs's influential work was empirical, scientific history, but it also carried assumptions about English personality and employed organic metaphors of national development. Interestingly, John Burrow opines that, insofar as Stubbs viewed 'constitutionalism' as an organic principle in English history, his 'underlying metaphysic [was] Hegelian' – a claim that is similarly made about Green's thought.[54]

A recurring theme through both Green's lectures on political obligation and the *Prolegomena to Ethics* concerns what is required for rule in a democratic society to be effective, and how individuals consent to governing institutions and practices that serve or create purposes with which they can identify.[55] Only through securing wide social consent to purposes of government could the state actuate and express the 'moral ideal'. And if the conception of a common good fails to make in the citizen of the ostensibly democratic state 'a loyal subject, if not an intelligent patriot', it is 'a sign that the state is not a true state'.[56] Only when 'the nation [is] organised in the form of a self-governing community', would large numbers of citizens develop a 'passion' for serving the national community, 'whether in the way of defending it from external attack, or developing it from within'.[57]

Again, it is in some of Green's statements about English religion that we find his most concrete illustrations of forms of self-governing community. In a speech delivered to an Oxford meeting of the National Church Reform Union in 1881, Green suggested how a free church polity could provide moral order while accommodating the need for

---

[52] John Coffey, 'Puritanism and Liberty Revisited: The Case for Toleration in the English Revolution', *HJ*, xli (1998), 984–5.

[53] First published in *Collected Works of T.H. Green*, ii.

[54] John Burrow, *A Liberal Descent: Victorian Historians and the English Past* (Cambridge, 1981), 147.

[55] See esp., T.H. Green, *Prolegomena to Ethics* (Oxford, 1883), secs 266–71; Green, *Lectures on the Principles of Political Obligation*, secs 114–22.

[56] Green, *Prolegomena*, sec. 270.

[57] Green, *Lectures on the Principles of Political Obligation*, sec. 122.

self-government.[58] Disestablishment of the national church, Green opined, was politically untenable, but its 'congregationalisation' would serve many purposes. The clergyman of the day (of whatever denomination) was already often a 'leader in useful social work, and *in the administration of such business as is not directly administered by [the] state'*. The reason for the low 'practical efficiency of clergy' in many districts was attributable to the fact that 'people have no share, direct or indirect in appointment of clergy, and are not associated with him in conduct either of worship, or of school, or of relief of sick and poor'. An elected clergy would be kept in line by bishops who would see that 'a certain elastic uniformity was maintained in order of worship', while a 'Congregational Council' might retain veto power over some local decisions. The 'success of any such plan manifestly depends on [the] possibility of restoring congregational life in the parishes'.

Green was primarily concerned here with reviving the national church, in keeping with other representatives of the clerisy idea, yet he believed that a salutary reform of English religion and national life might be brought about by a form of puritanisation. Canon Samuel Barnett, parish clergyman in St Jude's, London, and an active member (with his wife) in the Charity Organisation Society, heard Green's speech and found it 'full of doubts with drops of real thought floating in its midst'; the speech did not fall on deaf anglican ears.[59] However, the similarity of viewpoint between Green's recommendations and contemporary dissenting literature is striking. The congregationalist historian and editor, Robert Vaughan (1795–1868), the London barrister, William Mitchell Fawcett, and Green's friend, Robert William Dale, all proclaimed religious republicanism as contributions of dissent to English national life, and specifically recommended the model of congregational polity as a remedy for the problems and challenges of democracy and modern administration.[60]

There is more than meets the eye, then, in Green's rather innocuous but flattering observations in 1880 upon the opening of a dissenting private school in Oxford, for the simple reason that it accords with many other of his statements about what was, supposedly, distinctive about the English organisation of life. Whereas Coleridge, Carlyle, Thomas Arnold and Matthew Arnold all believed in the leadership role of the establishment in English moral life, Green believed that England's national faith cut across denominational boundaries; its national religious character was pluralistic. This was a particularly important progression for English (and British) liberal intellectuals and political leaders to make in an age of democracy. W.E. Gladstone's conversion to democracy during the mid 1860s coincided with his embrace of dissent, whose political leaders – John and Jacob Bright, Richard Cobden, Samuel Morley, R.W. Dale, and subsequently Joseph Chamberlain – both validated certain practices of political

---

[58] I quote from Charlotte Green's copy of this speech, Balliol College, Green Papers 1c: 'Notes for a Speech on Church Reform at Merton. Dec. 7? 1881' (emphasis added). The notes, with a report on the speech from the *Oxford Chronicle* (10 Dec. 1881), are printed in *Collected Works of T.H. Green*, v, 376–9.

[59] Henrietta Barnett, *Canon Barnett: His Life, Work, and Friends, by His Wife* (2 vols, 1918), quoted in Nicholson's introductory note to document cited in *Collected Works of T.H. Green*, v, 376–9.

[60] R. Vaughan, *Congregationalism: Or, the Polity of Independent Churches* (1842); *Religious Republicanism: Six Essays on Congregationalism*, ed. W.M. Fawcett (1869); R.W. Dale, 'Congregationalism', *Quarterly Review*, lxxiii (1881), 1–12, 265–88. Dale and Green were both on the governing board of the King Edward VI Grammar School Foundation, Birmingham, and Green gave encouragement to the foundation of Mansfield College, Oxford, of which Dale was prime mover. See Leighton, *Greenian Moment*, 207–10, 224–6.

mobilisation and harboured suspicion of the masses.[61] Through quite different paths, Green and Gladstone had concluded that a sort of free trade in christianity would advance more effectively the moralisation of English society than would the maintenance of an establishment, and this was a step that few liberal anglicans had contemplated.

Green's statements about English religion and free spiritual association contained his view of English national identity. While he did not have a 'strong' idea of the nation, compared to, for example, James Fitzjames Stephen or John Seeley, Green's idea of community was shot through with assumptions about the English national character and its historical development. This made his statements about community and nation rather more concrete than the teachings of Mazzini, of which Green and other Liberals of his generation were enamoured. While we may question the view shared by Mandler, Jones and Varouxakis that English nationalism during the 19th century was *exceptional* in being articulated in religious (rather than racial or ethnic) terms – was the same not true of Polish nationalism or German national sentiment at the time of the *Kulturkampf*? – it is clear that religion was rarely absent from the minds of English Liberals when they contemplated the nation past, present and future.[62] If Green was exceptional among establishment Liberals with regard to the idea of national character, it was in his identification of specific religious practices and principles that most clearly exemplified Englishness and in his appreciation of the dissidence of dissent.

[61] Vincent, *Formation of the British Liberal Party*, pp. xxx–xxxi; G.I.T. Machin, 'Gladstone and Nonconformity in the 1860s: The Formation of an Alliance', *HJ*, xvii (1974), 347–64; J.P. Parry, *The Rise and Fall of Liberal Government in Victorian Britain* (New Haven, 1993), 251–4.

[62] Of German nationalism in Green's time, David Blackbourn remarks, following Gangolf Hübinger, 'German culture *was* Protestant. The Reformation was never far below the surface of educated discourse': D. Blackbourn, *The Fontana History of Germany 1780–1918* (1997), 293; G. Hübinger, *Kulturprotestantismus und Politik* (Tübingen, 1994).

Een-Gonyama Gonyama!: Zulu Origins of the Boy Scout Movement and the Africanisation of Imperial Britain

TIMOTHY PARSONS

British imperialists in the late 19th century denigrated non-western cultures in rationalising the partition of Africa, but they also had to assimilate African values and traditions to make the imperial system work. The partisans of empire also romanticised non-western cultures to convince the British public to support the imperial enterprise. In doing so, they introduced significant African and Asian elements into British popular culture, thereby refuting the assumption that the empire had little influence on the historical development of metropolitan Britain.

Robert Baden-Powell conceived of the Boy Scout movement as a cure for the social instability and potential military weakness of Edwardian Britain. Influenced profoundly by his service as a colonial military officer, Africa loomed large in Baden-Powell's imagination. He was particularly taken with the Zulu. King Cetshwayo's crushing defeat of the British army at Isandhlawana in 1879 fixed their reputation as a 'martial tribe' in the imagination of the British public. Baden-Powell romanticised the Zulus' discipline, and courage, and adapted many of their cultural institutions to scouting.

Baden-Powell's appropriation and reinterpretation of African culture illustrates the influence of subject peoples of the empire on metropolitan British politics and society. Scouting's romanticised trappings of African culture captured the imagination of tens of thousands of Edwardian boys and helped make Baden-Powell's organisation the premier uniformed youth movement in Britain. Although confident that they were superior to their African subjects, British politicians, educators, and social reformers agreed with Baden-Powell that 'tribal' Africans preserved many of the manly virtues that had been wiped by the industrial age.

Keywords: Robert Baden-Powell; Boy Scout movement; Zulu; Cetshwayo; Ndebele; Anglo-Zulu War 1879; South African Scout Association; woodbadge; racism; British empire

In the 1920 edition of *Scouting for Boys: A Handbook for Instruction in Good Citizenship*, Sir Robert Baden-Powell explained the proper way to conduct a 'Scouts' War Dance'.[1] Directing the scouts to march single file into a circle while singing the 'Een-Gonyama song', he described how the boys should conduct themselves as Zulu warriors:

Into the centre of [the circle a scout] steps forward and carries out a war dance, representing how he tracked and fought with one of his enemies. He goes through

---

[1] The central ideas for this essay, which envision the British empire as a medium of cross-cultural exchange, come from a graduate seminar that I co-taught with Richard Davis entitled 'Britain in Africa'.

the whole fight in dumb show, until he finally kills his foe; the Scouts meantime still singing the Een-Gonyama chorus and dancing on their own ground. So soon as he finishes the fight, the leader starts the 'Be Prepared' chorus. . . . Then they commence the Een-Gonyama chorus, and another Scout steps into the ring, and describes in dumb show how he stalked and killed a wild buffalo. While he does the creeping up and stalking the animal, the Scouts all crouch and sing their chorus very softly, and as he gets more into the fight with the beast, they simultaneously spring up and dance and shout the chorus loudly.[2]

Although he claimed an expert knowledge of Africa from his service in colonial wars, Baden-Powell could hardly be considered an authority on Zulu customs. This mattered little as metropolitan Britons were almost entirely ignorant of African institutions. Nevertheless, they were fascinated by the romanticised and exoticised depictions of their new colonial subjects they read about in the popular press, juvenile literature, and memoirs of colonial war heroes.

The British public's growing interest in Africa in the late 19th century did not spring from respect or admiration for African culture. Rather, communities like the Zulu came to represent the simpler, savage, but nobler qualities that nostalgic observers worried were vanishing from Edwardian Britain. Politicians, clergymen, generals, and social commentators worried that industrialisation, urbanisation, and class struggle were sapping the vitality of British youth, thereby leaving the nation militarily and morally unprepared to defend its empire from overseas and continental rivals.

Baden-Powell incorporated 'tribal' elements into scouting to promote national fitness by inspiring young Britons to emulate what he interpreted to be the most praiseworthy aspects of African life. He drew on a diverse and eclectic mix of tribal peoples in designing the Boy Scout movement that included Amerindians, Arab Bedouins, New Zealand Maoris, and British youth gangs, but Africans occupied a central place in his thinking. Late Victorian and Edwardian British imperialists believed that their non-western subjects lived in primordial static tribal societies that were far down the evolutionary ladder in comparison to the 'modern' west. In truth, tribes were political units that usually formed in response to the expansion of imperial power, but the concept of the tribe was a useful category that allowed empire builders to make sense of the unfamiliar and confusing societies they conquered.[3] Regardless, Baden-Powell firmly believed tribal peoples preserved pure and noble institutions and traditions that could be recaptured by the west once they were shorn of inappropriate or 'immoral' underpinnings. More specifically, he sought to teach younger generations of Britons to embrace the self-discipline, obedience, and physical toughness that the soft comforts of western modernity had stripped away.

Most historical considerations of the later British empire emphasize that British rule introduced new values and customs into the non-western communities of the imperial periphery. Yet the processes of conquering and governing 'tribal peoples' also transformed the British metropole. Older histories of imperialism tended to assert that either the empire had no impact on metropolitan British history, or that it represented a set of

---

[2] Sir Robert Baden-Powell, *Scouting for Boys: A Handbook for Instruction in Good Citizenship* (9th edn, 1920).
[3] P.S. Well, 'The Barbarians Speak', in *Roman Imperialism*, ed. Craige Champion (Malden, MA, 2004), 254.

abstract ideas that politicians and public intellectuals used to promote national unity across class and party lines. More recent studies have moved beyond this debate to explore how the British public interpreted and internalised imperial ideas.[4]

In reality, however, the processes of becoming a global imperial power influenced metropolitan politics and society even more directly and profoundly. British imperialists may have denigrated non-western cultures to legitimise the violence of empire building, but they also had to assimilate their new subjects' values and traditions to govern them. Imperialists on the periphery brought these values back to Britain when they returned home, where the partisans of empire romanticised non-western cultures to convince the British public to support the imperial enterprise. In doing so, the imperial special interest groups introduced significant 'tribal' elements into British popular culture. For example, Nupur Chaudhuri has shown how western women returning from India made Kashmiri shawls and Indian curry staple elements of metropolitan British life in the 19th century.[5]

Similarly, Boy Scouting was not an African institution, but it taught British boys to 'act African'. Baden-Powell's idealised tribal institutions bore little resemblance to their African equivalents, but neither was British curry authentically Indian. Baden-Powell's vivid accounts of African tribal life were not mere topoi intended to critique the failings of metropolitan British society. Just as colonised peoples appropriated and reinterpreted western culture, Britons borrowed freely, albeit sometimes unconsciously, from their imperial subjects. In doing so, they did not create an alien colonial 'other'; rather, they were confident enough in their cultural superiority that they could appropriate and reinterpret what they considered to be the most virtuous aspects of 'tribal life'. Urban British boys embraced scouting, at least in part, because they found its anglicised African elements added adventure and stimulation to their increasingly mundane daily lives.

1. *Scouting and Colonial Soldiering*

The Scout movement's African characteristics reflected the expertise and biases that Baden-Powell acquired in roughly two decades of fighting in African colonial wars. As a member of the colonial military caste, he actively sought service in these campaigns to advance his career and win fame and fortune. Although his career began in India, he made his reputation during the Zululand campaign against Dinizulu in 1888, the 1895 Asante expedition in the Gold Coast (Ghana), and the suppression of the Ndebele (modern Zimbabwe) uprising one year later. Baden-Powell supplemented his income by publishing accounts of his exploits, which built his reputation and helped him win the rank of brevet colonel during what the British termed the 'Matabele expedition'. He made no apologies for his brutal treatment of the Ndebele and justified killing 200 African fighters on the grounds that 'any hesitation or softness is construed by them as

[4] Much of this work comes from the 'Studies in Imperialism' series of the University of Manchester Press. For examples see: *Imperialism and Juvenile Literature*, ed. Jeffrey Richards (Manchester, 1989); *Imperialism and Popular Culture*, ed. John MacKenzie (Manchester, 1992); Anandi Ramamurthy, *Imperial Persuaders: Images of Africa and Asia in British Advertising* (Manchester, 2003).
[5] Nupur Chaudhuri, 'Shawls, Jewelry, Curry, and Rice in Victorian Britain', in *Western Women and Imperialism: Complicity and Resistance*, ed. Nupur Chaudhuri and Margaret Strobel (Bloomington, 1992), 238–41.

a sign of weakness, and at once restores their confidence and courage'.[6] With his expertise in African warfare firmly established, Baden-Powell published a small handbook on frontier fighting and tracking called *Aids to Scouting for NCOs and Men* that would later serve as a key inspiration for the Boy Scout movement.

Although Baden-Powell won a measure of fame killing Africans, his reputation grew exponentially after his successful defence of the frontier town of Mafeking during the South African War. His leadership of the small garrison during the roughly yearlong siege by a much larger Afrikaner force made him a national celebrity in Britain. After the British victory, the war office put him in charge of a new paramilitary police unit called the South African Constabulary. The command gave Baden-Powell the opportunity to put his ideas on leadership, self-improvement, and character building into practice. The force's motto 'Be Prepared' would eventually become the scout motto, and its uniform of a Stetson hat and khaki shirt and shorts was the model for the scout uniform.

Baden-Powell was a fully-fledged imperial hero when he returned to Britain to become the inspector-general of the cavalry in 1903. His exploits captured the imagination of British boys, who helped push sales of *Aids to Scouting for NCOs and Men* over the 100,000-copy mark.[7] William Smith, the founder of the Boys' Brigade, asked him to rewrite the manual for his christian uniformed youth movement. The Brigade was Britain's first national organisation for boys, and Baden-Powell became one of Smith's vice-presidents. He parted ways with Smith, however, when Smith refused to give his scout programme a more central role in the Boys' Brigade curriculum.[8]

Scouting grew out of Baden-Powell's decision to found his own independent youth movement that would promote physical, moral, and imperial fitness among British youth by capitalising on their fascination with 'frontier scouting' and tribal life. The publisher of *Aids to Scouting* bankrolled the venture and brought out a new edition of the book for the youth market entitled *Scouting for Boys*, which is what Americans now call the 'Scout Handbook'. In 1909, over 11,000 uniformed boy scouts turned up for a rally at Crystal Palace. Scouting's growing popularity inspired Baden-Powell to retire from the army to devote his full attention to the movement.

Initially, Baden-Powell gave relatively little thought to developing a coherent ideology for scouting. Over time, several key themes emerged in his thinking and became the central core of the scout creed. Worried that urban slums, social unrest, and moral laxity had undermined Britain's national security, he sought to prepare younger generations to defend their nation and empire. Just as life on the imperial frontier taught virility, resourcefulness, and self-discipline, scouting was a 'school of the woods' that would save the empire by instilling these same ideals in British youth. Baden-Powell looked to the tribal peoples of the frontier to rediscover the vital martial qualities that materialism had expunged from 'civilised' western society. In explaining why Africa and Africans occupied

[6] Robert Baden-Powell, *The Matabele Campaign, 1896* (Westport, 1970), 63. Baden-Powell, however, failed to mention that he almost faced a court martial for his decision to make an example of captured Ndebele fighters by executing them without trial. For the official correspondence regarding the British government's decision not to prosecute him see: TNA (PRO), WO 32/5626: governor Cape Colony to colonial secretary, 22 Dec. 1896.

[7] Tim Jeal, *The Boy-Man: The Life of Lord Baden-Powell* (New York, 1990), 361.

[8] J.O. Springhall, 'The Boy Scouts, Class and Militarism in Relation to British Youth Movements, 1908–1930', *International Review of Social History*, xvi (1971), 131–2; John Springhall and Brian Fraser, *Sure and Steadfast: A History of the Boys' Brigade* (1983), 102.

a central place in scouting, he declared: 'Why do I like Africa? Well, because you can get away from cinemas and jazz, motor-buses and crowds, noisy streets, stuffy with petrol-exhaust fumes, and all the artificial life which we call civilization.'[9]

Historians have debated whether Baden-Powell secretly intended scouting to prepare young men for military service in the tense years before the First World War.[10] Baden-Powell always emphatically denied the charge, but the popular backlash against militarism stemming from the war in Europe in the 1920s led him to de-emphasize the movement's overt nationalism. Instead, he recast scouting as a force for promoting international peace and understanding. In later editions of *Scouting for Boys*, he declared that European frontiersmen like the North American trappers, Central American hunters, Australian drovers, and the South African Constabulary were in fact 'peace scouts' rather than agents of western imperialism.[11] His later writings still emphasized that scouting would strengthen the empire by preparing British boys to face the rigours of the frontier, but Baden-Powell also now acknowledged that non-Europeans could also be scouts. In this sense he believed that the movement could help convince colonised peoples to see things from 'the white man's point of view'.[12]

2. The African Roots of the Scout Movement

Although Baden-Powell believed firmly that Britons were racially and culturally superior to their colonial subjects, tribal peoples in general, and the Zulu in particular, loomed large in his imagination. He did not fight in the Anglo-Zulu War of 1879, but like most Britons he was impressed by King Cetshwayo's crushing defeat of the British army at the battle of Isandhlawana. It did not matter that the Zulu eventually lost the war. Their success in standing up to the imperial forces fixed their reputation as a prototypical 'martial tribe' in the eyes of both military elites and the general British public. Queen Victoria herself described the Zulu as 'the finest and bravest race in South Africa'.[13] As was the case with the Nepalese Gurkhas in South Asia, British imperialists reasoned that any non-western people who could defeat them in battle had to be particularly tough and noble.[14]

Over time, many British officers came to believe that the Zulu and related groups like the Ndebele preserved the virtues of loyalty, morality, and self-sacrifice that were

[9] Robert Baden-Powell, *African Adventures* (1937), 73.

[10] For a summary of the debate see: Michael Rosenthal, *The Character Factory: Baden-Powell's Boy Scouts and the Imperatives of Empire* (New York, 1984); Allen Warren, 'Sir Robert Baden-Powell, the Scout Movement and Citizen Training in Great Britain, 1900–1920', *EHR*, ci (1986); John Springhall, 'Baden-Powell and the Scout Movement Before 1920: Citizen Training or Soldiers of the Future', *EHR*, cii (1987).

[11] Sir Robert Baden-Powell, *Scouting for Boys: A Handbook for Instruction in Good Citizenship* (13th edn, 1920), 25.

[12] Sir Robert Baden-Powell, 'White Men in Black Skins', *Elders Review of West African Affairs*, viii (1929), 7.

[13] Carolyn Hamilton, *Terrific Majesty: The Powers of Shaka Zulu and the Limits of Historical Invention* (Cambridge, 1998), 112.

[14] In practice, the Gurkhas actually had diverse ethnic origins. Initially, they were a product of the British military imagination that viewed them as 'warrior gentlemen' who soldiered for the empire because they respected the equally brave British officer caste. Lionel Caplan, *Warrior Gentleman: 'Gurkhas' in the Western Imagination* (Providence, 1995), 10–12.

vanishing from the increasingly individualistic modern western society. With Zululand entirely pacified in the 20th century, Baden-Powell could comfortably claim: 'I loved the Zulus, even though I had to fight against them.'[15]

Yet Baden-Powell also had more practical reasons for giving Zulu cultural elements a central place in scouting. In the early years of the Scout movement he borrowed heavily from Ernest Thompson Seton's plan for using Amerindian culture and lore to train western boys in woodcraft. Seton was a British-born American naturalist who had a complicated relationship with scouting. Although he helped found the Boy Scouts of America and met personally with Baden-Powell on visits to Britain, he resigned from American scouting's executive board in 1915 on the grounds that the movement was becoming too militaristic.[16] Seton's books on the North American frontier fascinated the British public, but Baden-Powell was reluctant to incorporate too many American elements into scouting because he wanted sole authority to define the nature and character of the movement. He therefore implied that Seton had overstated the virtues of the Amerindians: 'I know a little about the Red Indian, and he is not (and was not in his prime) all he is pictured by some who write about him only on his sunny side.'[17]

By comparison, Baden-Powell claimed an expert knowledge of the Zulu. Stressing that his expertise in African tribal life came from personal experience rather than books, he implied that he had discovered, rather than invented, the Boy Scout movement during his travels and campaigns in Africa. The Zulu thus became prototypical scouts who could teach British youth the virtues of discipline, chivalry, friendship, and woodsmanship through their exemplary reading of the 'book of Nature'.[18] Yet Baden-Powell's self-declared respect for African 'savages', did not mean that he viewed them as equals. He referred to colonial campaigning as 'nigger fighting' and openly questioned whether African boys had the skull capacity to comprehend western education. Nevertheless, he paid the Zulu what he undoubtedly considered to be the supreme compliment by declaring that they were 'white men at heart'.[19]

Baden-Powell first introduced British boys to his version of Zulu customs in 1907 at a, now famous, experimental camp on Brownsea Island. Intended to test out the ideas in *Aids to Scouting for NCOs and Men* that he had adapted for youth work, the outdoor gathering marked the formal beginning of the Boy Scout movement. For approximately ten days, Baden-Powell led a mixed company of 22 public school and working class boys in camping, cooking, playing games, tying knots, and learning tracking and woodcraft. Every morning he blew an Ndebele kudu horn to wake the scouts, and in the evening he told them 'yarns' about his adventures in Africa. He also taught them his interpretation of a Zulu call and response chant that he called 'Een-Gonyama – Gonyama'.[20]

[15] Baden-Powell, *African Adventures*, 115.

[16] Jeal, *The Boy-Man*, 376–7, 381.

[17] Robert Baden-Powell, *B.-P.'s Outlook: Selections from the Founder's Contributions to The Scouter from 1909 – 1941* (Ottawa, 1979), 95: July 1920.

[18] Baden-Powell, *B.-P.'s Outlook*, 95; Robert Baden-Powell, *What Scouts Can Do: More Yarns* (Philadelphia, 1922), 74.

[19] Baden-Powell, *What Scouts Can Do: More Yarns*, 129; Robert Baden-Powell, *Scouting and Youth Movements* (New York, 1931), 101; Baden-Powell, 'White Men in Black Skins', 6.

[20] Jeal, *The Boy-Man*, 383–6.

Baden-Powell did not incorporate African elements into scouting in a systematic fashion. Instead, he fell back on his personal impressions of the various African societies he encountered during his military career and turned his personal mementos into scout artifacts. Collecting 'trophies' was a common practice in most of Britain's colonial wars, and the British victors in the Anglo-Zulu War of 1879 went home with spears, shields, clubs, wooden milk jugs, spoons, and even the dried sole of a foot of a dead Zulu.[21] None of Baden-Powell's African treasures were this grizzly. Most were fairly simple items that took on totemic qualities once he incorporated them into the Scout movement.

The kudu horn used at the Brownsea camp was a fairly innocuous keepsake of the Matabele campaign. It became the stuff of scout legend after he donated it to the British Scout Association for use in its scoutmaster training courses at Gilwell Park. John Thurman, the Gilwell camp chief, told generations of scoutmasters that Baden-Powell acquired the horn because he was impressed with how Ndebele warriors used it as a 'war horn' to send coded messages to each other.[22] In his later years Baden-Powell made a point of blowing the horn for rapt audiences at international scout jamborees.

Similarly, Baden-Powell incorporated carved willow beads from a 12-foot-long Zulu necklace into the badges, marking successful completion of the Woodbadge scoutmaster training course. He claimed to have captured the necklace from King Dinizulu in the 1888 Zululand campaign, but his biographer, Tim Jeal, asserts that it actually came from a dying Zulu girl that he happened across during the fighting. After Baden-Powell's death in 1941, the British Scout Association made the story more palatable by turning the necklace into a gift that an admiring Dinizulu bestowed on Baden-Powell. In fact, the Zulu king surrendered to the governor of Natal and there is no evidence that he ever even met the founder of the Scout movement.[23]

Nevertheless, official scouting now holds that the beads are symbols of loyalty and bravery. The South African Scout Association, which faced international condemnation for its unwillingness to speak out against apartheid, tried to use them to win allies in the world Scout movement. It commissioned four reproductions of the complete necklace and gave them to high-ranking officials of the American and British Scout Associations at the 1967 World Jamboree. Scout lore also holds that the Zulu royal family demanded the return of the remaining original beads until they learned of their esteemed place in the scout programme.[24]

Many of the other important African elements in the Boy Scout movement were largely products of Baden-Powell's imagination. Starting with actual Zulu institutions, he appropriated and reconfigured them as exotic tribal customs for consumption by impressionable British boys. Critics charged that scouting had a secret militaristic agenda because its members wore uniforms and advanced through military-style ranks.

[21] Michael Lieven, 'A Victorian Genre: Military Memoirs and the Anglo-Zulu War', *Journal of the Society for Army Historical Research*, lxxvii (1999), 119.

[22] John Thurman, *The Gilwell Book* (2nd edn, 1930).

[23] Jeal, *The Boy-Man*, 134; Malawi National Archives, 17/BSA/1/210: organizing commissioner Nyasaland Boy Scout Association to governor's private secretary, 16 Nov. 1951; Jeff Guy, 'Imperial Appropriations: Baden-Powell, the Woodbadge, and the Zulu *Iziqu*', in *Being Zulu: Contesting Identities Past and Present*, ed. Benedict Carton, John Laband and Jabulani Sithole (forthcoming).

[24] South African Scout Association Archives, Cape Town, BC 956/H/1967: Jamboree, Dinizulu's Necklace, South African Boy Scout Association, c.1967.

Baden-Powell, however, claimed that he got the idea for the scout ranks of tenderfoot through first class scout, which really do not conform to military norms, from Zulu age tests. In one of his standard 'yarns' he recounted how Zulus, Ndebeles, and other related peoples tested young candidates for warriorhood by painting them white before sending them alone into the 'jungle' armed only with a spear. These young men had to rely on their stalking and hunting skills to survive, and could be killed by any adult who discovered them while they were still white. If they survived the month it took for the whitewash to wear off, the tribe welcomed them back as warriors.[25] In recounting the story to British audiences Baden-Powell added: 'I don't suppose that very many British town boys could do it unless they were Boy Scouts, and I expect that a good many even of these would starve in the attempt. . . . I am supposing that you have nothing more than your shield and assegai with you. Think it over.'[26] Baden-Powell based the 'Een-Gonyama – Gonyama' praise song that he taught the Brownsea scouts on a song he heard in Zululand. Claiming that he at first confused massed singing Zulu warriors with a church organ, he tried to teach his boys to replicate what the novelist H. Rider Haggard, who was similarly moved by Zulu singing, called a 'chant never to be forgotten'.[27] Baden-Powell similarly drew on Zulu military dancing as inspiration for the scouts' 'war dance' mentioned at the beginning of this essay. He appears to have initially envisioned his adaptation of Zulu war songs and dances as entertaining campfire diversions, but later Scout authorities ruled that the 'Een-Gonyama' song was only for special occasions.[28]

Smaller examples of Baden-Powell's 'Zuluisms' are peppered throughout the traditions and literature of the Scout movement. He told them that scouts were to carry long walking sticks because Zulu boys acting as 'orderlies' for older warriors used similar staves to carry supplies and sleeping mats. Baden-Powell also adopted the Zulu title *Mhlala-paunzi*, 'the man who lies down to shoot', as the motto for the Scout 'marksmanship' proficiency badge on the grounds that it meant planning before taking action.[29]

3. Boy Scouting in an Imperial Context

Baden-Powell's appropriation and reinterpretation of 'tribal' tradition demonstrates the indirect influence of subject peoples of the empire on metropolitan British society. Scouting's romanticised trappings of African culture captured the imagination of generations of British boys and helped make Baden-Powell's organisation the premier uniformed youth movement in Britain. Although confident that they were superior to their African subjects, British politicians, educators, and social reformers agreed with Baden-Powell that 'tribal' Africans preserved many of the manly virtues that had been undermined by the industrial age.

[25] Robert Baden-Powell, *Young Knights of the Empire: Their Code and Further Scout Yarns* (Philadelphia, 1917), 204.

[26] Baden-Powell, *What Scouts Can Do: More Yarns*, 73.

[27] Baden-Powell, *What Scouts Can Do: More Yarns*, 75; H. Rider Haggard, *Cetywayo and His White Neighbors* (1882).

[28] Kenya Scout Archives, Nairobi, KBSA/C/54/34: Uganda Boy Scout Association Quarterly Newsletter, no. 5, Apr. 1948.

[29] Baden-Powell, *What Scouts Can Do: More Yarns*, 124, 164.

Baden-Powell and his allies were largely unaware of the broader implications of their cultural borrowing. Scouting was not simply a case of disenchanted western elites romanticising an exotic colonised 'other' to critique their own social failings. Just as Britons wore Kashmiri shawls and have come to love their version of Indian curry, the Boy Scout movement taught British boys to 'act African', albeit in an entirely western fashion. More to the point, scouting grew into an enormously successful institution because adventurous and imaginative British boys actually wanted to be African, at least in the way that Baden-Powell described being African. In the 1930s, several schoolboys embarrassed the segregated white South African Scout Association by asking how to join the Pathfinders, the segregated African branch of the movement, on the grounds that it was more authentically African.[30]

Popular British enthusiasm for 'tribal' Africa did not translate into respect for Africans any more than eating curry generated metropolitan support for Indian nationalism. Rather, scouting demonstrated how imperially-minded Britons appropriated desirable African cultural elements, reimagined them, and made them their own. In this the Scout movement had a great deal in common with African efforts to appropriate useful elements of British culture by founding their own independent schools and christian churches.[31]

Scouting was thus part of a larger hybrid imperial culture linking Britain with peripheral societies that transformed both the British and their colonial subjects. From the metropolitan standpoint, the British empire was much more than a set of ideas that could be invoked for political and social purposes by politicians and public intellectuals. It was instead an intimate embrace between Britons and the people they conquered and reigned over. The realities of imperial governance and indirect rule required British administrators first to understand and then to assimilate the cultural values of their subjects. Scouting's African origins demonstrate that, despite their overt cultural chauvinism and sometimes open racism, imperialists developed a tacit admiration for their colonial subjects that they imparted to the larger British public.

Finally, the cross-cultural dialogue between the coloniser and the colonised fed back on itself. Although scouting had its roots in Africa, both Baden-Powell and British colonial officials doubted whether Africans had the sophistication and intelligence to grasp the central message of the movement. In practical terms, the fourth scout law, which declared all scouts to be brothers, undermined the strict racial segregation in the settler societies of eastern and southern Africa. Although many African boys and their elders enthusiastically embraced the movement, during the transfer of power it appeared that scouting would die out along with the other trappings of British colonialism.[32]

Yet this did not come to pass. Scouting has survived and flourished in post-colonial Africa. Nationalist politicians seized on the African origins of the Scout movement to reimagine it as authentically African. President Julius Nyerere of Tanzania, who was

---

[30] Tammy Proctor, ' "A Separate Path": Scouting and Guiding in Interwar South Africa', *Comparative Studies in Society and History*, xlii (2000).

[31] E.g., see Derek Peterson, *Creative Writing: Translation, Bookkeeping, and the Work of Imagination in Colonial Kenya* (Portsmouth, 2004).

[32] For a full discussion of the Boy Scout movement in British Africa see Timothy Parsons, *Race, Resistance and the Boy Scout Movement in British Colonial Africa* (Athens, OH, 2004).

himself a former scout, claimed Baden-Powell simply learned scouting from the Zulu.[33] Similarly, Jeremiah Nyaggah, a Kenyan cabinet minister and scout chief commissioner, declared: 'Scouting is African in origin, it was FOUNDED in Mafeking (Africa), NURSED in the United Kingdom, SPREAD all over the world and the founder decided to be buried in Nyeri (Kenya). . . . Why, therefore, shouldn't we Africans feel part and parcel of Scouting? We should modernise and perfect it for others to learn and follow.'[34] In other words, the Scout movement is popular in many African countries because African boys are drawn to the anglicised version of their own cultural heritage.

[33] *Zambian Daily Mail*, 7 Oct. 1975.
[34] *Nation*, 27 July 1971.

'The Cow is Still the Most Important Figure in Indian Politics!': Religion, Imperial Culture and the Shaping of Indian Political Reform in the 1930s

ANDREW MULDOON

This essay assesses the impact of imperial culture, particularly constructions of India and hinduism, on British responses to the Indian nationalist movement in the 1930s. The essay draws on personal and governmental papers, paying special attention to the language and vocabulary employed by British policy makers concerned with Indian affairs. The major issue addressed here is the British presumption that the 1935 Government of India Act, a plan for a federated India with British central control, would defuse nationalist agitation. Such a sanguine view of this proposal seemed misplaced, given the popular success of the nationalists, especially Gandhi, and given the explicit demands of Indians for full self-government. However, such an optimistic assessment drew on presumptions about Indian political and social behaviour, and especially on conceptions of hinduism. Policy makers in Britain and India argued along well-established lines, that hinduism inculcated moral and physical weakness, among other deficiencies, and that a British offer of compromise would attract many Indians who feared continuing confrontation with the Raj. Moreover, colonial advisors relied on a belief that social and caste divisions within hinduism would recur within the nationalist ranks as well. This sense that Indians would respond to half-measures of reform persisted until the 1937 provincial elections. Though British administrators predicted only a moderate showing by the Indian National Congress, the polling proved otherwise, as Congress took power in the majority of the provinces. The Raj lasted another decade, but the confident cultural assumptions sustaining it took a fatal blow.

Keywords: British India; hinduism; Indian National Congress; orientalism; Sir Malcolm Hailey; M.K. Gandhi; Government of India Act 1935; Katherine Mayo; Indian political intelligence; christianity

It will come as little surprise to imperial historians that the debates of the 1930s over the future of British India were replete with religious references. On all sides, policy makers and observers invoked God, christian duty and imperial mission. Indeed, as Gerald Studdert-Kennedy has so persuasively argued, the public debate over Indian political reform demonstrated a notable reliance on such 'Christian discourse'.[1] However, there was another, perhaps even more important, discourse about religion and India which suffused British discussions about the best way to maintain the Raj in the face of an organised nationalist campaign. Historians have noted the presence of such a discourse, but have not explored its impact in much depth; to quote

---

[1] Gerald Studdert-Kennedy, *British Christians, Indian Nationalists and the Raj* (Delhi, 1991), esp. ch. 1.

Studdert-Kennedy again: 'The discourse or structure of ideas in terms of which the "India Public" in England interpreted India's distinctive fusion of religion and nationalism has not been fully explored.'[2] There existed something of a consensus about the fundamental religious foundation of Indian society, and specifically about the nature and practice of hinduism in India. Yet these conceptions of Indian religiosity and of hinduism were employed simultaneously both to support and to condemn the 1935 Government of India Act, a piece of legislation that granted provincial autonomy and a federal system to India, albeit with significant powers still reserved to British control. Those who opposed the reform proposals argued very publicly that a communally-divided and hindu-led India could not capably govern itself, while those who supported the reforms as a means of holding onto the Raj – although they could hardly say so publicly – believed that they could exploit what they saw as religious divisions and, even more so, the weaknesses of the 'hindu character' in order to undermine the nationalist cause. In essence, the architects of the 1935 act based their strategy not just on mechanical calculations of divide-and-rule, but also on specific cultural understandings about India, and hinduism in particular. They believed that this moderate reform would in fact de-fang the nationalists. As a historian of American foreign relations has reminded us recently, policy makers are human too: they 'are subjects of culture, not just policy-wonks who shed their images of others like raincoats at the office door'.[3] British cultural perceptions about India were certainly important in justifying colonial rule and in designing strategies of imperial governance and control; it should therefore not be a great surprise that these conceptions also influenced how the British played the imperial end-game.

As it had in debates over the future of British rule in Ireland, religion usually worked its way into the Indian controversy, and not only in rhetoric praising Britain's mission and duty in India. For example, Edwin Montagu, the architect of the Indian reforms of 1919, found himself the object of anti-semitic attacks that characterised him as an 'Asiatic' and not a true Briton.[4] That religious ideas and rhetoric surrounded the debate on the 1935 act is especially unsurprising, for those who gathered at the round table conferences, party conferences and parliamentary committees on India were collectively a fairly pious bunch. They included the high anglican viceroy, Lord Irwin, known at times as the 'Holy Fox'; stout churchmen like Stanley Baldwin and Samuel Hoare; the liberal-minded archbishop of Canterbury, Cosmo Gordon Lang; and christian imperialists like Henry Page Croft.[5] Gandhi, of course, occupied his own unique place on this crowded stage. This display of religiosity hardly went unnoticed, especially among the less devout, more acerbic set. One editor called Irwin 'his "Theological Excellency"', and a young R.A. Butler supposed that Irwin 'had dealt with [Gandhi] as one mystic with

---

[2] Gerald Studdert-Kennedy, *Providence and the Raj: Imperial Mission and Missionary Imperialism* (New Delhi, 1998), 47.

[3] Andrew Rotter, 'Saidism without Said: Orientalism and U.S. Diplomatic History', *American Historical Review*, cv (2000), 1205–17.

[4] Chandrika Kaul, *Reporting the Raj: The British Press and India, c. 1880–1922* (Manchester, 2004), 174–5.

[5] For reference, see, among others: Philip Williamson, *Stanley Baldwin: Conservative Leadership and National Values* (Cambridge, 1999), esp. ch. 9; Henry Page Croft, *My Life of Strife* (1948); Andrew Roberts, *The Holy Fox: A Biography of Lord Halifax* (1991).

another'.[6] An Indian politician, meanwhile, described the Irwin–Gandhi negotiations of early 1931 as a meeting of 'the two uncrucified Christs'.[7]

Christian ideas and rhetoric pervaded both public and private conversations about the future of the Raj. Irwin justified his efforts at placating nationalist opinion as a sort of atonement, a way of 'paying for the sins of past days', and was convinced that the 'salvation of India' from the immoderate Congress Party was the highest priority of the day.[8] Other proponents of the Government of India Bill argued that the British 'duty' to India consisted of following up on the pledges made for further political reform in 1919.[9] To the die hard opponents of further Indian reform, any transfer of responsibility for the Indian 'masses' to the nationalists meant, in the words of one, the desecration of 'the sacrifices of our ancestors' who had 'pour[ed] out their blood and their treasure to perform the miracle of the Pax Britannia in India'.[10] Another opponent of Indian reforms argued that supporters of these measures had ceased to believe in the 'moral duty' of an empire that had 'shown itself to be the greatest force of progress in the world next to the Christian Church'.[11] Opponents of the reforms congregated in the Indian Defence League and pledged 'to see the British mission in India faithfully discharged'.[12] These were vivid religious sentiments, then, cloaked to various degrees in the rhetoric of sin, expiation and sacrifice.

Nevertheless, it would not do to conclude that religious, or christian, ideals were the driving force behind all sides of the debate over India's future. Certainly with the passage of the India Act in 1935, some die hard opponents of it did feel, like the remnants of Cromwell's forces in 1660, that God had spat in their faces. Page Croft wrote that '[w]hen Britain leaves India this witness to the Cross will forever end and the whole power of Christian example will evaporate'.[13] Others, though, including Winston Churchill, had opposed the act for more directly political, not theological reasons, though his rhetoric was at times highly religious.[14] And while Irwin, and even Baldwin, had viewed the growth of Indian autonomy within a christian Hegelian framework, many others in their party had seen the act not as an exercise in ushering India towards an independent future, but as a way of out-foxing and bottling up Gandhi and the Congress Party.[15] Even Irwin conceded that the real aim of his efforts was to 'make the shop

---

[6] BL, India Office Library, Reading Papers, MS Eur. F118/24/15J.L: Garvin to Lord Reading, 17 Feb. 1930; Trinity College, Cambridge, Butler Papers, D48/840–2: R.A. Butler to Sir Montagu and Lady Butler, 24 June 1931.

[7] Srinivasa Sastri to Venkatarama Sastri, 17 Feb. 1931, in *Letters of the Right Honourable V.S. Srinivasa Sastri*, ed. T.N. Jagadisan (New York, 1963), 209.

[8] Lambeth Palace Library, Lang Papers, 41/257–63: Lord Irwin to Archbishop Cosmo Lang, 8 Apr. 1927; BL, India Office Library, Irwin Papers, MS Eur. C152/6: Irwin to Wedgwood Benn, 2 Jan. 1930.

[9] See Hansard, 5th ser., cclxxxiii, 197: speech by E. Campbell, MP, 22 Nov. 1933.

[10] Hansard, 5th ser., cclxxxiii, 225: speech by Page Croft; see also Gerald Studdert-Kennedy, 'The Christian Imperialism of the Die-Hard Defenders of the Raj, 1926–35', *Journal of Imperial and Commonwealth History*, xviii (1990), 342–62.

[11] Hansard, 5th ser., cclxxxiii, 134: speech by Viscount Wolmer, 22 Nov. 1933.

[12] BL, India Office Library, Willingdon Papers, MS Eur. E237/5: India Defence League leaflet, 1933.

[13] Page Croft, *My Life*, 249.

[14] Graham Stewart, *Burying Caesar: The Churchill-Chamberlain Rivalry* (1999).

[15] Studdert-Kennedy, *Providence and the Raj*, 52; Williamson, *Stanley Baldwin*, 270–1; Carl Bridge, *Holding India to the Empire: The British Conservative Party and the 1935 Constitution* (New Delhi, 1986).

window look respectable from the Indian point of view'.[16] He admitted to a colleague in 1929, that he had proposed the reforms to allow Britain 'to "get away with" some solution' which would give Indians some provincial autonomy, but allow Britain to keep hold of India itself at the centre.[17] R.A. Butler heard Irwin defend his ideas in 1931 and came away 'disturbed' that the supposedly moralistic viceroy had opted for the strategy of 'Divide to Rule', a maxim which is 'more Roman than British'.[18] In his memoirs, nevertheless, Irwin retreated to the language of the mystic, claiming that, regarding India, Britain had taken the moral high ground in the 1930s: 'Dimly, inarticulately, unconsciously, the instinct of the British people was as usual guiding them wisely.'[19] However, a more recent assessment of Irwin has concluded that he was 'more fox than holy and given to unconscious self-delusion'.[20]

The rhetoric of christian imperialism was, therefore, more widely disseminated than deeply felt, especially on the pro-reform side. This discourse of obligation and moral duty was not the only way in which religion figured in the Indian debates though. Ideas about the role, persistence and influence of religion in India pervaded the debate over the 1935 act on both sides. Three particular understandings were at the core of this discourse: the notion that India was a land still in thrall completely to religion and irrationality; the conflation of hinduism with India, and especially with the nationalists; and the conviction that belief fundamentally divided Indians and thus that the best way to understand the sub-continent was as an amalgamation of religious communities, from the superstitious hindu to the manly muslim and the loyal sikh.[21] Both the popular and the intellectual cultures of empire had produced and reinforced these conceptions about the sub-continent and its people. The foundation for these views was the widely-articulated belief that India was a backward land, one where religion dominated social organisation and popular consciousness. According to the ethnographer H.H. Risley, India was still in the throes of religious belief, as compared to the rationalism of modern Europe.[22] A land so dominated by religion must necessarily have retained other elements of pre-modernity as well, so the argument went. The larger picture that emerged, then, was of an India comprised of small agrarian villages and populated by a backward, parochial peasantry. One former Indian civil servant, writing after his return to Britain, asserted that 'the general pattern of Hindu society as we know it had been established by the seventh century B.C.' and had remained 'static' since the 4th century AD.[23] As practitioners of an ancient religion, the great majority of Indians also lived like the ancients, according to British experts. Indians lived in villages which resembled, in Henry Maine's

[16] BL, India Office Library, Irwin Papers, MS Eur. C152/18/219: Irwin to Lord Stonehaven, 12 Nov. 1928.
[17] University of Birmingham, Neville Chamberlain Papers, 2/22: Neville Chamberlain diary, 26 July 1929.
[18] Trinity College, Cambridge, D48/840–2: Butler to Sir Montagu and Lady Butler, 24 June 1931.
[19] Lord Halifax, *Fulness of Days* (1957), 151.
[20] The quote is from M.E. Yapp's review of H. Tinker, *Viceroy: From Curzon to Mountbatten* (Karachi, 1997), in *Bulletin of the School of Oriental and African Studies*, lxii (1999), 170–1.
[21] Thomas Metcalf, *Ideologies of the Raj* (Cambridge, 1995), 132–48. For an example of the persistence of this conception, see the remarks of Sir Philip Chetwode (commander-in-chief for India) on the potential for Indianising the army. (BL, India Office Library, Permanent Undersecretary Files, MS Eur. d714/17/96–101: Chetwode to Sir (Samuel) Findlater Stewart, 11 May 1932.)
[22] H.H. Risley, *The People of India* (Delhi, 1969), 216.
[23] P.J. Griffiths, *The British Impact on India* (1952), 23–4.

estimation, nothing so much as the earliest English communities.[24] The *Imperial Gazetteer* of 1909 estimated that 90% of Indians lived in communities with populations less than 5,000, and reckoned that nearly all those born in these villages remained there for their entire lives.[25] These communities remained largely isolated from the modern world and its concerns, with most Indians concerned only with matters of 'family, clan or village'.[26] Even an author who supported nationalist aspirations conceded that Indian immaturity had produced a 'naïve excitableness over trifles' and that 'this spirit of revolt has had little effect on India as a whole. The masses still dream on in the villages . . . The true Indian type will always be the same.'[27] Religious practices in these villages reinforced the notion of a backward society in the imperial mind.

Hinduism, the religion of the majority of Indians, occupied the British colonial imagination. The pervasive understanding of hindu India contained some basic, if at times contradictory, assumptions. The religion was synonymous with weakness, both physical and moral, but was also regarded as ancient – traditional and even hidebound – and therefore a metonym for Indian society as a whole. Katherine Mayo's *Mother India*, a must-read for Irwin and many others in British colonial circles in the 1920s – and elsewhere: it had 20 printings between 1928 and 1930 – had reinforced several stereotypes about hinduism, most particularly the notion that it was effeminate, governed by unrestrained sexual desire and led by 'broken-nerved, low-spirited, petulant ancients' whose followers were inevitably 'narrow-chested, near-sighted [and] anemic'.[28] Hindus were 'small weak and timid', according to an official source in 1909.[29] Hindu weakness expressed itself not just physically, but also very much in an Indian penchant for bribery, outlandish rhetoric and double-dealing. A popular study of India from 1934 concluded that: 'The Hindu is the talker, the Mohammedan the fighter.'[30] Such a conception informed the colonial creation of the stock figure of the 'babu', a western-educated hindu prone to excitability and extravagant phrase-making, but also unalterably Indian, lacking in physical and moral courage.[31] The retired Indian administrator Rushbrook Williams summarized this view in 1938, arguing that 'to many Hindus the duty owed to other members of the joint family appears something far stronger than any duty owed to the State; what Westerners call nepotism is in India a positive virtue'.[32] Moreover, to

---

[24] There is an extensive literature on this British belief. See Metcalf, *Ideologies of the Raj*, 68–72, 91; for examples, see the work of Henry Maine, Katherine Mayo, H.H. Risley and Richard Temple, among many others.

[25] *Imperial Gazetteer of India* (Oxford, 1909), i, 433–67.

[26] *Imperial Gazetteer*, i, 433; Risley, *The People of India*, 299–300.

[27] Barbara Wingfield-Stratford, *India and the English* (1922), 97.

[28] Katherine Mayo, *Mother India* (ed. and with an introduction by Mrinalini Sinha) (Ann Arbor, 2000), 92; for concise summaries of this view of hinduism, see Metcalf, *Ideologies of the Raj*, 92–112.

[29] *Imperial Gazetteer*, i, 447.

[30] Charles Sandford, *India: Land of Regrets* (1934), 111.

[31] Mrinalini Sinha, *Colonial Masculinity: The 'Manly Englishman' and the 'Effeminate Bengali' in the Late Nineteenth Century* (Manchester, 1995). For an example of such stock characters in Anglo-Indian literature, see Rudyard Kipling's short story, 'The Head of the District'.

[32] Quoted in Andrew Rotter, *Comrades at Odds: The United States and India, 1947–1964* (Ithaca, 2000), 129–30.

the British, hinduism appeared dominated, and riven, by caste.[33] Even Edward Thompson, father of the historian and normally sympathetic to Indian causes, admitted that caste had left India mired in 'Hindu social injustice'.[34] This sense that caste was such a fundamental force in India pervaded British governing circles to such a degree that, for example, India office intelligence reports on indigenous politicians began with a classification of these men's caste status: Malaviya was a 'Malwa Brahmin', Nehru a 'Kashmiri Brahmin', and even Jinnah was described as 'Mussalman (Khoja)'.[35]

The nationalist movement, furthermore, was in British eyes a hindu-dominated effort that drew mainly on the 'Hindu middle classes of the towns'.[36] Indeed, it had, by the 1930s, taken on some of the trappings of hinduism itself, with the use of religious symbols, hindu hymns, and especially the very public piety of Gandhi.[37] One British administrator recalled in the 1950s that there had been a 'close association of aggressive Hinduism with nationalism'.[38] The notion that the Congress was the party of hinduism strengthened one further British assumption about Indian society: that it was permanently and historically divided by religion, and by hinduism and islam specifically.[39] As the Anglo-Indian popular author, Flora Annie Steel, had put it, India was a 'vast category of races, creeds [and] customs'.[40] Lord Lothian, who toured India in 1932 as part of an effort to determine how to structure the Indian franchise, reported that 'Indian society . . . is essentially a congeries of widely separated classes, races and communities with divergencies of interests and hereditary sentiment which for ages have precluded common action or local unanimity.'[41] The 1934 report of the parliamentary committee which examined the proposed Indian political reforms concluded that 'Hinduism is distinguished by the phenomenon of caste . . . the religion of Islam on the other hand is based upon the conception of the equality of man.'[42] Irwin resorted to more decorative

[33] For discussions of the growth of British ideas about caste, see, among others: Bernard Cohn, 'Notes on the History of the Study of Indian Society and Culture', in his *An Anthropologist among the Historians and Other Essays* (Delhi, 1987); Nicholas Dirks, *Castes of Mind: Colonialism and the Making of Modern India* (Princeton, 2001), esp. chs 3, 10.

[34] Edward Thompson, *The Reconstruction of India* (1930), 262–3.

[35] For all three, see profiles in BL, India Office Library, Indian Political Intelligence files, L/PJ/12/201/2–4, 8–10, 27–9. 'Khoja' refers to a particular sect within shi'ite islam.

[36] Sir Michael O'Dwyer, *India as I Knew It* (1925), 39.

[37] For an incisive examination of some of the ways in which Congress politicians utilised 'hindu idioms and ideologies', see William Gould, 'Congress Radicals and Hindu Militancy: Sampurnanand and Purushottam Das Tandon in the Politics of the United Provinces, 1930–1947', *Modern Asian Studies*, xxxvi (2002), 619–55.

[38] P.J. Griffiths, *The British Impact on India* (1952), 486.

[39] There is now an immense literature on this British conception of a communally-divided India, and on the possible impact that such an understanding has had on Indian politics throughout the 20th century. For the former see: Metcalf, *Ideologies of the Raj*, and G. Pandey, *The Construction of Communalism in Colonial North India* (Delhi, 1990). For the debate on the latter, see among others, the essays by Amartya Sen and Ayesha Jalal in *Nationalism, Democracy and Development: State and Politics in India*, ed. Sugata Bose and Ayesha Jalal (Delhi, 1998), and the contributions of Mushirul Hasan and Sumit Sarkar in *Contesting the Nation: Religion, Community and the Politics of Democracy in India*, ed. David Ludden (Philadelphia, 1996).

[40] Quoted in Benita Parry, *Delusions and Discoveries: India in the British Imagination, 1880–1930* (2nd edn, 1988), 123.

[41] Quoted in Bidyut Chakrabarty, 'The Communal Award of 1932 and its Implications in Bengal', *Modern Asian Studies*, xxiii (1989), 493–523.

[42] Bodl., Conservative Party Archives (CPA), microform 1934/52: 'The Future of India', joint select committee on Indian constitutional reform, 1934.

language in 1935, recalling 'what a unique mosaic of humanity India is'.[43] Those charged with ruling India in the 1930s could hardly have ignored such thinking, for, of course, the idea of hindu–muslim separation had already been enshrined in Indian governance under the auspices of such reforms as the Morley-Minto programme of 1909 which instituted separate communal electorates for the Indian legislative council.

Supporters and opponents of what became the 1935 act invoked these ideas about India throughout the debates of the early 1930s, demonstrating just how effectively they had become embedded in the British imperial consciousness, through their diffusion through popular culture, in the syllabi of the public schools and universities, and in political discourse about everything from imperial justification to the debate over women's suffrage.[44] There was, indeed, a common discourse or vocabulary for discussing India, one based on widely-shared assumptions and beliefs about the sub-continent. The major difference between the supporters and opponents of the 1935 act was that the latter employed these tropes publicly, while the former used these conceptions of India mainly among themselves, as reassurance that their reform scheme would achieve its true purpose of thwarting nationalist aspirations.

Die-hard opponents of the reform legislation fell back on all of these descriptions of Indian behaviour in their efforts to derail the proposals. They argued that Britain could not abandon the vast Indian masses which remained locked into pre-modern modes of thinking and were thus virtually children: a 'hardy, patient, but inarticulate folk' in the words of the Conservative MP, Patrick Donner.[45] Opponents of the 1935 proposals brandished this image of India, a land of simple, illiterate and child-like peasants – the 'humble, silent millions', as Lord Curzon had put it – in their argument for continuing the British guardianship, or quasi-parental oversight, of India.[46] Die hards like Page Croft quoted approvingly in the house of commons from the work of both Mayo and Patricia Kendall, two Americans who had toured India and concluded that Indians were so trapped in their backward villages that only Britain could ensure the advancement of education, technology and sanitation in much of India.[47] Moreover, Croft, Churchill and their fellow die hards argued that the inherent provincialism and localism of the average Indian proved that no unified conception of 'India' even existed – thus making any case for an autonomous Indian central government completely moot. In their view, only Britain had been able to prevent the sub-continent's descent into a many-sided civil war.[48]

Ideas about an entrenched caste system, and about the hindu orientation of the nationalist party generally, combined with this notion of an unsophisticated Indian

---

[43] Viscount Halifax, speech of 4 Dec. 1934, reprinted as 'Indian Constitutional Reform', *International Affairs*, xiv (1935), 198–216.

[44] Antoinette Burton, *Burdens of History: British Feminists, Indian Women and Imperial Culture, 1865–1915* (Chapel Hill, 1994); Katherine Castle, 'The Imperial Indian: India in British History Textbooks for Schools, 1890–1914', in *The Imperial Curriculum: Racial Images and Education in the British Colonial Experience*, ed. J.A. Mangan (1993).

[45] Hansard, 5th ser., cclxxxiii, 154: 22 Nov. 1933.

[46] Nayana Goradia, *Lord Curzon: The Last of the British Moghuls* (Delhi, 1993), 177.

[47] See Page Croft speech in Hansard, 5th ser., cclxxxiii, 225; Patricia Kendall, *Come with Me to India!* (New York, 1931), 261.

[48] See, e.g., Churchill's Albert Hall speech, 18 Mar. 1931, in *Winston S. Churchill: His Complete Speeches, 1897–1963*, ed. R.R. James (8 vols, New York, 1974), v, 5003–9.

peasantry to intensify the criticism further. Given the aims and practices of the Congress, the creation of a 'hindu despotism' would be the only result.[49] According to the India Defence League (IDL), a die hard pressure group, political reform could only end up placing 'the dumb and helpless millions of India under the heel of their hereditary oppressors'.[50] The IDL's argument even invoked the Nazis in predicting the effect of such religious division in India: 'We have seen the results of similar conditions in Germany. The results will be far worse in India.'[51] Without British guidance, the die hards claimed, India would slip back into a 'barbarism' in which the lower castes and untouchables would suffer under the rule of a rapacious Brahmin elite.[52] A clergyman opposed to the reforms argued that they would leave India in the hands of a corrupt 'priestly' caste.[53] The editor of the right-wing *Morning Post* saw a capitulation to the 'timorous Hindoo'.[54] At Manchester's Free Trade Hall in 1933, Lord Lloyd combined all of these elements into a sweeping condemnation of the reforms, declaring that they would leave 'several hundreds of millions of people . . . to be handed over to the tender mercies of the Brahmin oligarchy, of Bombay monopolists, of Ahmedabad millowners, of usurers more exacting than Shylock, and priests more zealous than Torquemada'.[55] The emphasis on the hindu domination of the Congress underpinned yet another aspect of the die hards' criticism: the claim that without the benevolent presence of the British, India would devolve into communal violence and the repression of muslims, sikhs and other non-hindus. Lloyd warned that 'we know the strength of religious and communal feeling in India and the danger to the general security which it constantly threatens'.[56] Churchill thundered that even earlier Indian reforms had not brought 'peace between jarring races and rival religions . . . they have only wakened old passions which were slumbering under the Pax Britannica'.[57] The *Indian Empire Review*, the house organ of the die hards consistently predicted that without British protection, muslims would disappear from India entirely.[58] On a comparative note, it is also worth adding that this was not the first time that arguments about priestly despotism had been used by opponents of colonial self-rule. After all, one recurring theme throughout the debates over Irish home rule had been that home rule meant 'Rome rule' with nefarious and scheming jesuits in control of a superstitious and backward Irish peasantry. The Ulster Unionist, Colonel Edward Saunderson, for example, predicted only doom if Ireland 'bowed down to the sacerdotal yoke'.[59]

[49] Winston Churchill speech to Indian Empire Society, 12 Dec. 1930 in Winston Churchill, *India: Speeches and an Introduction* (1931), 40–7.

[50] BL, India Office Library, MS Eur. E237/5: India Defence League pamphlet: 'Pure Folly (The White Paper Proposals for India)', July 1933.

[51] BL, India Office Library, MS Eur. E237/5: India Defence League leaflet, 1933.

[52] See Churchill, *India: Speeches and an Introduction*, 30–5, 122–6.

[53] Quoted in Studdert-Kennedy, *Providence and the Raj*, 211.

[54] Cambridge University Library, Baldwin Papers, 104/71–4: H.A. Gwynne to S. Baldwin, 24 Nov. 1930.

[55] *Manchester Guardian*, 13 May 1933.

[56] Lord Lloyd speech of 4 July 1933, reprinted as 'The Problem of Constitutional Reform in India', *International Affairs*, xii (1933), 593–610.

[57] Quoted in R.A. Butler, *The Art of the Possible: The Memoirs of Lord Butler* (1971), 47.

[58] See Studdert-Kennedy, 'Christian Imperialism', 359.

[59] Quoted in Alvin Jackson, *Colonel Edward Saunderson: Land and Loyalty in Victorian Ireland* (Oxford, 1995), 131.

However, these ideas about Indian religious divisions, political behaviour and social organisation also formed part of the calculations of those Conservatives who wished to kill Indian nationalism with kindness. That these administrators saw some real potential for the reforms to undermine Congress could be seen in the remarks of Malcolm Hailey, writing from India to the permanent undersecretary at the India office, on the plan for federation: '[A]s I remember remarking to you at the time, we thought at first that it was at least a good red herring, but afterwards we came to believe that it was really something much more substantial.'[60] Not only did these notions shape these tories' strategies for containing the Congress, but they also, significantly, appeared to influence how these politicians and administrators interpreted events in India, allowing them to maintain a belief in the efficacy of their actions even when the available evidence seemed to argue otherwise. These colonial stereotypes seemed to have a profound effect especially on the viceroy, Irwin, shaping his assessment of, and response to, the nationalists.

From 1926, the first year of his viceroyalty, Irwin argued that the hindu-dominated nationalist movement was not a great threat, drawing on various colonial conceptions of Indian and hindu behaviour as immature, sentimental and unmanly. He claimed that Indian politicians, even those more moderate than the Congress, were 'lacking in qualities of vigour and constructive statesmanship', while Indians on the whole seemed 'to lack the quality of perseverance'.[61] Irwin was therefore convinced that many Indian agitators were deeply uncomfortable with, and even fearful of, the prospect of long-term conflict with the British, with the personal and political prices that might exact. These Indians were only concerned now to 'save face' and 'extricate themselves from a line of action that promises little result'.[62] Moreover, he assured colleagues in London of the fundamental naïveté of the Indian political classes, who believed that 'if they go on shouting something favorable to them will happen . . . I think it is very much like a child refusing to eat its supper. There comes a point when it is no good pleading or reproaching any longer and when its tempers are ignored it may return to eat it on its own.'[63] Irwin noted that 'dealing with the Indian mentality is rather like riding a young horse, some of whose antics are the result of youth rather than vice'.[64] There was little depth or rationale to the nationalist stance: it was, in the end, the product of an 'Indian hypersensitive psychology' and thus 'more psychological than political'.[65] Irwin's solution to the anti-colonial challenge lay in his sense that India was a land where '[t]he heart mesmerizes the head and words reign supreme . . . [and] as one would expect, sentiment looms very large'.[66] To friends in London, he was quite explicit about how he might take advantage of Indian sensibilities: 'The Indian habit of phrase-making is really the limit.

[60] BL, India Office Library, Findlater Stewart Papers, MS Eur. D890/9/41–7: Sir Malcolm Hailey to Findlater Stewart, 15 June 1931.

[61] BL, India Office Library, MSS Eur. C152/17/103: Irwin to Lord Reading, 13 Sept. 1926; Eur. C152/17/320: Irwin to N. Chamberlain, 16 Aug. 1927; Eur. C152/17/354: Irwin to Sir Samuel Hoare, 31 Oct. 1927.

[62] Cambridge University Library, Baldwin Papers, 102/177–80: Irwin to Stanley Baldwin, 27 Dec. 1927; BL, India Office Library, MS Eur. C152/18/101: Irwin to Geoffrey Dawson, 2 June 1928.

[63] BL, India Office Library, MS Eur. C152/29: Irwin to Lord Birkenhead, 23 Feb. 1928.

[64] BL, India Office Library, MS Eur. C152/6: Irwin to Wedgwood Benn (Indian Secretary), 22 Oct. 1930.

[65] BL, India Office Library, MSS Eur. C152/18/190: Irwin to earl of Crawford and Balcarres, 6 Oct. 1928; Eur. C152/17/33: Irwin to Dawson, 18 May 1926; Churchill College, Cambridge, Churchill Papers, 2/164/4–5: Irwin to Winston Churchill, 25 Feb. 1929.

[66] Cambridge University Library, Baldwin Papers, 102/78–83: Irwin to Baldwin, 28 Apr. 1926.

I am convinced in my own mind, that 85 out of 100 people who use these big words would not detect any inconsistency in some modification of the policy that to our minds, would make it something quite different.'[67] He proposed that he announce in late 1929 that Britain's ultimate intention was to see India given dominion status, a promise that Irwin saw as nothing more than a more grandiloquent restatement of British policy as laid down in earlier Indian reform plans.[68] He was convinced that such a gesture would have a great effect on 'Indian mind[s]' which were inherently susceptible to such blandishments.[69] The administration in Bombay, at least, agreed, reporting that while Congress had attracted a crowd of 30,000 to a rally in January 1930, the bulk of those attending were 'ignorant masses and [a] particularly youthful element . . . impressed by demonstrations and influenced by violent speeches delivered with impunity'.[70] Sir Frederick Sykes, governor of Bombay, lamented that his problems there were exacerbated by the emotional 'Gujarati mentality' that possessed even Gandhi.[71]

By early 1931, the viceroy believed he had succeeded. It was a conviction, however, that relied on some misreading of Indian politics, especially concerning the potential for splits within the nationalist movement, and the discomfort of some politicians with Gandhi's strategy of civil disobedience. Some well-known Indian politicians, albeit with only a few from within the Congress ranks, had indeed accepted Irwin's pledge on dominion status and had agreed to come to London for what would prove to be the first of three round table conferences.[72] Irwin concluded that his pledge had:

> undoubtedly rallied all moderate opinion [in India], and I feel very little doubt that they will remain thus rallied for some time to come . . . It is of course hopeless to expect people in England to understand that Indian politicians are greatly surprised if their utterances are taken quite seriously, and that the Indian, almost more than anybody else is concerned to try and save his face.[73]

The round table conference that convened in November 1930 produced the plan for an Indian federation of autonomous provinces and the princely states. This scheme, too, attracted some prominent Indian support, including that of Indian 'moderates' like T.B. Sapru and M.R. Jayakar, and muslim and princely representatives, but again not that of the Congress. On the contrary, the year 1930 saw the inauguration of the most co-ordinated Congress action in India to date, including Gandhi's salt march, boycotts of

[67] BL, India Office Library, MS Eur. C152/18/273: Irwin to J.C.C. Davidson, 18 Jan. 1929.

[68] Cambridge University Library, Baldwin Papers, 103/81–6: Irwin to Baldwin, 8 Oct. 1929.

[69] BL, India Office Library, Templewood (Hoare) Papers, MS Eur. E240/76/83–7: Irwin to Hoare, 10 June 1930.

[70] BL, India Office Library, Sykes Papers, MS Eur. F150/2a/5–6: Bombay Government (Home Department) to Government of India (Home Department), 30 Jan. 1930.

[71] BL, India Office Library, MS Eur. F150/3b/198–200: Sir Frederick Sykes to Willingdon, 12 Nov. 1931.

[72] See T.B. Sapru to Irwin, 24 May 1930, in *Crusader for Self-Rule: Tej Bahadur Sapru and the Indian Nationalist Movement: Life and Selected Letters*, ed. R. Hooja (Jaipur, 1999), 143–4. For an account of the intra-Congress debates over the viceroy's statement, see D.A. Low, *Britain and Indian Nationalism: The Imprint of Ambiguity 1929–1942* (Cambridge, 1997), 41–71.

[73] BL, India Office Library, MS Eur. c152/27/170: Irwin to Lord Halifax, 3 Dec. 1929.

British cloth and other goods, and large-scale demonstrations in major Indian cities.[74] Malcolm Hailey, governor of the United Provinces, noted that the demonstrations had overcome even social barriers and 'arous[ed] very deep sympathy among every class of Hindus', a remarkable development for British administrators who saw caste as an insuperable barrier to Indian co-operation.[75] Even those indigenous politicians who had welcomed Irwin's declaration on dominion status were not as moderate in their demands as the viceroy might have wished. Sapru, for example, continued to explain that he would expect full dominionhood for India after a period of only 'temporary safe-guards'.[76] Sapru and the Congress differed over tactics, but not very much over the goal of Indian autonomy.[77] Irwin himself conceded that the nationalist movement was enough to cause 'considerable' strain on the Raj's resources.[78] Yet the viceroy continued to view Indian politics overall in the same way he had throughout his time there. He still felt that Indians were, at heart, reluctant to follow the path of confrontation, but were, never-theless, hesitant to voice their views out of 'the Indian unwillingness to pass condem-nations on those who at the moment seem to have the shouts of the crowd with them'.[79] Irwin also predicted that even those most committed to these nationalist protests would reconsider their position once the Indian government cracked down, noting that 'if we had beaten [such protests] once, the Indian character being what it is, there would not be the same enthusiasm for early revival'.[80]

From 1932 through 1935, and even up to the provincial elections held as part of the reforms in early 1937, other British officials, in India and at the India office, echoed and reinforced Irwin's claim that some very limited concessions might go a long way in India. Again, these arguments relied on colonial conceptions of Indian, especially hindu, character and behaviour, but they also dwelled on the importance of communal and caste divisions for Britain's long-term strategy in India. Malcolm Hailey, the dean of the Indian civil service, governor of the United Provinces, and a key adviser to the India office in this matter, saw the nationalists as inherently weak, or at least weak-kneed, and opined that many Indian politicians had realized that they had bitten off more than they could chew. He sensed among Indians that '[t]he nearer we get to [giving India] any practical measure of responsibility, the greater seems to be the hesitation to assume it.'[81] In New Delhi, Lord Willingdon, Irwin's replacement in 1931, argued that all 'the Indian' really wanted was 'to be able to say before the world that he is administering his own country',

---

[74] See D.A. Low, 'Anatomy of a *satyagraha*, Lucknow, May 1930', in *Britain and Indian Nationalism*, 72–118; also Gyanendra Pandey, *The Ascendancy of the Congress in Uttar Pradesh: Class, Community and Nation in Northern India, 1920–1940* (2nd edn, 2002); R. Kumar, 'From Swaraj to Purna Swaraj: Nationalist Politics in the City of Bombay, 1920–1932', in *Congress and the Raj: Facets of the Indian Struggle 1917–1947*, ed. D.A. Low (1977), 77–107.

[75] Quoted in Pandey, *Ascendancy of the Congress*, 88.

[76] Quoted in R.J. Moore, *The Crisis of Indian Unity, 1917–1940* (Oxford, 1974), 125; see also Sapru to D. Graham Pole and H.S.L. Polak, 10 Oct. 1929, in *Crusader for Self-Rule*, 120–2.

[77] BL, India Office Library, Sapru Papers (microfilm), 1st ser. /26/115–21: Sapru to M.R. Jayakar, 12 July 1930.

[78] BL, India Office Library, MS Eur. E240/76/83–7: Irwin to Hoare, 10 June 1930.

[79] BL, India Office Library, MS Eur. C152/19/63: Irwin to George Lane-Fox, 5 May 1930.

[80] BL, India Office Library, MS Eur. C152/19/64: Irwin to Wedgwood Benn, 8 May 1930.

[81] BL, India Office Library, Hailey Papers, MS Eur. E220/25a/50–3: Hailey to Geoffrey de Montmorency, 12 Nov. 1932; see also MS Eur. E240/52a/7: Hailey to Findlater Stewart, 26 Sept. 1932.

while, in truth, leaving the heavy lifting to the British.[82] Hailey reckoned that these Indians would accept something much less than self-rule rather than take over the rigorous tasks performed by the British administration, a sentiment conveyed to the Indian secretary, Samuel Hoare, by the governor of Madras as well.[83] There also remained the belief that even the prospect of provincial autonomy alone in India would be enough to pull many away from the national Congress movement through the 'prospects' of offices, jobs and patronage.[84] An India office administrator summed up this approach to the nationalists thus: 'The Bengali is an emotional creature with a bad inferiority complex . . . Anything which goes to persuade him that great opportunities are open to him is all to the good.'[85] Willingdon was convinced that the lure of patronage would draw Indians into the provincial assemblies, telling a former Indian governor – and in religious terms at that – that 'in the end [the Congress] will come in – the loaves and fishes are too tempting!'.[86] In the last days before the passage of the 1935 bill, John Anderson, the governor of Bengal, reported that there was 'very little conviction' behind continued Indian criticism of the proposed reforms.[87] Thus informed, the Indian secretary found confirmation, at the end of 1932, of his 'impression that Indian public opinion . . . is prepared to accept a scheme provided that we keep the initiative and do not delay too long about it'.[88]

Hailey also introduced the notion that sectarian considerations, not ideas about self-rule, would dominate Indian discussion of the reforms. In India, a place where religion was supposedly paramount, 'it will be the Communal Award which will be the touchstone, not questions of federation, or franchise and the like'.[89] As Hailey noted to a former Indian civil service colleague, 'the cow is still the most important figure in Indian politics!'[90] From Calcutta, the British governor reported that 'what really rankles in Bengal is the Communal Award [and] the Poona Pact', and that local politicians had told him they would work the reform scheme 'for it is realized that non-cooperation will only serve to consolidate the position of the Muslims [and] Depressed Classes'.[91] The idea of a hierarchical and caste-dominated India further bolstered the arguments of those who thought it would be possible to deflect Indian political aspirations with a few well-chosen and calculated concessions. They viewed the nationalist movement as inevitably hindered by social division and stratification, with a large gulf between a small cadre of elite leaders and the ordinary Indian peasants who had been coaxed into following them. In early 1934, with Nehru imprisoned, a frustrated Willingdon noted that Gandhi continued to draw crowds, but only 'because these stupid people still look upon him as

[82] BL, India Office Library, Willingdon Papers, MS Eur. F116/54/46–7: Willingdon to Sir Harcourt Butler, 26 May 1933.
[83] BL, India Office Library, Erskine Papers, MS Eur. D596/12/11–12: Lord Erskine to Hoare, 22 Dec. 1934.
[84] Bodl., copy at Sir John Simon Papers, 71/146–54: Hailey to Hoare, 28 Feb. 1932.
[85] BL, India Office Library, Anderson Papers, MS Eur. F207/5/2–5: Findlater Stewart to Sir John Anderson, 9 Mar. 1932.
[86] BL, India Office Library, MS Eur. F116/54/116–17: Willingdon to Harcourt Butler, 25 Nov. 1935.
[87] BL, India Office Library, MS Eur. F207/5/355–7: Anderson to Hoare, 25 Mar. 1935.
[88] Bodl., MS Simon 75/57–8: Hoare to Simon, 30 Dec. 1932.
[89] BL, India Office Library, MS Eur. E220/27c/350–4: Hailey to J. Crerar, 14 June 1934.
[90] BL, India Office Library, MS Eur. E220/27c/463–7: Hailey to F.H. Brown, 19 July 1934.
[91] BL, India Office Library, MS Eur. F207/5/348–9: Anderson to Hoare, 10 Dec. 1934.

a holy man'.[92] Hailey summed up the situation thus: 'in the East democracy is being demanded not by the great mass of the people themselves, but by an intellectual class which hopes thereby to gain control of the people'.[93] Hailey and others predicted therefore that the more 'conservative' Indian masses had only a weak loyalty to the Congress 'babus' and their 'revolutionary' ideas, and that the British might profitably deepen this split by providing some moderate political reforms.[94] For Madras, both Willingdon and the governor, Lord Erskine, saw the reforms as reinvigorating the provincial Justice Party which would attract the votes of newly-enfranchised 'non-Brahmins' who opposed the Brahminical Congress.[95] According to these arguments, then, the proposed reforms would ensure British control in India by, first, weakening nationalist resolve through the promise of office-holding and, second, by providing a political system which would encourage an Indian tendency towards localism and social division.

Events in India between 1932 and 1935 did in some way seem to confirm, if only superficially, what Hailey and others had argued about the future prospects of the nationalist movement. With Indian representatives unable to agree over representation under the proposed reforms, the British government published its communal award for India in August 1932, a step that both reinforced the notion that Indians identified themselves fundamentally by their religion, and seemed to indicate the continued presence of communal antipathy, something the reforms' supporters counted on for their strategy's success. Moreover, the controversy over separate representation for untouchables under the award, and the split between Gandhi and some high-caste hindus over the question of untouchability, made more credible the idea that caste division would ultimately prevent any real hindu political unity.[96] Finally, the decision by significant numbers of Congress followers to re-enter Indian electoral politics in 1934 and 1935, a step that coincided with Gandhi's decision to halt the civil disobedience campaign, seemed to indicate a fracture within the Congress, and also might be interpreted as showing the inevitable triumph of the Indian attraction to office and its opportunities over ideological commitment. This view of Indian politics survived even in the face of Congress successes in the 1934 elections to the existing Indian legislative assembly, a largely consultative body, but one with symbolic value as well. Hailey reassured the India office that 'few people in the provinces' paid close attention to these elections, reserving their real interest for local politics.[97] Willingdon wrote off the results as the work of a 'so uninstructed and so emotional' Indian electorate, without seeming aware that this assessment presented the possibility that the reforms would not go as he planned.[98] The

[92] BL, India Office Library, MS Eur. F116/54/71–2: Willingdon to Harcourt Butler, 21 Feb. 1934.

[93] BL, India Office Library, MSS Eur. E220/21b/399–403: Hailey to J.T. Gwynn, 13 Aug. 1931; Eur. E220/24e/587–90: Hailey to Sir Dinshaw Washa, Sept. 1932.

[94] Bodl., Davidson Papers, MS Eng. Hist. c556/55–6: J.C.C. Davidson memorandum on Indian tour, 28 Mar. 1933; BL, India Office Library, MS Simon 77/64–71: Willingdon to Simon, 15 Oct. 1933.

[95] BL, India Office Library, MS Eur. D596/8/8: Erskine to Willingdon, 23 Apr. 1935.

[96] For reports emphasizing Gandhi's strained relationship with some hindu elites, see those from the Indian police, district commissioners and others for 1933–4 in BL, India Office Library, L/PJ/7/595.

[97] BL, India Office Library, MSS Eur. E220/28A/74–9: Hailey to Hoare, 1 Oct. 1934; see also Eur. E220/28a/115–16: Hailey to Willingdon, 10 Apr. 1934; Eur. E220/27c/350–4: Hailey to J. Crerar, 14 June 1934; Eur. F207/5/348–349: Anderson to Hoare, 10 Dec. 1934.

[98] BL, India Office Library, MS Eur. E240/8/591–3: Willingdon to Hoare, 19 Nov. 1934.

viceroy claimed that once real provincial autonomy was at stake, the Indian elector would 'genuinely' cast his vote, rather than indulge in 'sentimental considerations'.[99]

However, developments in 1937 demonstrated clearly that these earlier events had not foreshadowed a Congress break-up, despite much wishful British thinking to the contrary. Nineteen thirty-seven saw elections to responsible provincial legislatures, the first step ordained by the successfully-passed 1935 act. These provincial bodies were supposed to redirect Indian political attention away from the national and toward the local, encouraging provincial rivalry and the development of regional political parties. As one aide to the governor of Madras predicted in 1934: 'Provincial jealousies will play an important part in future and will probably adversely affect Congress as an All-India party.'[100] Instead, Congress embarked on a campaign of 'intense and carefully organized electioneering' in all the provinces of British India.[101] When provincial governors undertook to explain the Indian political situation in 1936 to Willingdon's successor, Lord Linlithgow, they continued nevertheless to underestimate Congress's prospects and its cohesion. Nearly every governor forecast that Congress might get some seats in the new assemblies, but not enough to gain control of them. One notable example was Hyde Gowan, governor of the Central Provinces, who saw Congress gaining only 34 out of 104 seats, largely due to the fragmentation of local politics.[102] Even when a local Indian notable warned the governor that Congress would take over 60 seats, both Hyde Gowan and one of his district commissioners disagreed, predicting only half that number.[103] In the end, the Congress picked up 70 seats in the Central Provinces, demonstrating the limits of the British political intelligence system that relied more on cultural assumptions and less on indigenous reporting. This was not an isolated incident either. The district officer in Koraput in Orissa had estimated that Congress might take one of the district's three seats; they took all three in fact.[104] British hopes for a revival of the Justice Party in Madras also proved in vain, as Congress took the vast majority of the seats. The overall result was Congress ministries in seven of 11 provinces under co-ordinated party control. In their efforts to explain the party's success, British officials turned to the very cultural assumptions that had led them to think that Indian hindus, in particular, were incapable of such a feat. The fault lay with the 'greatly enlarged and very ignorant electorate', one gripped by 'extreme sentimentality and timidity', and one that had fallen for all of Congress's 'absurd promises'.[105] The governor of Bihar believed that 90% of the voters there saw the ballot box simply as a 'letter box for Gandhi'.[106] There was some grudging

---

[99] BL, India Office Library, L/PJ/7/752/90–5: Willingdon to Hoare, 23 Nov. 1934.

[100] G.T.H. Bracken, chief secretary to the Madras governor, quoted in David Arnold, *The Congress in Tamiland: Nationalist Politics in South India, 1919–1937* (Delhi, 1977), 188.

[101] David Arnold, *Gandhi* (2001), 203.

[102] BL, India Office Library, Linlithgow Papers, MS Eur. F125/12: Sir Hyde Gowan to Lord Linlithgow, 10 Nov. 1936. Hyde Gowan was quite ill as well, another limitation on his ability to gather information in his province. In fact, he left office early in 1938, and died in March, just after his voyage home.

[103] BL, India Office Library, MS Eur. F125/12: Hyde Gowan to Linlithgow, 17 Dec. 1936.

[104] BL, India Office Library, MS Eur. F125/12: John Hubback (governor of Orissa) to Linlithgow, 1 Feb. 1937.

[105] BL, India Office Library, MSS Eur. D596/8/108–12: Erskine to Linlithgow, 1 Mar. 1937; Eur. F125/12: Hubback to Linlithgow, 1 Feb. 1937.

[106] BL, India Office Library, MS Eur. F125/12: James Sifton (governor of Bihar) to Linlithgow, 9 Feb. 1937.

acknowledgment of the party's organisation, but this was often couched in the complaint that other hindu parties had not prepared themselves at all for the elections.[107] A few months after this election, only a few British officials seemed to have noted the larger lesson learned: 'There are fissiparous tendencies in the Congress, which superficial observers are inclined to think must soon break the movement, but past history shows that any such idea is an illusion.'[108]

The public and private debate over the 1935 Government of India Act did revolve around a shared understanding of Indian religious beliefs and practices, though proponents and opponents of the reform plan differed in their interpretations of what these practices meant for the possibility of strategic political concessions in India. The consensus view was that religion divided India, both communally and socially, while hinduism in particular demonstrated Indian backwardness and immaturity. The unsurprising conflation of hinduism and the nationalist movement in particular, governed many Britons' assumptions as to how to meet and disrupt this threat to the continued stability of the Raj. Like many imperial assumptions, these ideas about Indian religion often found just enough superficial confirmation to achieve resonance. And, also like many of these cultural perceptions, these notions contained some notable contradictions, albeit ones that allowed for some explanatory flexibility. The idea of Indian immaturity supported the claim that the Congress could not sustain itself, yet also provided a convenient explanation when Congress failed to fall apart. In the end, what the debate over Indian reform may have represented was the last gasp of British pretensions to 'know' and thus to be able to manipulate India. This attitude was a hallmark of Victorian rule in India, but could not survive the events of 1937. British control of India lasted a decade further, but the Raj had reached its end. Indeed, Lord Irwin had been more prescient than he knew in 1931 when, upon his departure from New Delhi, he warned a colleague that 'everything in this country always turns out in the opposite sense to that which you might expect'.[109]

[107] E.g., see BL, India Office Library, MS Eur. F125/12: Michael Keane (governor of Assam) to Linlithgow, 18 Feb. 1937.

[108] BL, India Office Library, L/PJ/12/235/38: J.M. Ewart memorandum, Intelligence Bureau of Home Department (India), 1 May 1937.

[109] BL, India Office Library, MS Eur. F150/3a/140–2: Irwin to Sykes, 31 Mar. 1931.

Sir John Coxe Hippisley: That '*Busy* Man' in the Cause of Catholic Emancipation

SUSAN MITCHELL SOMMERS

The late 18th and early 19th centuries represent a critical time for the emergence of modernity in western political life. Of particular interest is the confluence at that time of increased religious toleration with political reform. Research for an earlier study, *Parliamentary Politics of a County and its Town: General Elections in Suffolk and Ipswich in the Eighteenth Century* (Westport, 2002), led to an examination of Sir John Coxe Hippisley, MP (1747–1825). In many ways, his political career is an exemplar of the broader conflicts of contemporary English political life writ small.

Set between 1790 and 1818, Hippisley's parliamentary career is fascinating, for while he was an active and precocious supporter of catholic emancipation, he represented Sudbury in Suffolk, a borough with a high proportion of protestant dissenters. His constituents found Hippisley's enthusiasm for catholic emancipation repugnant, but not so much so that they could not be convinced to continue to vote for him if the price was right. Consequently a constant and expensive wooing of his constituents marked his parliamentary career.

On a national level, Hippisley's constant and public pursuit of catholic emancipation, coupled with his equally avid quest for preferment, led to a series of quixotic contradictions in his political behaviour. Hippisley and his political adventures thus represent a crucial development stage in the movement for religious freedom in England and the west, as well as providing an illuminating case study on the dynamics of local politics in the time leading up to the first great age of reform.

Keywords: John Coxe Hippisley; catholic; emancipation; Henry Benedict Stuart, Cardinal York; catholic committee; Catholic Relief Act; Sudbury; William Windham

Despite, or perhaps on account of, the powerful issues involved in Irish catholic emancipation, the history of English catholics in the decades prior to 1829 has been comparatively neglected. English catholics were neither as numerous, nor as desperate as their Irish co-religionists, and prior to the conflation of their cause with that of the Irish following the Act of Union, scholars have shown relatively little interest in them. In the early 19th century, when emancipation of any sort was still uncertain, there was a flurry of scholarly excitement, mostly amongst catholic scholars, to document the sufferings and loyalty of English catholics, and to allay protestant fears. The most currently useful examples of this sort of apologetic are by Charles Butler and John Milner.[1] A century later, the centennial of catholic emancipation was celebrated by a new generation of

---

[1] Charles Butler, *Historical Memoirs of the English, Irish, and Scottish Catholics since the Reformation* (4 vols, 1819–21); John Milner, *Supplementary Memoirs of English Catholics* (1820).

scholars, such as Denis Gwynn and Bernard Ward, though at both of these junctures little distinction was made between Irish and English catholic concerns.[2] The 1950s brought a modest rise in scholarly attention, as historians commemorated the centenary of the restoration of catholic hierarchy in England and Wales. In this instance, works such as the volume of essays edited by George Andrew Beck, did focus more directly on English catholics, though emancipation was no longer the event of note.[3]

Scholarly inattention to English catholics, especially in the second half of the 18th century, is also due in part to the success of the community in making itself virtually invisible to its non-catholic neighbours. Granted, the number of catholics in England was relatively small, perhaps reaching 80,000 by the late century, with a concentration of around 20,000 in London and its environs.[4] However, times were changing, and with them, educated opinion about religion changed as well. Monsignor Caprara, papal nuncio in Cologne, travelled secretly to London in 1772 to explore the possibility of establishing diplomatic relations with the British government. While this end was not achieved until 1914, Caprara reported he found old prejudices against catholicism waning.[5] Waning, perhaps, but still quite real, and a palpable presence in British popular politics for decades to come.

Lay leaders in the catholic community worked quite deliberately to integrate catholicism into the mainstream of English dissent in late 18th-century England, attempting to further ameliorate their improved, but still legally precarious position. In the 1770s, leading catholic laity found an unexpected ally in the government of George III, which, with the outbreak of the American revolution, was badly in need of troops. Catholics had been barred from military service, at least officially, since the 17th century, though common soldiers had of necessity frequently passed unremarked.[6] In 1775 the Irish parliament enacted legislation permitting catholics to take a simple oath of allegiance to the crown, clearing the way for extensive recruiting in the kingdom. The ministry hoped to find similar accommodation elsewhere, in Scotland and perhaps England. While the English catholic bishop, Richard Challoner, was reluctant to work with the administration on this point, his lay co-religionists were not.[7]

Facing clerical ambivalence, the catholic gentlemen of England, accustomed by their social standing to assuming leadership, established the Catholic Committee in 1778.[8] This was a distinctly lay organisation, dominated by gentry and aristocrats, and led by a lawyer, William Sheldon. The committee took upon itself responsibility for representing the

---

[2] Denis R. Gwynn, *The Struggle for Catholic Emancipation, 1750–1829* (1928); Denis R. Gwynn, *A Hundred Years of Catholic Emancipation* (1929); Bernard C. Ward, *The Eve of Catholic Emancipation: Being the History of the English Catholics During the First Thirty Years of the Nineteenth Century* (2 vols, New York, 1911–12); Bernard C. Ward, *The Sequel to Catholic Emancipation* (1915); George E. Anstruther, *A Hundred Years of Catholic Progress* (1929).

[3] *The English Catholics, 1850–1950: Essays to Commemorate the Centenary of the Restoration of the Hierarchy of England and Wales*, ed. George A. Beck (1950).

[4] Ernest G. Rupp, *Religion in England, 1688–1791* (Oxford, 1987), 190.

[5] Ilario P. Rinieri, *Il Congresso di Vienna e la S. Sede, 1813-15* (Rome, 1904), 145.

[6] 7 Jac. I, ii; 25 Car. II, ii.

[7] Richard Challoner (1691–1781), bishop of Debra, vicar apostolic of the London District; influential writings include *Garden of the Soul* (1740), and *Meditations for Every Day of the Year* (1753). Rupp, *Religion in England*, 196–7.

[8] John Bossy, *The English Catholic Community, 1570–1850* (1975), 330–3.

English catholic community in a political capacity, at a time when relief from legal disabilities seemed likely for both catholics and protestant dissenters. Military necessity, the spread of religious toleration, and sympathy of well-placed individuals like Edmund Burke, all acted in the committee's favour. The resulting Catholic Relief Act of 1778, while not granting full emancipation to English catholics, did remove many potentially ruinous penalties, particularly against catholics with property.[9]

Despite progress, hostility against catholics, and especially against the pope, was still entrenched in English popular politics, flaring periodically as in the Gordon Riots of 1780. Nonetheless, catholics moved forward cautiously, re-forming the Catholic Committee in 1782, this time under the leadership of Lord Petre, with the lawyer, Charles Butler, as secretary.[10] The committee worked closely with William Pitt to devise an acceptable loyalty oath that would effectually grant emancipation to jurors. This time the committee seems to have gone too far in attempting to erase or deny distinctions between catholic and protestant dissenters, referring to jurors as 'Protesting Catholic Dissenters', as though they might be some sort of anglican off-shoot. While the resulting Catholic Relief Act of 1791 addressed many remaining legal penalties against catholics, controversies surrounding committee efforts led to deep divisions within the community itself.[11]

The outbreak of the French revolution and ensuing hostilities between Britain and France made it desirable for the government to establish at least informal lines of communication with Rome, despite what more progressive English catholics may have thought of such an overture. This was accomplished in 1792, when John Coxe Hippisley went south, ostensibly for his health and to promote Suffolk woollens, but actually under commission to see to British interests, and to act as a liaison between the Papal States and London.[12]

Hippisley was born John Cox Hipisley around 1746 in Bristol, and despite his later political causes, was baptised an anglican in 1747. His father, William Hipisley (1718–1800) was a prosperous haberdasher, and his mother Anne was the daughter of Robert Webb of Cromhall in Gloucestershire. John was socially ambitious, as evidenced by later strategic alterations to his name.[13] Hipisley attended Bristol grammar school, then Oxford. He was awarded an honorary doctorate of comparative law by Oxford in 1779, and in 1811 took an MA from Cambridge. He read law at the Inner Temple beginning in 1766, and was called to the bar in 1771.

Hippisley had high aspirations. He wished to become a renowned barrister. He hoped to marry into nobility. He sought wealth and preferment. Hippisley's tireless pursuit of credentials, titles, and offices led contemporary wit, Joseph Jekyll, to refer to him as 'Sir

---

[9] Financial rewards for informers were abolished; catholics were now permitted to buy, sell, and inherit property. Priests were no longer subject to life imprisonment.

[10] Robert Edward Petre, 9th Baron (1742–1801). Charles Butler (1750–1832).

[11] The Catholic Relief Act of 1791 permitted open worship in registered chapels. Registration of wills and the double land tax were abolished. For more on the Cisalpine movement in English catholicism, see Joseph P. Chinnici, *The English Catholic Enlightenment: John Lingard and the Cisalpine Movement, 1780–1850* (Shepherdstown, 1980).

[12] Aidan Gasquet, *Great Britain and the Holy See, 1792–1806: A Chapter in the History of Diplomatic Relations between England and Rome* (Rome, 1919), 15.

[13] The Hippisley Coxes were a wealthy family, vaguely connected to John Coxe Hippisley through his second marriage.

John Coxe Hippisley MP FRS SAS XYZ etc'.[14] Hippisley simultaneously manifested genuine sympathy for those less fortunate, and devoted considerable time and energy to ameliorating the sufferings of constituents, various worthy individuals, and an entire class of English subjects, catholics. He seems to have rather fallen into what became his life's calling, the quest for catholic relief and emancipation, in 1779, when he ran out of money pursuing a reluctant countess across Germany. Having failed to convince Countess Percy, daughter of Lord Bute, to marry, Hippisley went on to Italy, to soothe his soul and restore his finances.[15]

How Hippisley came to be the British government's man in Rome is not entirely clear. It seems likely, that ever with an eye to self-promotion, he proffered his services, and was accepted. For two years, Hippisley hosted visiting British dignitaries, acting as *cicerone* and introducing them to the proper people in Rome. He revelled in the life of an expatriate, visiting ruins and cultivating artists. Brinsley Ford notes Hippisley had, 'the generosity, or some might say, the vanity to commission four of the less fashionable artists to paint his portrait'.[16] It was probably a combination of vanity and thrift, as he would surely have commissioned more famous artists had he been able to afford them. In Rome he met expatriates of a bohemian bent, including Welsh memoirist and artist, Thomas Jones, and young gentlemen on the grand tour like George Augustus, Lord Herbert.[17] Amongst his most influential acquaintances from that period was William Windham, who introduced Hippisley in 1789 to the Sudbury constituency he represented in parliament, with only a brief hiatus between 1796 and 1799, until he retired from politics in 1818. While still in Rome in 1780, Hippisley took as his first wife, Margaret Stuart, daughter of Sir John Stuart and his wife, Margaret Agnes Smith. The couple had three daughters and a son before her death in 1799.[18]

Hippisley brought his bride back to England in 1781, but it was a brief stay. Anxious to repair his finances permanently, Hippisley appealed to well-placed friends for assistance. With help from both Lord Bute and Windham, Hippisley secured a position in the East India Company (EIC), and removed to Madras. He held a number of posts within the EIC between 1782 and 1787, including company writer and factor, finally becoming paymaster and acting resident at Tanjore.[19] Hippisley's connection with both the EIC and India provided one of his lifelong causes, as he remained interested in India legislation, and frequently spoke in the House on India affairs. His career with the EIC also provided a fortune, and Hippisley reputedly returned to England in 1789 with in excess of £100,000, and political ambitions.[20]

[14] 'Sir John Coxe Hippisley', *Oxford Dictionary of National Biography* [*ODNB*], xxvii, 308; 'Sir John Coxe Hippisley', in R.G. Thorne, *History of Parliament: The House of Commons, 1790–1820* (5 vols, 1986) [hereafter cited as *HP, 1790–1820*], iv, 202–7.

[15] She was divorced from Hugh, Earl Percy, later 2nd duke of Northumberland, in 1779.

[16] Brinsley Ford, 'Sir John Coxe Hippisley: An Unofficial Envoy to the Vatican', *Apollo*, xcix (1974), 440.

[17] Ford, 'Sir John Coxe Hippisley', 442. *Henry, Elizabeth, and George (1734–80): Letters and Diaries of Henry, Tenth Earl of Pembroke and his Circle*, ed. Sidney Herbert (1939).

[18] In 1801, Hippisley married Elizabeth, widow of Henry Hippisley Coxe. They had no children, but through her he acquired Ston Easton Park. He apparently altered the spelling of his name about this time.

[19] BL, Add. MS 41622.

[20] 'Sir John Coxe Hippisley', *ODNB*, xxvii, 307.

Hippisley's hopes were realized when Windham encouraged him to pursue an interest in Sudbury, a decayed wool town in Suffolk – not an obvious choice as he had no prior connections.[21] Nonetheless, in 1789 Hippisley duly became borough recorder and declared himself a candidate for parliament at the next election.[22] Sudbury's numerous and impoverished electorate made it a volatile and fractious borough.[23] Exacerbating the situation in the 18th century was the absence of formal local parties, which encouraged unstable interests and brought on frequent contests. Established Suffolk gentlemen thus left Sudbury to rich strangers with deep pockets and strong constitutions, and encouraged Sudbury electors to become passionately addicted to the largesse accompanying a contested election. The 1790 election alone was reported to have cost Hippisley £6,000, and he was sharing expenses![24] Subsequent contests in 1806, 1807, and 1812 were similarly costly – and that does not take into account the constant expenses Hippisley faced maintaining his interest between campaigns.[25] Good stewardship of the interest included everything from contributing toward the Sunday school and annual mayor's feast, to providing employment for electors who would otherwise become a charge on the parish, and lose their right to vote.[26]

To make Sudbury even more interesting, the borough provides one of the best-documented examples of dissenting political activities in Suffolk politics.[27] Despite similarities in their legal status, most 18th-century protestant dissenters felt little sympathy for their catholic brethren. This meant that while a Sudbury vote was expensive, it became even more costly for Hippisley over the course of his tenure in the borough, since he had additionally to overcome constituents' reluctance to come to terms with his pro-catholic activism.

Hippisley's concern for religious and civil liberty did not at first extend to Ireland. Sympathy for English catholics was, in the last quarter of the 18th century, a relatively comfortable cause for gentlemen like Hippisley – it was simply a question of justice and tolerance, not one of race, class, or national identity. His sympathies were additionally aroused by the plight of French clergy at the hands of revolutionaries, and of exiled English catholics on the Continent, especially Henry, Cardinal York. At home, Hippisley took up the cause of English catholics by supporting the Catholic Relief Bill in 1791.[28]

With the onset of the French revolution, Hippisley also adopted a loyalist line, using his position in the chair to thwart a Whig Club attempt in 1791 to unite with the Revolution Society in celebration of Bastille day. He also followed Windham in

---

[21] BL, Add. MS 37849: Correspondence of Windham and Hippisley, 1781–1810.

[22] *Ipswich Journal*, 14 Mar., 18 Apr., 9 May, 4 July, 22 Aug. 1789, 12, 26 June 1790.

[23] Susan M. Sommers, 'Politics in Eighteenth Century Suffolk', Washington University in St Louis PhD, 1992, 255–309. In 1814, roughly 25% of the population of 3,628 had the right to vote. BL, Davy Collection (Papers relating to Suffolk), 10351.i.24.

[24] *ODNB*, xxvii, 307.

[25] 'Sudbury', *HP, 1790–1820*, ii, 374–7.

[26] Sommers, 'Politics in Eighteenth Century Suffolk', 290–301.

[27] W.W. Hodson, *The Meeting House and the Manse: Or, the Story of the Independents of Sudbury* (1893), 73; Michael Watts, *The Dissenters from the Reformation to the French Revolution* (Oxford, 1978), 509, appendix, table xii. Estimate of dissent in Suffolk. In 1710–18, there were 370 to 400 presbyterian and independent hearers in Sudbury.

[28] 'Hippisley', *HP, 1790–1820*, iv, 202–7.

collaboration with Pitt's administration. Hippisley took a hard line against seditious meetings and practices in Suffolk, and in 1792 used his influence as recorder and member for the borough to forcibly extract a loyal address from a recalcitrant, and largely Foxite, Sudbury corporation. Leaving a disgruntled borough behind, he then went abroad that December, not returning to Sudbury for several years.

Hippisley went first to Paris, to attend the trial of Louis XVI. The experience confirmed the more conservative trend of his political thinking, which had he returned to England would no doubt have led to an open rupture with Fox.[29] Other opportunities waited, and he went on to Rome, claiming the climate helped restore his frequently precarious health, and where he still had friends and family.[30] In Italy, Hippisley looked for ways to be useful to the British government. His first opportunity came in 1793, as revolutionary wars spilled steadily across Europe, and Great Britain declared war on France.[31] At about the same time, the anti-clerical nature of revolutionary ideology was asserted, and as many as 8,000 exiled French religious persons were eventually welcomed into Britain.[32] The presence of these sympathetic victims did much to lessen popular fear of catholicism, and convinced the government that regular, if unofficial, communications with the Papal States would be necessary, especially for ease of naval operations in the Mediterranean.[33]

Hippisley was Pitt's man on the ground, as he enthusiastically took up a quasi-ambassadorial role, engaging in a variety of negotiations.[34] Notwithstanding the utility of having a representative in Rome, Lord Grenville complained that Hippisley exceeded his brief, and even Edmund Burke was critical of Hippisley's attempts to instruct the pope on Irish affairs.[35] Working from earlier contacts, Hippisley became an important liaison, helping to arrange Charles Erskine's posting to England as a similarly unofficial envoy, from 1793 to 1801.[36] Hippisley also procured supplies for British ships in the Mediterranean at advantageous prices.[37] The times were exciting, and Hippisley was in his element serving privately at a level to which he would never rise through regular channels. In recognition of Hippisley's efforts, the Roman senate granted him use of its insignia, which he subsequently displayed with his coat of arms.[38] He continued to represent British interests until he went home in 1796, at which time responsibility shifted to Thomas Jackson, minister to Sardinia. Based on the practical experience he gained in Rome, Hippisley became a persistent advocate of establishing formal diplomatic relations with the Papal States. [39]

---

[29] 'Hippisley', *HP, 1790–1820*, iv, 202–7. Hippisley's connections with Portland and Windham go back at least to 1789, when they recruited him to stand for Sudbury.

[30] 'Hippisley', *HP, 1790–1820*, iv, 202–7.

[31] BL, Egerton MS 2401: Diplomatic and other letters and papers, 1790–1822.

[32] John T. Ellis, *Cardinal Consalvi and Anglo-Papal Relations 1814–1824* (Washington, 1942), 8.

[33] Ellis, *Cardinal Consalvi and Anglo-Papal Relations*, 7–9.

[34] 'Hippisley', *HP, 1790–1820*, iv, 202–7.

[35] 'Hippisley', *HP, 1790–1820*, iv, 202–7.

[36] Charles Erskine, cardinal (1739–1811).

[37] Desmond Keenan, *The Grail of Catholic Emancipation 1793 to 1829* (no place, 2002), 79.

[38] Ford, 'Sir John Coxe Hippisley', 444–5.

[39] Ellis, *Cardinal Consalvi and Anglo-Papal Relations*, 9.

While he was delighted to be of service, Hippisley also desired recognition of that service, and in 1794 began lobbying Pitt for a baronetcy. Hippisley was anxious for high office, and laboured in the belief that if he were useful abroad, he would be more likely to achieve what he desired at home. Hippisley, described by George III as 'That *busy* man', and 'the grand intriguer', became an omnipresent gadfly, bombarding ministers and influential persons with letters, requests, and advice.[40] His persistence led one historian to permanently attach 'ubiquitous' to Hippisley's name.[41] Sir Gilbert Elliot commented on his persistent ingratiation and self-aggrandisement, in reference to a 1792 letter to Lord Chancellor Thurlow: 'It is quite in Hippisley's manner – very laborious and industrious, and meddling and intriguing and every line meant for a purpose of his own or some friend or other – but it contains some matter that may be useful. He has *made himself* a sort of minister at Rome and corresponds with all the generals and admirals, and with the cabinet at home, and the Prince of Wales, etc. etc.'[42] In March 1795 Hippisley wrote from Rome to Alderman William Strutt, his staunchest supporter on the Sudbury corporation, declaring his desire to stand again in the upcoming election. Hippisley apologised for his long absence, explaining that his health had been such he could not have attended parliament even if he had been home. Mindful of corporation concerns, he assured Strutt he had been assiduous in distributing samples of Sudbury wool in Italy, in the hope of encouraging trade. Perhaps most importantly, Hippisley finally revealed what had long been rumoured: he was persuaded of the justice of emancipation of English catholics, and intended to pursue it in parliament when re-elected. This last bit was really too much for some back in Sudbury, where rumours of Hippisley's conversion to Rome became a perennial irritant.

By the time of Hippisley's return to England in December 1795, the political situation in Sudbury had become quite complex, and not just because of his declared intent to relieve English catholics. In the eyes of his constituents and the corporation, Hippisley had changed political colours, from a reform-minded whig, to something other. His time abroad convinced him of the dangers of popular radicalism, and he further weakened his local position by openly clashing with fellow Sudbury member, Thomas Crespigny, on the floor of the house of commons. At issue was a recent Sudbury petition against the Seditious Meetings Act and the Treasonable Practices Act. Both of these measures were intended to discourage radical meetings and demonstrations, which were feared might spark general disturbances. With Hippisley in Rome, the corporation and Crespigny had felt free to submit a petition more to their liking than the Hippisley-induced loyal address of 1792. Hippisley questioned the propriety of this second petition, referring to 'the ignorance of the lower orders of freemen, the distress of the woollen manufacturers and the dissenting element in the borough', all of which might tend to inflame the populace.[43] This all proved too much for Hippisley's allies in Sudbury, who withdrew their support.[44] Facing overwhelming opposition, Hippisley retired from the contest.

---

[40] 'Hippisley', *HP, 1790–1820*, iv, 202–7.

[41] Ellis, *Cardinal Consalvi and Anglo-Papal Relations*, 52, 84, 137.

[42] 'Hippisley', *HP, 1790–1820*, iv, 202–7.

[43] 'Hippisley', *HP, 1790–1820*, iv, 202–7.

[44] Suffolk RO, Bury St Edmunds, HD 744/194b: 25 July 1795.

In the ensuing three-year hiatus from parliament, Hippisley busied himself in other ways. His repeated attempts to be considered useful bore fruit, and Hippisley was called upon to negotiate the marriage between Prince Frederick of Württemberg (1754–1816) and Charlotte, the princess royal (1766–1828), eldest daughter of George III.[45] Bringing the negotiations to a successful conclusion resulted in partial success of Hippisley's own ambitions, and he received a baronetcy in 1796 through the good offices of the duke of Portland, then home secretary.[46] It is perhaps worth noting that despite Hippisley's enthusiastic service, Pitt could not bring himself to recommend Hippisley for the honour.[47]

Hippisley is frequently remembered for his 1799 role in securing a pension for Henry Benedict, cardinal duke of York.[48] During the French revolution, York, the last of the Stuart princes, was left financially embarrassed by the loss of his French benefices and Frascati possessions. Through Hippisley's efforts, George III granted York a pension of £4,000 per year. In gratitude, the cardinal gave Hippisley several family portraits, a cameo ring with the cardinal's portrait, and other tokens.[49] York also willed James II's crown jewels and numerous Stuart papers to the Prince of Wales, effectively restoring them to England.[50] Hippisley's activities in Rome attracted the grateful attention of the catholic hierarchy in Ireland, and gave Hippisley reason to hope for an Irish peerage, though nothing came of his lobbying.[51] Undaunted, he continued to seek both official positions and grander titles for the next two decades, with no success.[52]

Throughout his parliamentary career Hippisley was reliable only on those topics to which he was committed – India, catholic emancipation, and prison reform. By 1800, Hippisley was firm and public in his support for emancipation of English catholics. He began writing on pet topics, especially catholic emancipation, and his prolific publication won him a reputation as a political author.[53] About the same time Hippisley began to

[45] Duke Frederick III of Württemberg assumed the title 'elector' in 1803, and was recognized by Napoleon as king of Württemberg in 1805. Frederick took part in the Confederation of the Rhine, but later joined the allies. His kingly title was subsequently confirmed at the Congress of Vienna.

[46] William Henry Cavendish Cavendish-Bentinck, 3rd duke of Portland (1738–1809).

[47] 'Hippisley', *HP, 1790–1820*, iv, 202–7.

[48] Walter W. Seton, 'The Relations of Henry, Cardinal York, with the British Government', *Transactions of the Royal Historical Society*, 4th ser., ii (1919), 94–112. Brian Fothergill, *The Cardinal King* (1958).

[49] Ford, 'Sir John Coxe Hippisley', 445.

[50] 'The Will of Henry Cardinal, Duke of York, and Some Supplementary Papers', ed. H.C. Stewart, *The Stewarts*, x (1955), 3–28.

[51] 'Hippisley', *HP, 1790–1820*, iv, 202–7; *ODNB*, xxvii, 307: Fothergill, *The Cardinal King*, 231. George III eventually authorised a pension of £4,000 a year. The cardinal's claim was based on money owed to his family from Mary of Modena's jointure of £50,000 plus accrued interest.

[52] *ODNB*, xxvii, 307. He sought, and failed to win, governorship of the Cape Colony, a privy councillor-ship, a position on the board of trade, an India appointment under Lord Minto, an ambassadorial posting to Württemberg, as well as the elusive Irish peerage.

[53] Sir John Coxe Hippisley, *Letters from the Cardinal Borgia and the Cardinal of York, 1799–1800* (1800); Hippisley, *Observations on the Roman Catholics of Ireland* (1806); Hippisley, *Begin: From the Globe News-paper. 15 June, 1811* [A Report of Sir J. C. Hippisley's Speech in the House of Commons, 31 May 1811] (1811); Sir John Coxe Hippisley, *Statement of Facts Presented to the Sovereign Pontiff P. Pius VII., 1818.* [In Reference to the Catholics of England and Ireland.]; Sir John Coxe Hippisley, *A Letter to Cardinal Litta . . . 1818.* [In Respect to the Re-establishment of the Order of Jesuits in England.] *Few MS. notes* (2 pt, 1818); Sir John Coxe Hippisley, *A Letter to a Noble Lord, One of His Majesty's Ministers, and a Member of Parliament, Relative to*

take a more pointed interest in the Irish hierarchy, though his advocacy for private Irish catholics lagged, only developing into a broader concern after the 1801 Act of Union made dealing with their disabilities unavoidable. Although he nominally followed Windham into opposition in 1804, this was evidence merely of personal loyalty – he was not a party stalwart, becoming even less reliable after Windham's death in 1810. After 1807, Hippisley voted very irregularly with the opposition, and supported the government on questions of public order.[54]

Once the Act of Union necessitated the eventual normalisation of the civil status of Irish catholics, Hippisley's approach to the question of emancipation changed. Emancipation of a small and mostly respectable English catholic community was one thing, removing a layer of the controls keeping the Irish in order was something else entirely. In France, Hippisley had seen first-hand the dangerous results of dramatic change in the political and social *status quo*, and had no desire to replicate such disorder in a suddenly unencumbered catholic Ireland. He argued before the Commons that in Ireland, reform must be managed carefully to prevent, 'the first ambitious knave, or unsuccessful demagogue, who wished to convulse' it 'anew, to seize it, and direct it against his country'.[55] 'The application to the case of Ireland was but too obvious', Hansard adds.[56]

A renewed Catholic Committee, the Board of British Catholics, formed in 1808 with whig encouragement. Hippisley immediately felt a kinship with the members, and offered to act in parliament on their behalf.[57] He was, he reported, 'expressly charged with the interest of a most respectable body of English Catholics'.[58] By then, the political terrain on catholic issues was transformed, and parliamentary debates were inevitably taken up with questions of greater concern to Irish than to English catholics.[59] Hippisley recognized the shift, and adapted his arguments accordingly. Nonetheless, he regretted the change in paradigm, and opposed Irish catholic relief efforts later on, when they did not conform to his personal programme.[60]

From the outset, Hippisley's presence in parliament left something to be desired. His voice was never strong, and he was occasionally unable to make himself heard, though he continued to prepare and attempt to deliver long speeches. Both contemporaries and biographers allude to Hippisley's lugubrious and elaborate addresses. His parliamentary colleagues found him tiresome, even by the standards of the day, and Hippisley was frequently forced to publish what he would have said in parliament, had he not been cut short.[61] Jekyll remarked in 1810, that when Hippisley rose to call for the creation of a

[53] (continued) Sir J. C. Hippisley's Late Conduct at Rome (1819); Sir John Coxe Hippisley, Prison Labour, etc. Correspondence and Communications Addressed to His Majesty's . . . Secretary . . . for the Home Department Concerning the Introduction of Tread-Mills into Prisons; with Other Matters Connected with Prison Discipline (1823).

[54] 'Hippisley', HP, 1790–1820, iv, 202–7.

[55] Hansard, 1st ser., xi (1808), 600.

[56] Hansard, 1st ser., xi (1808), 600.

[57] Bossy, The English Catholic Community, 331; Ward, Eve of Catholic Emancipation, i, 99–157; Hansard, 1st ser., xx (1811–12), 386–7.

[58] Hansard, 1st ser., xx (1811–12), 386.

[59] Bossy, The English Catholic Community, 333.

[60] In 1813, 1816, 1817.

[61] See, e.g., Sir John Coxe Hippisley, The substance of additional observations intended to have been delivered, 14th May, 1805, Substance of the Speech of Sir John Cox Hippisley, Bart . . . 18th May, 1810.

select committee on catholic claims, 'the House coughed him down five times in vain, and the catarrh lasted two hours'.[62]

Hippisley's political publications, dating from 1800 to 1823, fall into three main categories: published speeches on emancipation, correspondence with eminent persons about emancipation, and prison reform. The most significant are speeches and annotations of speeches he either delivered or intended to deliver in parliament.[63] Hippisley considered it his personal obligation to inform the Commons annually, at length, about the necessity for catholic emancipation. With time, he was increasingly convinced that his expertise in the area far exceeded that of his colleagues, and he became progressively more rigid in his prescriptions for resolving the situation. Indeed, his conviction was so firm that in 1813 he worked to halt the Catholic Relief Bill, hoping instead to create a committee on securities.[64] Lord Melgund observed, 'Hippisley, after having represented the Pope for so long in this country, is going to do everything in his power to mar the success of the measure because it is not introduced in the precise manner which suits his taste.'[65] Finding it inconceivable that a rational person would deviate from his carefully laid out and well-publicised plans, Hippisley exasperated his catholic supporters and pro-emancipation colleagues by voting against measures he found unacceptable.[66] Hippisley steered an increasingly fine course, seeking catholic emancipation while guaranteeing both public order and the protestant constitution that he believed was its safeguard. He was convinced that from a political point of view, the anti-clericalism of the Catholic Committee of the 1770s and 1780s was well-founded, and argued strenuously in favour of measures that would both limit Rome's ability to interfere in Irish affairs, and guarantee the crown a veto over Irish episcopal appointments. He also remained nervous about the unpredictability of the crowd, and hoped for government action to ameliorate the 'prejudices and ignorance of the masses' in matters of religion.[67] Ultimately Hippisley argued if the passions of the crowd could be done away with, catholicism would be as compatible with the English constitution as with that of any country in Europe. Touching on two of his primary concerns, national security and

---

[62] 'Hippisley', *HP, 1790–1820*, iv, 202–7.

[63] Sir John Coxe Hippisley, *The substance of additional observations intended to have been delivered in the House of Commons in the debate on the petition of the Roman Catholics of Ireland on the 13th and 14th May, 1805. With notes, and an appendix, containing letters from Dr. Troy, etc.* (1806); *The speech of Sir J. C. Hippisley, Bart., in the House of Commons, on the Catholic question in 1808; Substance of the Speech of Sir John Cox Hippisley, Bart. . . . 18th of May, 1810. The second edition, corrected: with an appendix greatly enlarged, and additional notes. MS. notes.* (1810); *Substance of the speech of Sir J. C. H., on seconding the motion of Henry Grattan to refer the petition of the Roman Catholics of Ireland to a Committee of the House of Commons.* (1810); *Correspondence respecting the Catholic Question, with various additions printed and MS.* (1812); *Catholic Question. Substance of the speech of Sir J. C. Hippisley, Bart., on the motion of . . . Henry Grattan . . . on the 24th April, 1812; for a committee of the whole House, on the state of the penal laws now in force against the Roman Catholics of Ireland . . . With supplementary notes, etc.* (2 pt, 1812); *Letters to the Earl of Fingall, on the subject of the 'Catholic Claims'. With supplementary documents.* (1813); *The Substance of a Speech . . . in the House of Commons, on Tuesday, May 11, 1813, for the appointment of a select committee on the subject of the Catholic claims; with notes, and an appendix containing the pontifical rescripts of P. Clement XIV, and P. Pius VII. respecting the abolition and restoration of the order of Jesuits.* (1815); *A sketch of proposed regulations, concurrent with the establishment of a state provision for the Roman Catholic clergy* (1823).

[64] Hansard, 1st ser., xxiv (1812–13), 850–4, 1215–27; xxvi (1813), 1–68.

[65] Lord Meglund, Gilbert Elliot-Murray-Kynynmound later 2nd earl of Minto (1782–1859). 'Hippisley', *HP, 1790–1820*, iv, 202–7.

[66] Hansard, 1st ser., xxix (1814–15), 395–7, 931–9, 1018–19.

[67] 'Hippisley', *HP, 1790–1820*, iv, 202–7.

safeguards against the divided loyalty of catholic subjects, Hippisley argued in 1811: 'Neither the dispensing doctrine, as to oaths of allegiance, nor the deposing doctrine, which naturally springs out of it, were ever declared by any general council, as a canon or decree of faith: but the contrary has been maintained by œcumenical councils, – by provincial synods, – by the faculties of theology in the universities of the continent, – and by the rescripts of Popes.'[68] Despite this conviction, Hippisley became increasingly insistent about the necessity for a select committee to investigate and recommend the best procedure for guaranteeing both the liberty of catholics, and security for the constitution. He was unconvinced that successive administrations were adequately appreciative of the nuances of either catholicism or confessional diplomacy, and bemoaned the lack of parliamentary interest: 'In questions involving the integrity of the civil and political principles of a fourth, or fifth part of our fellow subjects, arraigned, as they have been, by proceedings in this House, at successive periods, since the reformation, we have not a single page, on parliamentary authority.'[69] While Hippisley successfully retained his Sudbury seat until his retirement from politics in 1818, his speeches and especially his pamphlets, were a source of growing friction between the member and his more zealously protestant constituents. He appears to have deliberately provoked what he considered useful controversy by liberally distributing his pro-catholic pamphlets across the borough. These pieces played a significant role in the politics of the borough, no doubt causing his agents additional trouble in keeping up Hippisley's interest. In 1812, his agent, Stephen Poder, wrote about the Sudbury freemen: 'They are angry with you. They say because you are for the Catholicks – But mainly because they are not treated & c.'[70]

Hippisley maintained his position in the borough largely through gifts and careful stewardship. Freemen were free in their demands on him, and Hippisley's correspondence with government men and EIC officers was consequently full of requests for assistance for his constituents. Many thought it prudent to include not only statements of their political loyalty, which would be easy enough to verify by a glance at the poll books, but also avowals of their persuasion of the justice of catholic relief. This is illustrated nicely by an 1811 letter from constituent John Must, asking Hippisley to use his influence to secure Must's promotion in the EIC indigo warehouse. Must writes:

> I take up my pen for the 8th time, to [ask] the favor of you to make me a Commodore, which you kindly promised in April 1810 . . . Pray Sir, let my poor Wife Family & self have cause to bless the worthy name of Sr J Hippisley, adding a little comfort to our sphere in life . . . I have one thing to add ere I close this Epistle that is, many evil disposed persons have asserted, you do not intend Representing our Borough any more, & that . . . you are a friend to Catholicism! What then Sir, if you are . . . [71]

[68] Hansard, 1st ser., xx (1812), 394.

[69] Hansard, 1st ser., xx (1812), 395.

[70] Suffolk RO, Bury St Edmunds, HD 744/51: Stephen Poder to Hippisley, 1 Oct. 1812. See also 'Hippisley', *HP, 1790–1820*, iv, 202–7.

[71] Suffolk RO, Bury St Edmunds, HD 744/128: John Must, sr to Hippisley, 28 May 1811.

Similar correspondence from constituent Isaac Duce is both typical, and typically ungrammatical. He initially writes to Hippisley on 20 February 1812: 'I purswade myself you will pardon me (making so free) when you consider that the whole family have allways supported your Interest at Sud[bur]y, I shall not withhold my vote from you Because you voted for the Catholick Question . . . I am certain that Its the only step that government can take to do away [with] religious prejudice.'[72] Five days later, the reason for the initial correspondence becomes clear as Duce writes he has, 'Devis'd a plan to Improve some of the Old Branches (of manufacturing) and have also invented one or two more Entirely new'.[73] Deuce goes on to request Hippisley's support in bringing his schemes to fruition.

The meaning of these letters is clear: Hippisley's constituents would send him to parliament, and they would tolerate his stand on the 'catholick question', but he would pay, and pay dearly, for both their votes and their forbearance. In December 1812, agent J. Burkitt, wrote:

> I am sorry to find that some of your friends here, have profited so little, by your repeated endeavours to enlighten their understandings, and bring them to a just view of the subject – but the Clergy, many of whom look but to one side of a question and are tremblingly alive to the fear of consequences; fill the minds of the Public with apprehensions. Mr. Wilkinson compared the Catholics to the Lions in the Tower, safe whilst confined to their dens, but once let loose their ferocity would soon shew itself in all the horror of past times.[74]

Following the general election of 1812, which Hippisley led against a stranger to the borough by only 18 votes, his agent Robert Frost wrote:

> I know that you were much hurt at not having a much greater Majority on the Poll, but when it is considered with what violence your opinions with Respect to the Catholic Question were opposed, by a very great Number of Men, who are active in Elections, it is not much to be wondered at, for it was [only] by the address of some of your Friends which prevented the General outcry of No Popery, that your Election was secured.[75]

Another supporter, John Addison, gives us a peek at politics out-of-doors, or perhaps on doors, in Sudbury. Writing to Hippisley in December 1812, he observes, 'the old subject of No Popery still prevails among some and continues to be written on the Walls & is uttered from the mouths of others'.[76]

Finally, letters to Hippisley from constituent William Earl illuminate the electors' take on the relationship between Hippisley and Sudbury freemen. Earl writes: 'my most sincere thanks for your pamphlet you was so good to give me when I see you last. I have

---

[72] Suffolk RO, Bury St Edmunds, HD 744/77: Isaac Duce, sr to Hippisley, 20 Feb. 1812.

[73] Suffolk RO, Bury St Edmunds, HD 744/78: Isaac Duce, sr to Hippisley, 25 Feb. 1812.

[74] Suffolk RO, Bury St Edmunds, HD 744/19: J. Burkitt to Hippisley, 26 Dec. 1812.

[75] Suffolk RO, Bury St Edmunds, HD 744/37: Robert Frost to Hippisley, 23 Aug. 1813. Outcome of the general election of 1812: Hippisley 489; Charles Wyatt 471; Emanuel Felix Agar 363.

[76] Suffolk RO, Bury St Edmunds, HD 744/16: John Addison to Hippisley, 14 Dec. 1812.

read the whole of it and have received a great deal of information so much so that I am perfectly convinced of the propriety of granting to the catholics every right and privileged that belong to the constitution equally the same as protestants.'[77] In the next letter, though, Earl notes, 'I find being frequently with different freemen that most of them possess contrary principles to yours.'[78]

Sir John Coxe Hippisley retired from politics in 1818, moving temporarily to Rome for a well-deserved rest. Sudbury had provided a fairly reliable, if consistently expensive, political platform, and Hippisley made a parting gift of £100 to be distributed amongst the poor. Former mayor, Lachlan Maclean, remarked: 'This parting token of his regard for the poor is the more honourable to him, since he has no vote, – no favour to solicit, in return.'[79] Hippisley spent his last years advocating prison reform. His particular concern was the use of the treadmill in prison workshops, which he thought unusually cruel, advocating handcranks instead. His 1823 pamphlet, *Prison Labour*, was devoted to, '*The Introduction of Tread-Mills into Prisons; with Other Matters Connected with Prison Discipline*'.[80] Hippisley was also an active magistrate in Somerset, where he had considerable property, including his Ston Easton estate. Hippisley died in London in 1825, and was buried in the crypt of the Inner Temple church.

Hippisley was a mixed blessing for catholics. His decision to repeatedly stand for and represent Sudbury, with its considerable, corruptible, and pugnaciously anti-catholic constituency, makes all the more curious his concomitant decision to make catholic relief and emancipation the focus of his political career. While Hippisley spoke on India affairs early in his parliamentary career, and prison reform late in life, it was the plight of catholics that motivated him to become a political writer, and informed his apparently interminable speeches before the House. Hippisley was thus remarkable for his precocious advocacy of catholic emancipation, as early as the 1780s, and his dogged persistence in the face of both his constituents' resistance and his parliamentary colleagues' indifference. He put catholic issues out in public and kept them there, decades before it became either necessary or fashionable. This was not an easy task to take on, and he has not been sufficiently acknowledged for his efforts.

On the other hand, Hippisley's character was such that, once convinced of the righteousness of his cause, and indeed the correctness of his particular approach, he was immovable. Thus, rather than downplaying his legislative agenda, he flaunted it, hoping to persuade his constituents to support him because of, rather than in spite of it. Hippisley regularly sent pro-catholic pamphlets to his Sudbury agents to distribute, which eventually led to rumours of his religious conversion, and heightened discontent amongst the freemen. He did not make things easy for himself at home.

Hippisley's conduct was no less quixotic in parliament. He spent decades cultivating the trust of influential catholics, his colleagues' forbearance, and grudging support of his constituents. But when the iron was hot, Hippisley dithered, and transformed himself into an obstacle to change rather than an instrument of it. He allowed his personal flaws,

[77] Suffolk RO, Bury St Edmunds, HD 744/27: William Earl to Hippisley, nd.
[78] Suffolk RO, Bury St Edmunds, HD 744/28: William Earl to Hippisley, nd.
[79] Allan W. Berry, *Sudbury's Freemen: A Chronicle of 900 Years* (1987), 42.
[80] *Prison Labour, etc. Correspondence and Communications addressed to His Majesty's . . . Secretary . . . for the Home Department concerning the Introduction of Tread-Mills into Prisons; with Other Matters Connected with Prison Discipline.* (1823).

which were substantial, to obscure his very laudable goal of not just emancipation for catholics, but removal of common religious bigotry. So despite decades of work toward normalisation of the civil status of catholics and cultivation of the papacy, Hippisley became, in the end, so rigidly prescriptive that he had to turn away from the cause entirely, taking up in retirement the more modest issue of prisoners sentenced to work on treadmills.

'With All My Oldest and Native Friends'. Joseph Parkes: Warwickshire Solicitor and Electoral Agent in the Age of Reform[1]

NANCY LOPATIN-LUMMIS

Joseph Parkes, Birmingham solicitor, electoral agent, whig party advisor and secretary to the Parliamentary Municipal Corporation Commission was a modern master of exposing corrupt and fraudulent electioneering and using it as a catalyst for the election of reform and Liberal politicians immediately following the 1832 Reform Act. Warwickshire's own political and legal history was the foundation for Parkes's understanding of how politics worked in Britain and what was wrong with it, and helped forge his vision for an effective reform in parliamentary and local government. This essay examines Joseph Parkes's understanding of national electoral politics, informed by his work in Warwickshire. As a local solicitor, Parkes gained the wisdom of controlling electoral registration, canvassing in a routine and orderly manner and establishing a network of professionals to secure that registrations turned into votes at elections. This experience would culminate in the formation of the Reform Club, a national organisation of whigs, Liberals and radicals, that would, eventually, become the base of the Liberal Party in modern British politics. In short, Joseph Parkes was a man who could not, and did not wish to, escape where he came from, at least in terms of his political education. His Warwickshire experiences and lessons learned, solidified a series of political reform goals that he pragmatically approached as a political advisor, operative and attorney, rather than an elected public servant, and marked the direction of politics for the rest of the century.

Keywords: Joseph Parkes; Warwickshire; parliamentary reform; Municipal Reform Act 1835; Great Reform Act 1832; Lord Brougham; Warwick Borough Bill; electoral management; voter registration; corporation reform

Joseph Parkes, Birmingham solicitor, electoral agent, whig party advisor and secretary to the Parliamentary Municipal Corporation Commission was a modern master of exposing corrupt and fraudulent electioneering and using it as a catalyst for the election of reform and liberal politicians immediately following the 1832 Reform Act.[2] His work in Warwickshire – electoral, legal and journalistic – is a perfect example of how the man worked in politics and why he was so valued by the whig party and its leadership.

---

[1] Lambton MSS, Lambton Castle, Co. Durham: Parkes to Durham, 22 Aug. 1834.

[2] There is general recognition, though no specific analysis, of Parkes's work on the Reform Bill in the literature of the period. See Michael Brock, *The Great Reform Act* (1973); E.A. Smith, *Lord Grey, 1764–1845* (1990); Ian Newbould, *Whiggery and Reform 1830–41: The Politics of Government* (1990); Robert Stewart, *Party and Politics, 1830–1852* (1989); Nancy LoPatin, *Political Unions, Popular Politics and the Great Reform Act of 1832*

Warwickshire's own political and legal history was the foundation for Parkes's understanding of how politics worked in Britain, and what was wrong with it, and helped forge his vision for an effective reform in parliamentary and local government. Specifically, his work with Warwickshire MP, Charles Tennyson, to attain a household franchise based upon rate payments (scot and lot) would be the foundation of his proposals for parliamentary reform in the two major pieces of legislation which would define the age and the reform movement: the Great Reform Act of 1832 and the Municipal Corporations Act of 1835. His Warwickshire experiences also taught Parkes that there were limits on how far he could go and that compromise was a valuable tool for accomplishment, rather than a defeat, allowing him to direct the work of the Birmingham Political Union to the government's (and his own) political advantage. As a Warwickshire solicitor, Parkes gained the wisdom of controlling electoral registration, canvassing in a routine and orderly manner and establishing a network of professionals to secure that registrations turned into votes at elections. This experience would culminate in the formation of the Reform Club, a national organisation of whigs, liberals and radicals, that would, eventually, become the base of the Liberal Party in modern British politics. In short, Joseph Parkes was a man who could not, and did not wish to, escape where he came from, at least in terms of his political education. His Warwickshire experiences and lessons learned, solidified a series of political reform goals that he approached pragmatically as a political advisor, operative and attorney, rather than an elected public servant, and marked the direction of politics for the rest of the century.

There is very little historical work on Joseph Parkes. The only biography on the man was by Jessie Buckley, written in 1926.[3] The influence of Jeremy Bentham and James Mill was the key to other studies of Parkes's political work, according to G.B.A.M. Finlayson, Joseph Hamburger and William Thomas. While examining the Municipal Corporation Bill and the use of the press during the Great Reform Bill agitation, these studies argued that Parkes's commitment to the teachings of Jeremy Bentham and James Mill (known as the philosophic radicals) shaped all his political reform work and the creation of important ties to the whig governments of Lords Grey and Melbourne.[4] Finlayson's work also examined some of the electoral agent work Parkes did following the passage of the Municipal Corporation Act, connecting new voters with existing political party definitions.[5] Most recently, Philip Salmon has picked up this line of study, examining Parkes as the electoral registrar for the whigs and the interconnection between local and national elections.[6] This study is meant to make connections between these earlier examinations rather than reinterpret Parkes's true role in 19th-century politics. Rather,

---

[2] *(continued)* (1999); Philip Salmon, *Electoral Reform at Work: Local Politics and National Parties, 1832–41* (2002). For Parkes and his Birmingham Political Union ties, see Carlos Flick, *The Birmingham Political Union and the Movements for Reform in Britain, 1830–39* (1978); David J. Moss, *Thomas Attwood: The Biography of a Radical* (1990).

[3] See Jessie Buckley, *Joseph Parkes of Birmingham* (1926).

[4] Joseph Hamburger, *James Mill and the Art of Revolution* (1963); William Thomas, *The Philosophic Radicals: Nine Studies in Theory and Practice, 1817–1841* (1979), ch. 6.

[5] G.B.A.M. Finlayson, 'The Municipal Corporation Commission and Report, 1833–35', *Bulletin of the Institute for Historical Research*, xxxvii (1963); Finlayson, 'Joseph Parkes of Birmingham 1796–1865: A Study in Philosophic Radicalism', *Bulletin of the Institute for Historical Research*, xlvi (1973).

[6] Salmon, *Electoral Reform*.

it argues that Parkes's world – son of Midland manufacturer, unitarian, law student, philosophic radical, election solicitor and resident of a closed corporation and pocket borough – *all* contributed to the foundation of his reform programme, his political pragmatism, and his success in shaping the direction of the politics of the modern whig. By examining Parkes's work – contesting elections in the courts in 1826 and 1832, drafting reform legislation in 1828 and 1834, working behind the scenes to assist the government in attaining the Reform Bill in 1831–2, and managing parliamentary elections in Warwickshire in 1835 – he demonstrated his ideological commitment to radical reform as he sought to eliminate political corruption, require aristocrats as well as elected public servants to obey the law, both on the national and local level, his political pragmatism in knowing how far he could go and what was too much, and always remembering that he was working for equality for his 'old playmates and personal friends' in a new political age.[7]

Joseph Parkes was born in the provincial town of Warwick in 1796. Raised by a father who was a staunch supporter of Lord Grey and the whigs, Parkes studied at Warwick Free Grammar School and entered the University of Glasgow with some basic committed principles: that parliamentary reform was essential to all economic and social change in England. He soon decided that the study of law would be the best means towards this end. His studies revealed to him that Warwick's operating political charter of 1694 was that of an incorporated scot and lot borough.[8] In other words, voting privileges were granted to those paying church and poor rates.[9] But the reality, the one that explained his father's stalwart support of whig reformers, was quite different. The dominating aristocratic force, the earl of Warwick's family, had converted to toryism generations earlier and changed the election and operation of Warwickshire governance through his influence. Warwick was, in essence, an aristocratic pocket borough of the earl, who, by Parkes's young adulthood, was also the lord-lieutenant of the county, recorder of Warwick, and the one responsible for appointing the town clerk.[10] The earl's solicitor was the treasurer of the corporation. As he used patronage and bribery to place tories in positions of local government, the courts and the house of commons, the necessity for parliamentary and municipal reform became the core of Parkes's ideological political views.

Parkes finished his law degree and moved to Birmingham, beginning his practice as a solicitor by taking cases that dealt with contested elections and accusations of electoral corruption. He represented the interests of local businessmen and manufacturers in negotiating land deals with railroad companies for access in and around Birmingham.[11] By 1826, his reputation as a reformer and successful solicitor had moved beyond Warwickshire, and he was hired in Leicester to serve as election agent. He also began

[7] University College London, Brougham MSS: Parkes to Denis Le Marchant, 8 Aug. 1834.

[8] See Joseph Parkes, *The Governing Charter of the Borough of Warwick, 5 William and Mary, 18 March 1694, with a Letter to the Burgesses on the Past and Present State of the Corporation* (1827).

[9] P. Styles, 'The Corporation of Warwick, 1660–1835', *Transactions and Proceedings of the Birmingham Archaeological Society,* lix (1938).

[10] *VCH, Warwickshire,* vii, 270–97.

[11] Finlayson, 'Joseph Parkes', 188.

researching the history of the chancery.[12] It was the legal fight within his own home town of Warwick that same year, which garnered him real political influence.

This legal case was for the election of Warwick's mayor. The charter of Warwick had empowered the burgesses of the town to elect a new mayor. The reality of this arrangement was that the earl of Warwick's influence had maintained mayors in office for as long as seven consecutive years and aldermen were often non-residents. Frequently, no election had even been held. When, in 1826, John Wilmshurst was made mayor for the third successive term, and put supporters into the aldermanic openings, Warwick's whig opposition retained the services of Parkes.[13] Parkes took the case to court, accusing the corporation of violating the charter and demanding that the mayoral results be tossed out.[14] Parkes won a *mandamus* from king's bench and a second election.[15] In order to make this success meaningful, Parkes decided to take on the burgesses. In February 1827, he published a pamphlet, *The Governing Charter of the Borough of Warwick, with a Letter to the Burgesses on the Past and Present State of the Corporation.*[16] He summarized the law in regard to what the charter had to say about charities and franchise rights and found, 'no printed or manuscript document, or particle of information'.[17] He called upon the citizens of Warwick to take advantage of 'the great political principal of civil freedom'.

The court win in 1826 had certainly been noticed by whigs and others who were now choosing to fight demonstrations of corruption and abuses at both the corporate and parliamentary level. The same year that Parkes won the *mandamus* in Warwick, he worked hand-in-hand with Warwickshire MP, Charles Tennyson, on drafting legislation to nullify the elections of Penryn and East Retford, disenfranchise both boroughs, and transfer the seats to Birmingham. The East Retford Bill proposed to, 'limit the poll to two or three days duration. The town is in natural division of twelve districts for the parish purposes of assessment, therefore we propose under one booth twelve district poll places where the rate payers are to poll in the perspective division. And various enactments of a local nature and against bribery, treating, etc.'[18] Public support in Birmingham was overwhelming, and enormous public rallies were held and petitions circulated for submission to parliament. Parkes became the joint secretary of the Birmingham committee to secure political representation. He corresponded with other radicals on the

---

[12] Parkes studied the history of the chancery as a way to understand the political implications for the legal system. In describing his findings on the eve of publication, he told Francis Place: 'the volume in fact will be the *History* of the grievances of the Court; at the same time practical collections for its reform'. It was in writing this book that Parkes became acquainted with Henry, Lord Brougham, reformer and rising star in the whig party. In the course of public discussion of reform within the court of chancery, Brougham drew Parkes into national alliances by mentioning 'the respectable solicitor of Warwickshire' and his work in glowing terms. See Joseph Parkes, *A History of the Court of Chancery* (1828).

[13] *Parliamentary Papers* (1835), xxvi: *First Report of the Royal Commission of Inquiry into Municipal Corporations of England and Wales,* part V, 665; Buckley, *Joseph Parkes,* 34.

[14] Styles, 'The Corporation of Warwick'. This was considered a huge victory in the courts as *mandamus* was rarely decreed and this was the first time since Parkes started practising law that he successfully handled a contested election in which the results were not just favourable, but established legal precedent that the courts would evaluate evidence suggesting corruption and fraud.

[15] *Warwick Advertiser,* 8 Dec. 1826.

[16] He dedicated this to Henry Brougham, for his distinguished advocacy of 'honest administration of the Charters'.

[17] Joseph Parkes, *The Governing Charter of the Borough of Warwick* (1827).

[18] BL, Add. MS 35148, ff. 19–20: Parkes to Place, 7 Jan. 1828.

parliamentary legislation. Francis Place and Joseph Hume advised the committee to
include ballot voting in their demands and hoped the bill would launch a larger and
national demand for extensive parliamentary reform. Parkes and Tennyson were more
realistic, fully aware that the problems of corporations such as Warwick would need
attention before a national parliamentary reform scheme would have meaning.

But in May 1829, parliament voted not to disfranchise East Retford, but rather extend
the parliamentary borough to include the hundred of Bassetlaw. Though unsuccessful,
Parkes and Tennyson seemed pleased that the longer-term campaign had begun, as it was
the beginning 'of a great national question'.[19] Thus, the interests of Birmingham were at
the foundation of the first parliamentary reform work in which Parkes engaged. The
failure of the East Retford Bill did little to change Parkes's drive. He continued to work
on Warwickshire political concerns, writing on the state of crime and prisons in the
county.[20] And Parkes continued his association with Tennyson, managing the latter's
election bid for a seat during the 1830 general election.

Tennyson opted to stand for Bletchingly rather than Warwickshire. Parkes wanted him
to stay within the county and voicing concerns over corporation activity and electoral
fraud. To this end, Parkes tried to get Tennyson to stand for Coventry, along with Edward
Ellice. 'I could have insured your return from about £2,000 by a conjunction of
circumstances.'[21] Tennyson opted for the more secure and less expensive (and less
corporation controlled) contest in the borough of Stamford. Parkes advised his client to
contribute to local charities in order to secure his return for years to come. 'I know the
evil of once beginning this system – and I know that you neither was invited or entered
on the principle of a purse contest. But still I think it will ultimately be a certain and
most economical seat to you.'[22] Parkes's success with this election was packaged to other
radicals and reformers as the beginnings of a successful campaign which could, if handled
correctly, result in a parliamentary reform measure. Tennyson's election warranted a
communication from Parkes to Lord Brougham informing him of his return.[23] Tennyson's was not the only election in Warwickshire in which Parkes had an interest.[24] In
Warwick itself, the ruling party was divided as to supporting the government in a reform
measure. John Tomes and Edward Bolton King were returned as 'independent' candidates, in an election that Parkes scrutinised for undue influence of the earl of Warwick
and another opportunity to go to court.

Parkes's direct connection with Warwickshire was complicated during the Reform
Bill campaign which began even before Lord Grey had committed his new whig

[19] Lincolnshire RO, Tennyson D'Eyncourt MSS, 4 TDE h/53/1: Parkes to Tennyson, 13 May 1829.

[20] Joseph Parkes, *State of the Court of Requests and Public Office of Birmingham, with considerations on the increase and persecution of crime in the County of Warwick, the expedience of an extended and improved jurisdiction of the recovery of small debts, and the establishment of a local prison with petty sessions and gaol delivery for Birmingham and its environs, Deritend, Ashted and Edgbaston* (1829).

[21] Lincs RO, 4 TDE H/53/5: Parkes to Tennyson, 4 Aug. 1830.

[22] Lincs RO, TDE H/31/25: Parkes to Tennyson, 16 Oct. 1830; 4 TDE H/53/20: Parkes to Tennyson, 16 Mar. 1831; TDE H/31/30: Parkes to Tennyson, 27 Mar. 1831; 4 TDE H/53/21: Bessie Parkes to Tennyson (on behalf of her husband), 26 Apr. 1831.

[23] The vote was Cecil 390, Tennyson 356 and Chaplin 302. University College London, Brougham MSS: Parkes to Brougham, 3 Mar. 1831.

[24] He worked for his friend, Colonel Gregory, in the Warwick county election as well. Lincs RO, 4 TDE H/53/23: Parkes to Tennyson, 21 May 1831.

government to introducing such a measure. Thomas Attwood founded the Birmingham Political Union (BPU) in January 1830, an event that Parkes described to Tennyson as 'ill contrived and worse timed'.[25] While he would never actually join the organisation, claiming he was 'a Reformer but not a Unionist', he recognized the good that would come from public support of the Grey ministry from extra-parliamentary organisation such as the BPU. The bill was certainly worth supporting, although it called for a property qualification rather than the ratepayer householder franchise that Tennyson and he proposed in 1829:[26]

> The thorough honesty of the Reform Billl, as against the Boroughmongers, drowns all objections to the details of the substituted electoral system. Of course numbers of persons object to the £10 as too high and too low; others think the Landed Interest has too great a proportion; the majority regret that the duration of Parliaments is not shortened; the larger majority wish the Ballot – but all agree that more than the Measure introduced could not have been expected of Ministers. A very strong objection exists against the Scot and Lot being terminated with the lives of the present electors – and see no reason for limiting our franchise to £10. But every soul unites in the confidence that such a Reformed Parliament as the new Bill will create would fairly from time to time, as occasion required, adapt the Electoral System to the rights of the People.[27]

But Parkes also realized that the BPU could do harm as well. 'On Monday the Union has convened all the neighbouring Unions to a Public Meeting in the open air', Parkes wrote to Tennyson just prior to the October 1831 defeat of the bill. 'Most extreme language and Resolutions will be passed, but as I am not a member and they attend to me I think I shawl attend and moderate . . . Great harm or great good may result from the meetings.'[28] Always critical of Attwood, from his motives to his abilities, Parkes stepped into what he saw as a void in leadership among the people after the bill's defeat. 'Viewing the increasing and numerically imposing public meetings in the three kingdoms since the loss of the bill, I am confident that the feeling [of instances that the bill must pass] increases in force and quantity; but it has no direction; it is an inundition [sic] which it carries off. The people seeing their leaders, like their ministers, without a plan or direction, are getting sulky and sullen – they are brooding a storm.'[29]

But as the fortunes of the Reform Bill ebbed and flowed, Parkes looked forward, again based upon his experiences as a Warwickshire man. He suggested local government reform as the next step for the whigs, going so far as to offer Lord Melbourne his thoughts on the subject in the winter of 1832: 'Some general improvement of the municipal system is becoming daily more necessary, not only in all the large manufacturing towns, but in the Corporation Towns . . . every where (or with few exceptions)

[25] Lincs RO, 4 TDE H/53/2: Parkes to Tennyson, 2 Feb. 1830.
[26] Lincs RO, 4 TDE H/53/19: Parkes to Tennyson, 7 Mar. 1831.
[27] Lincs RO, 4 TDE H/53/19: Parkes to Tennyson, 7 Mar. 1831.
[28] Lincs RO, 4 TDE H/53/32: Parkes to Tennyson, 26 Sept. 1831.
[29] BL, Add. MS 35,149, ff. 117–19: Parkes to George Grote, 26 Oct. 1831.

the Corporations possess and exercise political influence directly adverse to the principles of the present ministry.[30]

The Reform Bill's success in June 1832 meant both rejoicing and getting ready for an onslaught of work for Parkes. He immediately began working on the 1832 general election with enthusiasm and confidence. 'The field is all our own', he wrote to Tennyson.[31] While Tennyson and others returned to the first reformed parliament without incident, it was Warwick and the 1832 borough election that would rise to national infamy and, ultimately, the discrediting of one of the cabinet members. Parkes's role in Warwickshire politics would be significant for the next stage of his career and the future of political reform.

In December 1832, the earl of Warwick's brother, Sir Charles Greville, and Edward Bolton King stood for election as tories. The earl gave £3,000 to the town clerk to distribute for Greville. He was, not surprisingly, returned at the head of the poll. William Collins, the defeated candidate, hired Parkes to petition parliament and have the election thrown out in court. By then, Parkes had been appointed secretary of the commission on corporation reform and was a valued political appointee for the whig government. But Parkes was also a Warwickshire man and he took the case. First, he saw it as compelling evidence to all that his work collecting information on corporations in order to reform them, was warranted, if not the essential companion to the Reform Act. Second, this would, if the case succeeded, be a humiliating blow to the power of the aristocracy, or at least the earl of Warwick. Finally, he was personally tied to the case, Warwick being his home, 'the calendar of my nativity', and the town of 'his oldest and dearest friends'.[32]

Parkes eagerly, and immediately contacted whig party whip and friend, Edward Ellice, to explain his course of legal action, as this contested election was of great interest to the whigs. It reflected everything wrong with the old political practices and everything that the Reform Bill was supposed to eliminate. In essence, it was a litmus test for whether any real reform had occurred. Parkes reported in excruciating detail:

I went there for two days to investigate narrowly all the facts and evidence connected with the return of King and Sir Charles Greville. From breakfast till midnight on Monday at [William] Collins' house King's legal men and I studiously scrutinized the whole matter. First as to King – there is not a shadow of bribery imputable to him, his agents or Committee. All treating was rigidly suppressed on the issue of the writ. There has been no illegal application of money . . .

As to Greville – We have distinct indisputable proof of the grossest bribery ever perpetrated. Thirty cases are beyond all doubt; many of them are, 10–16 [are] paid by Committee men [i.e., bribed], and even in the Committee room. The men themselves have come forward and deposed in writing to the receipt of the money. – Secondly, the treating went on every poll day unlimited. – Thirdly we do not doubt that we can trace all the money paid up to this time to Lord Warwick's private Bank account.

[30] Lincs RO, 4 TDE H/53/48: Parkes to Tennyson, 15 Feb. 1832.
[31] Lincs RO, 4 TDE H/31/5: Parkes to Tennyson, 10 July 1832.
[32] University College London, Brougham MSS: Parkes to Denis Le Marchant, 8 Aug. 1834; Parkes to Durham, 22 Aug. 1834.

Fourthly we can show that his agent Brown [his Steward] previous to the Registration, colourably rated Lord Warwick's agricultural tenants for Lord Warwick's lands with in the Borough in his occupation.[33]

Parkes, having decided in consultation with 'twelve of the oldest and wealthiest of our [Warwick's] Burgesses', determined 'that we should never catch Lord Warwick in such a noose again as being virgin bribery it was barefaced'.[34] Not only would Parkes, representing William Collins, petition parliament to overturn the election for cause, but he would use the opportunity to draft legislation which would alter the boundaries of Warwick borough to include Leamington – a move which he and the burgesses believed would eliminate Warwick's ability to buy voters and 'cure everything'.[35] Parkes indicated that without the earl of Warwick's money, there would have been no question that King and Collins, the whig candidates, would have been returned as 'all the men bribed voted in 1831 for King and Tomes (a Whig), promised on the canvas of 1832 (November last) and voted Greville at the December poll!'.[36]

Parkes called upon Ellice to help with the estimated £1,000 towards the expense of bringing a petition to parliament, both personally and in his capacity as a party leader. 'Now surely for Warwick which on the Reform Bill election returned two after a desperate struggle – and for the county town of Warwickshire which has been the great focus of the Reform spirit of 1831 and 1832 – the London Magnates of the Upper Story ought to aid a little town'.[37] A petition was sent forward and heard before a parliamentary committee.[38]

When Lord Brougham appointed William Collins to the Warwickshire commission of the peace, Parkes wrote to clarify how Collins received the appointment. 'Mr. Collins' name was suggested at the House of our County member Sir George Philips', Parkes wrote to Denis LeMarchant, the chancellor's secretary. Collins, resident of Warwick and of liberal opinion, was to be placed on the Warwickshire commission of the peace. He was recommended by Warwick county MP, Sir George Philips. Sir Eardley Wilmot, MP, questioned whether this appointment was a gesture of thanks by the government that Collins had challenged the return of a tory MP. Parkes assured Brougham that the nomination of Collins 'has been generally mentioned to our county and other local members . . . [and Brougham's] communication to me this afternoon of the delicacy of an immediate issue of Mr. Collins's fiat, pending the case against Lord Warwick – Mr. Collins being the Petitioner – was the first intimation I had of any delay of the fiat'.[39] Parkes was concerned more that the appointment of the commission would be delayed than the appearance of a sinecure by the government. Collins, according to Parkes, 'would be perfectly satisfied as respects the Chancellor and yourself by the assurance that it is solely from propriety to Lord Warwick pending the proceedings in the House of

[33] Lambton MSS, Lambton Castle: Parkes to Ellice, 25 Apr. 1833.
[34] Lambton MSS, Lambton Castle: Parkes to Ellice, 25 Apr. 1833.
[35] Lambton MSS, Lambton Castle: Parkes to Ellice, 25 Apr. 1833.
[36] Lambton MSS, Lambton Castle: Parkes to Ellice, 25 Apr. 1833.
[37] Lambton MSS, Lambton Castle: Parkes to Ellice, 25 Apr. 1833.
[38] *Parliamentary Papers* (1833), xi, paper 295: *Report of the Select Committee on the Warwick Borough Election Petition.*
[39] University College London, Brougham MSS: Parkes to LeMarchant, 27 July 1833.

Commons. But his friends and the Public, who expect him to qualify on Thursday at Warwick, with the other gentlemen, may interpret the delay of the fiat as conveying an imputation on him, his character may be locally prejudiced.'[40]

The petition passed through the Commons and the parliamentary committee concluded that Greville had not taken any part in the bribery:

> the earl of Warwick did unconstitutionally apply . . . by his agent and steward . . . £3,000 and upwards towards the election expenditure, and promotion of the political interest of the candidate Sir Charles John Greville, in the transfer of such sum of money to James Tibbetts, town-clerk of the said borough, who appropriated the same to various corrupt and illegal practices at the last election . . . and the steward of the earl of Warwick, caused numerous persons, many of them non-resident in the borough, and dependents of the earl of Warwick, to be fictitiously rated to the poor of the two parishes of the said borough.[41]

Those guilty of bribing electors were fined £1,000 penalties at the Warwick assizes. Parkes mused to Edward Elllice that such 'good cash towards our expences and confirmatory of the Report' was welcome.[42]

Parkes not only secured a new election for his Warwickshire clients, but also shaped the Warwick Borough Bill. The bill was reminiscent of the East Retford Bill. The franchise was to be based on household suffrage and the payment of poor and church rates, reiterating the men's conviction that the scot and lot was best securing an expanded electorate and limiting the Conservative and landed interests of freemen. The borough of Warwick itself would be extended to include the householders of Leamington Spa, a point specifically referred to in the parliamentary debate against it.[43]

Parkes wasted no time offering Lord Brougham 'our best thanks . . . to good to the government and my local friends and much for the Warwick cause'. He also made him aware of the potential for additional change.[44] 'I do not like to send up a Pilot Balloon on this subject without your assent', he wrote to Brougham, 'but if you approve . . . nothing would serve the Cabinet at this juncture more than in the large Counties doing similar favour throu' the popular County members'.[45] The bill passed quickly through the Commons and Parkes was ready for others to take over. 'I . . . had proved and could prove a mass of corruption and the Lords might deal with it as they liked', he wrote to the earl of Durham.[46] The bill headed for the house of lords in March 1834, but between delays in interviewing witnesses and opposition by the tories, the bill was in trouble when taken up on 5 August.[47] By then the government had changed significantly. Edward Stanley, among others, resigned in May. Lord Grey appointed

[40] University College London, Brougham MSS: Parkes to LeMarchant, 27 July 1833.
[41] *Annual Register* (1833), 211–12.
[42] Lambton MSS, Lambton Castle: Parkes to Ellice, 15 Apr. 1834. This was evidently forwarded by Ellice to Durham.
[43] *Parliamentary Papers* (1833), iv, 633–4; *Parliamentary Papers* (1833), xi, 197; *The Times*, 6 Aug. 1834, p. 3.
[44] University College London, Brougham MSS: Parkes to LeMarchant, 31 July 1833.
[45] University College London, Brougham MSS: Parkes to LeMarchant, 5 Aug. 1833.
[46] Lambton MSS, Lambton Castle: Parkes to Durham, 19 June 1834.
[47] A short discussion on the bill's progress was mentioned in *The Times*, 24 May 1834, p. 5.

moderates to fill the cabinet vacancies and Durham was not among those invited to join the government. Then Grey resigned, after the schism within the government over Irish church rates became public knowledge. With the Irish question dividing the government, and the London dailies divided in their support and condemnation of its policies, Parkes found himself in an odd position. *The Times* had begun attacking the chancellor some months before the Warwick Bill, primarily over the government's poor law proposal. Parkes had been defending Brougham via the *Morning Chronicle*.

This, however, became nearly impossible for Parkes when Brougham spoke against the Warwick Bill in August, particularly as he had indicated personally to Parkes that he would support the measure. Brougham declared that the case was one 'of strong suspicion, but it was impossible for their lordships to legislate merely on suspicion . . . and it would be most unjust to visit with punishment an entire body because a few of them had acted corruptly'.[48] Durham was absent from a poorly attended house of lords, and the chancellor himself proposed that the bill be read in six months, essentially killing the legislation.

Parkes was outraged at the loss of the legislation, which he had fought for, in one form or another, since 1826. But he felt betrayed by Brougham, with whom he had worked, defended in the press, and whom he considered a friend. 'I am heartily glad you were absent from the Funeral [of the Warwick Bill]', he wrote to Durham. 'Your "virtuous indignation" never could have been restrained on the indecent and scandalous mode of burial adopted by Burke Brougham.'[49] In his view, Brougham had set the whole hearing up for a defeat of the bill, commencing with the time called for arguments to 'a three quarters of an hour rambling Oration – he was wrong on all the points of Law and Fact'.[50] Parkes was so angry, he claimed not to 'trust myself to comment on these mad and vulgarly dishonest proceedings . . . [but was] heartily glad' that Durham was not there 'to get into "collision" with him [Brougham]. You would have had a regular row.'[51]

The attack on the lord chancellor was immediate and harsh. *The Times* accused Brougham of strangling the bill as a personal attack on Durham, claiming the legislation was the latter's 'favourite ward . . . his *cheval de bataille* in the House of Peers'.[52] The chancellor thought that the Lords would be irresponsibly 'altering the franchise . . . and cause an alteration in the constitution of a borough'.[53] It was a severe enough political attack that LeMarchant asked Parkes to defend the chancellor in the press. 'I think you might say what we want without giving offence to your Warwick friends [in Warwickshire].' Parkes responded: 'On the subject of Warwick', he wrote to LeMarchant:

I will be frank and plain. My public character has been and is deeply committed in the case. I am not only responsible as Agent but greatly as co-originator of the proceedings. It is my native town . . . and all the capital Reformers of the Borough are my old playmates and personal friends. I was greatly responsible in advising the struggle of 1831, when we sent up two good men on the Reform Bills. I must under

---

[48] *The Times*, 6 Aug. 1834, p. 3.

[49] Lambton MSS, Lambton Castle: Parkes to Durham, 6 Aug. 1834.

[50] Lambton MSS, Lambton Castle: Parkes to Durham, 6 Aug. 1834.

[51] Lambton MSS, Lambton Castle: Parkes to Durham, 6 Aug. 1834.

[52] *The Times*, 7 Aug. 1834, p. 2.

[53] *The Times*, 7 Aug. 1834, p. 2.

such circumstances, and indeed it is my nature, go independently straight. I must frankly tell you and I speak not of the Warwick party alone but of the members of the House of Commons who have witnessed the conduct of the Lords on the Warwick Bill, that our case has been very ill treated from first to last . . . I have however no alternative but to discharge fully my professional duty and act politically independent which I will do unless my nature alters in a court atmosphere from which God protect me.[54]

Parkes's identity as a Warwickshire man guided his political actions once again.

But Parkes did not despair completely. He had two avenues left to continue his quest for household suffrage. He was working steadily on the commission for corporation reform, aware that Warwick's political problems could be solved permanently with the proper legislation to undermine the coercive power of the corporation and the freemen electors. But simultaneously, Parkes had new problems in Warwick that demanded his skills – this time, those as an election agent. Lord Melbourne's resignation meant another election to secure a government and Warwick was fertile ground for his skills in registering and canvassing voters to return MPs supportive of household suffrage.

The January 1835 general election was a busy one for Parkes. He managed three difficult elections in Warwickshire. The first was the logical continuation of his work in the removal of the earl of Warwick's influence in the borough of Warwick. In spite of the Greville scandal and the Warwick Borough Bill, the general election immediately followed the successful by-election of Edward Bolton King and Michael Collins. In addition to Warwick, Parkes managed the election in Coventry. Edward Ellice had sat for Coventry since 1818 (with a brief hiatus from 1826 to 1830 when a mob organised by the corporation and mayor attacked his supporters and prevented voting).[55] But the reform measure had changed the electorate (freemen retained their votes, but still outnumbered the newly enfranchised £10 property owner) and the corporation remained neutral in the December 1832 election, though Ellice and his fellow whig candidate, Henry Lytton Bulwer (formerly representing Wilton), hired their own bullies 'who were paid 5s. a day and as much to drink as they wished'.[56] Ellice and Bulwer won the election, but the corporation responded by swearing in 1,000 new constables in 1833, anticipating renewed violence at the next election.[57]

Disenchanted with the failures and schisms of an anaemic whig government, the Coventry radicals opted to run their own candidate in 1835. William Williams, a long-standing advocate for parliamentary reform and a member of the Coventry Political Union which had worked for the passage of the Reform Bill since its formation in the summer of 1830, decided to challenge Ellice.[58] Williams, a self-made cotton broker, had

[54] University College London, Brougham MSS: Parkes to LeMarchant, 8 Aug. 1834.

[55] Peter Searby, 'Coventry Politics in the Age of the Chartists, 1836–1848', *Coventry and North Warwickshire History Pamphlets*, i (1964), 9.

[56] Searby, 'Coventry Politics in the Age of the Chartists', 9.

[57] T.W. Whitley, *The Parliamentary Representation of the City of Coventry* (1894), 254.

[58] For the creation and the objectives of the Coventry Political Union, see Nancy LoPatin, 'Popular Politics in the Midlands: The Coventry Political Union and the Great Reform Act', *Midland History*, xx (1995), 103–18.

entered the Coventry common council in 1833 as a radical, and was an aquaintance of
Parkes through the London radical community.[59] While Ellice rarely visited Coventry,
Williams had steady contact, and his proposals to abolish church rates and support the
ballot were extremely popular. Parkes was not 'managing' Ellice's campaign as much as
watching over it while his friend recovered from an illness in Italy, and he was concerned
that a third candidate would harm both men's chances for re-election. Splitting the Ellice
and Bulwer ticket that had succeeded in 1832 could jeopardise the whole borough.
'Bulwer is very essential to the Ellice-ites . . . they split all Whig and Radical votes',
Parkes wrote to Durham. 'But little H. Bulwer is playing fast and loose. First he will, then
he will not go down; then he looks after a cheaper return – in fact I suppose they have
not a sous [sic]. In the meanwhile Ellice's party without the advantage of his presence
and pluck are alarmed; and being obliged to oppose Williams (the second Radical) a feud
political is brewing to the natural advantage of the Tories.'[60] Parkes hoped to convince
Bulwer to stand down so that he could stage an election between Ellice and Williams,
whom he liked as 'a good City Common Council man . . . but is tarred with Cobbe-
titeism' primarily because he had 'plenty of cash'.[61] Bulwer had none and Parkes was a
practical man. By the end of December, Bulwer had retired and Parkes had high hopes
that, 'the Ellicites ought to support Williams now and the Williamites Ellice. I want to
lick the Common Enemy and would coalesce with the Devil, on a French partnership,
to effect *that*.'[62] The strategy worked and Bulwer got the safe seat of Marylebone, but
Parkes complained that, 'It was sweating work in Coventry and nothing but getting
Bulwer to elope to Marylebone and incessant exertions saved Ellice. His absence, Free
Trade, and the rascally cross splitting between Williams's Cobbett men and the Tory
Thomas, nearly bilged Ellice.'[63]

Finally, he worked to return his friend, Arthur Gregory, to the North Warwickshire
seat. Gregory, a country gentleman who owned a small amount of property, shared
Parkes's support of the whigs and longer-term reform plans. But Gregory lost the
election and Parkes learned a valuable lesson from it. Gregory's limited funds did not
allow him to compete with the large landowners, as the expense of registering new
electors was staggering. 'Dr. Arnold, Headmaster of Rugby School, came two hundred
miles from Cumberland to plump for Gregory', Parkes wrote, but 'the PREMIER [sic]
arrived with Edmund Peel, polled Dugdale and Wilmot and posted on to London. Did
you ever know anything so indecent?'[64] The problems of pre-1832 electioneering had
not gone away, but merely changed. It made the need for more organised voter
registration efforts very clear to Parkes. 'We see that we lose by our own neglect and
pre-arrangement. In a fortnight, without one paid legal agent, and with only £1,300 and
Gregory paying legal expenses, we canvassed the whole of this division of Warwickshire
at a cost less than £300 and we polled 1,847 electors and moreover treated them well

---

[59] Daniel Evans, *The Life and Work of William Williams, M.P.* (1939).
[60] Lambton MSS, Lambton Castle: Parkes to Durham, 22 Dec. 1834; 15 Dec. 1834.
[61] Lambton MSS, Lambton Castle: Parkes to Durham, 22 Dec. 1834; 15 Dec. 1834.
[62] Lambton MSS, Lambton Castle: Parkes to Durham, 22 Dec. 1834; 15 Dec. 1834.
[63] Lambton MSS, Lambton Castle: Parkes to Durham, 18 Jan. 1835.
[64] Lambton MSS, Lambton Castle: Parkes to Durham, 18 Jan. 1835.

with cold meats and barley corn, being two hundred and ninety-seven votes for the Reform Cause beyond our poll of 1832.'[65]

Parkes did serve as an electoral agent for some midland seats in the 1837 and 1839 general elections, and one or two select seats in 1841, but his work for the whigs was quite limited after the Municipal Corporation Commission and the legal work imme-diately following the reform measures. He remained active in the Reform Club and was long concerned with the issues involving electoral registration, and his correspondence with leading radical, whig and even Conservative Party leaders was quite prolific. But Parkes never participated in backroom political work - doing the necessary day-to-day monitoring of money, votes, and the details of legislative application in the boroughs and corporations – either qualitatively or quantitatively, after 1835. Had he achieved all he could in the way of reform for his 'oldest and native friends'? In some ways, he had. By the later 1830s, the whigs, for whom he had worked diligently, were in crisis over what they hoped to achieve in terms of political reform. They were divided on issues, and the alliance formed with the radicals in politics, of whom Parkes and many Warwickshire men considered themselves, was breaking apart. But while the whigs floundered on the national level, beginning to lose seats in parliament to an emerging Conservative Party that understood the importance of party registration as well as Parkes, the new municipal governments in the midlands – Warwick being the chief example – now saw themselves governed by aldermen, charity commissioners, mayors and MPs who had been the excluded whig opposition to the closed corporation a decade earlier. Reform, though not the householder suffrage and ballot version of reform that Parkes hoped to secure, had been achieved, and the midlanders were benefiting from it, politically as well as economically. Parkes had opened the door for his 'old playmates' and the necessity of working with the whigs was waning with each successful election and shift of local power. Parkes had accomplished many of his goals by pragmatic political work. He aided the candidacies of aristocratic whigs, compromised on ideological programme of reforms when necessary, using the courts and the press for generating 'the steam' of public opinion, and guided and monitored elections through registration and canvassing as no other political operative at the time did. He also recognized when he could no longer assume he had the support of the whigs, either in terms of legislation or money for parliamentary campaigns. His skills at compromise and his patience allowed for the evolution of reforms that grew out of his personal and provincial experiences as a young solicitor. He left politics (or at least lessened his political activity) knowing that his considerable abilities, refined in Warwickshire, made an enormous difference in the development of the politics of his nation.

[65] Lambton MSS, Lambton Castle: Parkes to Durham, 20 Mar. 1835.

'Meddling with Politics': The Political Role of Foreign Missions in the Early Nineteenth Century

MICHAEL A. RUTZ

The proper character of the relationship between missionaries and politics shaped one of the most contentious debates within the first century of the modern missionary movement. While the leadership of the missionary societies repeatedly insisted upon the separation between the work of the gospel and politics, missionaries in the field frequently found it difficult to remove themselves from political controversies. John Philip and James Read served with the London Missionary Society in the Cape Colony for most of the first half of the 19th century. Their persistent defence of the interests of the colonial Khoi made them controversial figures in the debates over the social, political and economic structures of the Cape Colony. Missionaries like Read and Philip, rarely described their activities as 'political', and certainly did not conceive of their work as in any way related to the patronage-ridden political system of the early 19th century. Nonetheless, in their promotion of the ideas of religious and civil equality, and in their effective use of public opinion to shape government and public perception of colonial policy, their actions reflected many of the important changes taking place in contemporary British politics. Dissenting political activity focused on the issues of the defence of religious liberty, the struggle to secure their own civil equality, and the debate over the proper relationship between church and state. These issues also played a crucial role in colonial politics throughout the period. This essay will illustrate the important role of the foreign missionary movement in this process. Examining the work of Philip and Read enables us to identify the ways that issues of domestic politics helped to shape the political debates emerging in Britain's expanding empire.

Keywords: missions; Cape Colony; dissent; evangelicalism; politics; John Philip; London Missionary Society; James Read

During the summer of 1836, the parliamentary committee investigating the condition of the aboriginal peoples of the British empire took up the matter of the conflict on the eastern frontier of the Cape Colony, and the treatment of the Xhosa. Among those who gave testimony before the committee was John Philip, superintendent of the London Missionary Society's (LMS) missions in southern Africa. Philip brought with him two African converts, Andries Stoffels, a deacon in the independent congregation at the government sponsored Kat River settlement, and Jan Tshatshu, a Xhosa chief. Appearing before the committee, and audiences throughout the country, the Africans 'aroused much interest' and provided excellent publicity for the LMS.[1] Stoffels and Tshatshu were more than missionary trophies, however, and their presence with Philip had a deeply political

---

[1] School of Oriental and African Studies [hereafter SOAS], Council for World Mission/London Missionary Society Archive [hereafter CWM/LMS], Africa Odds, 9: *Jan Tzatzoe and the African Witnesses* (1836).

purpose. Their testimony constituted a crucial component of Philip's long campaign against the colonial government's policies in South Africa. Their manner and appearance testified to the benefits of the religious freedom, civil equality, and commercial opportunity, that Philip had helped to secure for them with the enactment of ordinance 50 in 1828. The onset of legal equality for the colonial Khoi had set the foundation for the experiment of the government sponsored Kat River Settlement, and Philip's hope for the future of a prosperous and productive colony based upon principles of equality and freedom of opportunity.[2]

Also with Philip was James Read, an LMS missionary who served as minister to the Khoi congregation at the Kat River Settlement. Read had arrived in South Africa in 1800, at the age of 23 years. He had worked as a carpenter in his native Essex before volunteering for the LMS, and served first as an artisan, before being ordained by Johannes van der Kemp, the first LMS superintendent at the Cape, in 1806. During his more than three decades in South Africa Read had worked beside van der Kemp and Philip in their struggle against the ill-treatment of the colonial Khoi. He was a controversial figure, both in and outside of the LMS. Colonists denounced him for encouraging Khoi to bring charges of abuse against their masters to the colonial courts. He clashed with fellow missionaries over the role of native agents in the missions, and was suspended by the LMS for a period because of sexual misconduct. During the first half of the 19th century, however, there was no more consistent advocate of African rights in all of southern Africa.

Throughout their careers, Read and Philip were key participants in vigorous debates over the role of the missionary, and the propriety of their actions on behalf of Africans. While critics, at the time and subsequently, accused them of engaging in 'politics' and stepping beyond the suitable activities of mission work, Read and Philip defended their advocacy as essential to the goal of spreading christianity among the non-christian peoples of South Africa. This essay considers one of these disputes, and suggests the importance of these debates for understanding the place of the missionary within the colonial context, and their connections to the changing nature of British politics during the first half of the 19th century.

In the midst of the escalating tensions on the colonial frontier that were the subject of the parliamentary committee's investigation, the LMS in South Africa faced internal controversies as well. Throughout the 1830s and 1840s, missionaries debated questions of church government and authority, the relationship between ministers and congregations, and the role of the missionary superintendent, John Philip. James Read was also an important figure in these contests, which both mirrored religious and political controversies underway in early-Victorian Britain, and also reflected genuine differences in attitudes towards race and the status of Africans that were specific to the colonial context. The conflict in the South African mission pitted Philip and his allies, especially Read and his son, against the legendary Robert Moffat and a group of newer missionaries on the eastern frontier, led by Henry Calderwood.

[2] The ordinance provided basic civil equality for all free Africans in the colony, ending the system of pass laws and granting Africans the right to own land. Afterwards, the government sponsored the establishment of an independent Khoi settlement at Kat River on the eastern frontier. The colonial administration hoped that the settlement might help to defuse the tensions between colonists and the Xhosa on the frontier.

Moffat had arrived in southern Africa in 1817, and had established his reputation at the Kuruman mission among the Tswana far to the north of the colonial border.[3] Moffat's relationships with Read and Philip were marked by the clash of their strong personalities and by disputes over the social and political role of missionaries within the colonial arena. In Kuruman, far removed from the centre of Cape society and government, Moffat was fiercely independent. He expressed a strong distaste for Philip's and Read's involvement in the political controversies over the status of the colonial Khoi. While Moffat condemned the superintendent's politicking, Philip complained of what he saw as the missionary's arrogant and self-serving attitude. Moffat 'would lay destitute the whole country', Philip wrote to the LMS leadership in London, 'rather than it should bear a plant not of his own watering'. James Read was even less charitable, calling Moffat an 'ambitious, arbitrary, self-important narrowminded man'.[4] The latter's participation in the 1817 synod, which had condemned Read for his sexual misconduct and his advocacy of Khoi rights, had especially embittered the relationship between the two missionaries.

During the 1820s and 1830s, Philip and Moffat quarrelled over the relationship between the LMS and the Griqua, who lived between the northern border of the colony and Moffat's outpost among the Tswana at Kuruman. A collection of predominantly mixed-race Africans, organised under the leadership of powerful 'captains' such as Adam Kok, Barend Barends and Andries Waterboer, the Griqua were important political and economic actors on the colony's northern frontier. The Griqua accepted mission christianity as a means of shaping a cultural identity among their diverse communities, and welcomed LMS missionaries as mediators between themselves and the colonial authorities. In the Griqua, Philip saw the potential of the civilizing influence of christianity to assist the formation of independent African communities. He lobbied the government to protect the Griqua against the expansion of white settlement, either through the incorporation of their territory into the Cape Colony or the establishment of a protectorate. In 1834, Governor D'Urban concluded a treaty with Andries Waterboer of Griquatown recognizing the status of the Griqua, and promising protection against 'intrusive white settlers'.[5]

This did not suit Moffat, whose assessment of the Griqua differed significantly from that of his colleagues. Among the most significant consequences of the development of the Griqua communities was their promotion of christianity north of the Orange River through an extensive network of native evangelists. Griqua captains also expected this missionary work to extend their political power within the region, but Moffat saw this expansion as a threat to his work among the southern Tswana. The Griqua, in turn,

---

[3] See C. Northcott, *Robert Moffat: Pioneer in Africa, 1817–1870* (1961); J.S. Moffat, *The Lives of Robert and Mary Moffat* (1886); Robert Moffat, *Missionary Labours and Scenes in Southern Africa* (1842).

[4] SOAS, CWM/LMS, South Africa, 16/1/C: Philip to Ellis, 29 July 1838; *The Kitchingman Papers,* ed. B. Le Cordueur and C. Saunders (Johannesburg, 1976), 206: Read to Kitchingman, 11 Mar. 1839.

[5] T. Keegan, *Colonial South Africa* (1996), 180–2; A. Ross, *John Philip: Missions, Race and Politics in South Africa* (Aberdeen, 1986), 156; For more substantial treatment of the relations between the Griqua and the missionaries, see M. Legassick, 'The Griqua', University of California Los Angeles PhD, 1969; M. Legassick, 'The Northern Frontier to c. 1840: The Rise and Decline of the Griqua People', in *Shaping of South African Society, 1652–1840,* ed. R. Elphick and H. Giliomee (Cape Town, 1989); R. Ross, *Adam Kok's Griquas: A Study in the Development of Stratification in South Africa* (Cambridge, 1976).

feared Moffat's interference in their affairs, and on one occasion even attempted to have him suspended by the LMS on allegations of adultery. In such circumstances, Moffat viewed Philip's championing of the Griqua as unwarranted meddling that endangered the interests of his own mission.[6]

In an effort to counter Philip's influence in the colony and over the missions, Moffat advocated the creation of a district committee system, whereby councils of ordained missionaries would oversee and govern the missions in place of a single superintendent. In 1839, he left for an extensive tour of Britain, and spent part of his time there trying to convince the society's directors to adopt the system. Moffat's proposal, at least, would have emasculated Philip's power. James Read supposed, with some good reason, that Moffat intended to convince the society to remove Philip from the office of superintendent. 'You are aware that Moffat is doing everything in his power in England to injure Dr. Philip', he wrote to the missionary, James Kitchingman, 'calling him a tyrant, and trampling the missionaries under his feet, and trying to get him removed.' Read continued that he feared there was 'a majority of our Brethren here who are of the same feelings and who would rejoice to see [Philip] home tomorrow'. From his perspective, the mission could not afford to lose Philip, 'for he is a check to those who would willingly enslave the Hottentots again, and other coloured peoples'.[7]

Upon his return from Britain, Moffat did find supporters for the committee system among a group of new missionaries on the eastern frontier, led by Henry Calderwood. A Scotsman, Calderwood set sail for South Africa in 1838. Having met Calderwood prior to his departure from Britain, Read described him as 'a fine man . . . a Presbyterian, but an excellent man, almost a radical'.[8] As missionary to the Xhosa at Blinkwater, near the Kat River settlement, Calderwood was to prove something less than a radical. He and Read found themselves quickly at odds over their attitudes towards the Africans and their views on church governance. The two men became central figures in a bitter dispute that nearly split the LMS mission in two.

Shortly after his return from Britain in 1843, Moffat assisted Calderwood in establishing a committee of missionaries for the eastern district. He then returned to Kuruman and organised a second committee for the northern region. Conflict over the purpose of the committees, and their authority, ensued almost immediately following their formation. Read saw in Moffat's plans for the committee system a desire to gain control over the northern missions and to limit the influence of Griqua evangelists among the southern Tswana. From the beginning, Read denounced the committees as nothing more than tools for restricting the participation of Africans in the mission churches and limiting the influence of their strongest advocate, John Philip.

In the same year, the LMS-supported congregation at Grahamstown became the centre of a dispute over the authority of African congregations to choose their own ministers.[9] The town contained an auxiliary missionary society that had sponsored the construction of a chapel in which both mission Khoi and white nonconformist settlers

[6] Elbourne, 'Vagrancy at Issue', *Slavery and Abolition,* xv (1994), 134–5; Ross, *John Philip,* 44–5.

[7] *Kitchingman Papers,* 217: Read to Kitchingman, 2 Dec. 1840.

[8] *Kitchingman Papers,* 196: Read to Kitchingman, 15 Feb. 1838.

[9] R. Ross, 'Congregations, Missionaries and the Grahamstown Schism of 1842–43', in *The London Missionary Society in Southern Africa, 1799–1999,* ed. J. de Gruchy (Athens, OH, 2000), 120–31.

worshipped. Over more than a decade, John Monro, the first LMS agent in Graham-stown, had built up the congregation paying special attention to the education and christianisation of the Khoi. However, in 1838, the LMS approved the appointment of the Rev. John Locke as Monro's successor. Locke established a very different relationship with the Grahamstown congregation. According to James Read, jr, Locke's 'ideas of the [Khoi] were begotten and matured in Graham's Town society', and he devoted the majority of his attention to the white parishioners.[10] The spiritual needs of the Khoi fell primarily to Nicholas Smit, the mission's young schoolteacher. Smit worked enthusiastically with the Khoi community, but his relationship with Locke soured following Smit's ordination as a full missionary in 1842. A power struggle ensued, and within a year, Smit decided to leave Grahamstown. In 1843, he moved to the Kat River settlement where he began work with the Reads as a printer.

This was hardly the end of the matter, however, as a significant portion of the Grahamstown Khoi (about 100) refused to accept Locke and seceded from the church. '[S]ince Mr. Monro left, Mr. Smit was our schoolmaster and our preacher', their representatives protested in a letter to the Society's directors, 'and since Mr. Lock [sic] began to build his church for the English people we began to talk together that we will have Mr. Smit for our minister for then we will have a church for ourselves.'[11] The Grahamstown Khoi's claim to the traditional congregationalist right to call their own minister incited a heated debate between the rival factions emerging within the LMS.

Moffat and Calderwood convened a meeting of the eastern district committee, which defended Locke and the status and authority of ordained ministers against the interference of their congregation. 'If these people, through unreasonable and wicked opposition, had succeeded in their object', Locke contended, 'would it not have furnished a precedent for others to follow when any dispute may occur between them and their missionaries.'[12] Moffat, Calderwood, and Locke all saw the machinations of James Read, behind the complaints of the Grahamstown Khoi. Locke insisted to the directors that the influence of Smit and 'other parties' (almost certainly a reference to Read and his son) had worked upon the Grahamstown Khoi, cultivating in them 'the manifestation of a most improper spirit towards me and their fellow members'.[13]

The Reads did weigh in on the controversy as the most vocal defenders of Smit's supporters. James Read rejoiced in the initial protests of the Grahamstown Khoi as 'the commencement of voluntaryism among the Hottentots . . . in this country and of independency or congregationalism'.[14] He had no doubts about the propriety of the

---

[10] SOAS, CWM/LMS, South Africa, 19/3/A: Read, jr to Philip, 17 July 1843. James Read, sr seems to have been a rather poor judge of the attitudes of prospective missionaries. In a letter to Kitchingman (*Kitchingman Papers*, 176, 11 Apr. 1837), he refers to Locke as 'one of our sort'. Locke, like Calderwood, proved to be anything but. Ross attributes Locke's character to his origins in 'the disciplinarian background of British Nonconformity', although it is not at all clear what he means by this (Ross, 'The Grahamstown Schism', 126).

[11] SOAS, CWM/LMS, South Africa, 19/1/C: deacons and subscribers, Graham's Town, to the directors, nd 1843.

[12] SOAS, CWM/LMS, South Africa, 19/3/A: Locke to Philip, 8 July 1843.

[13] SOAS, CWM/LMS, South Africa, 19/3/A: Locke to Philip, 8 July 1843.

[14] *Kitchingman Papers*, 240: Read to Kitchingman, 11 Dec. 1843. Philip openly supported Read's conviction that Africans should have a voice in choosing their missionaries. In a letter to Read, he noted the appearance of similar controversies among the missions in the West Indies. ' 'Tis rather singular', he observed, 'that the subject here should be agitated at the same time.': *Kitchingman Papers*, 236.

Africans' claims, or their desire to select their own pastor. 'It certainly is a right', Read argued, 'as much as they have a right to choose their own elders and deacons.' His opponents claimed that the Grahamstown Khoi had no right to call their own minister unless possessed of the resources 'to pay him'. This argument Read dismissed out of hand: '[The] white people gave Mr. Locke a call and he accepted it without a word about salary, but now that the coloured people give Smith [sic] a call they are told it cannot be, that they [cannot?] have a choice without they can pay him, and they are abused and called everything . . . because they dare prefer Smith to Locke.'[15] Read based his opinion on the foundation of his own religious and egalitarian principles. At the outset of the controversy, he had confessed to Kitchingman that although he had 'never [taken] any party' to that point, he would now 'declare [himself] to be an Independent or Congregationalist'. He also clearly recognized the racial outlook of his adversaries and concluded that their object was 'not to have native agents or native churches to have a voice in anything'.[16] Remarking that William Thompson had been welcomed by a meeting of the Dutch reformed ministers at Graaf Reinet with one of his 'black elders', Read expressed his fears that the LMS would fall 'behind the Dutch church [because] our Brethren say they will not have a black or Native Agent to present at our meetings!!'.[17]

In the midst of the Grahamstown controversy, the proponents of the committee system also intensified their criticisms of John Philip, and the office of superintendent. Philip had expressed to the directors his serious reservations about the committee system, which drew a harsh reply from missionaries on the eastern frontier under Calderwood's direction. For their part, Moffat and Calderwood argued that decisions made by a majority of ordained missionaries in committee would be more democratic than the potentially arbitrary or tyrannical decisions of an individual superintendent. Calderwood went so far as to compare superintendents (like Philip) to 'Bishops or mock-bishops', and to suggest that for 'congregational Dissenters' (like the Reads) to prefer them to 'an association of brethren' was 'something new under the Sun'. Another primary complaint was a concern that the superintendent might be unduly influenced by information 'from improper sources'.[18] This clearly reflected an objection, on the part of the Calderwood party, to the close relationship between Philip and the Reads, and Philip's reliance on them as his primary source of intelligence from the mission field. The controversy over the committee system ultimately came down to a struggle over the control of the missions and the ability to influence mission policy.

Calderwood's circle also pressed the directors to dismiss the Reads, sr and jr, on the grounds that they had sought to undermine the position and authority of the society's missionaries. As evidence, they pointed to a series of letters, discussing the recent controversies, between the Reads and two Khoi deacons at Calderwood's Blinkwater congregation. At bottom, Calderwood's complaint was that the Reads chose to put trust

[15] *Kitchingman Papers*, 241: Read to Kitchingman, 22 Jan. 1844.
[16] *Kitchingman Papers*, 236: Read to Kitchingman, 17 July 1843.
[17] *Kitchingman Papers*, 239–40: Read to Kitchingman, 11 Dec. 1843.
[18] SOAS, CWM/LMS, South Africa, 20/2/D: Brownlee, Kayser, Merrington, Locke, Birt, Calderwood and Gill to LMS, 10 Oct. 1844.

in and to side with the interests of the Africans against their missionary brethren. This issue loomed large in Calderwood's charges against them:

> It should . . . be here considered that there is an important difference between Missionaries conversing however freely among themselves . . . and this kind of intercourse which the Messrs Read have with the Native people. To speak or write of his Brethren secretly, in this manner to any one even the most intelligent Europeans would be highly dishonourable, . . . but to do so to the Natives is cruel to them & unfairness towards his Brethren in no common degree. . . . while Mr. J.R. speaks with the greatest disrespect & affected scorn & . . . in the lowest terms of the Missionaries, he speaks to & of the people in terms of marked respect and affection.[19]

Proponents of maintaining an appropriate social distance between the white missionaries and their African congregations, Calderwood's faction objected strongly to the familiarity of James Read's relationships with the mission Khoi. The theological and ideological influences that accorded Africans a fundamental humanity and equality in the missionary thinking of the early 19th century, personified by Read and Philip, was fading in the generation of Calderwood and Locke.

In a long letter to James Kitchingman, Read condemned the committee system's implications for the LMS, and the progress of African participation in the mission churches. 'Tis a sorry affair', he lamented, 'it strikes at the very root of the fundamental principle of our Society. It is establishing Presbyterianism.' Which was a true enough charge, for Calderwood was, of course, a Scottish presbyter. Read argued further, that the committee system was 'worse than Presbyterianism' because it made no provisions for lay representation. 'In the system proposed the churches are entirely at the mercy of the reverends.' In spite of having returned only once in the previous 40 years, Read kept himself well abreast of events in Britain. He recognized the parallels between the controversies over the rights of congregations there and the strife within the Cape mission. 'To force a pastor upon a church without in any way to consider its judgment would be to hand over God's heritage', he stated. 'This has given rise to the struggle in the Scotch Church that has proved to [be] fatal.'[20] The struggles between the missionaries of the LMS reflected debates over churches and authority that were driving the religious controversies in Britain itself. On a more fundamental level, however, in the contest over control of the missions, differences in ecclesiastical loyalties reflected deeper divisions in attitudes towards race and the status of Africans in colonial society.

In the midst of all this strife, Philip began to think of leaving Africa, especially as the directors had given approval to the creation of a committee system. Tiring of the

[19] SOAS, CWM/LMS, South Africa, 20/2/D: Calderwood and Birt to LMS, 26 Sept. 1844.

[20] *Kitchingman Papers*, 242–3: Read to Kitchingman, 22 Jan. 1844. Illustrative of how keenly missionaries kept informed of such developments at home, the representatives of the Glasgow Missionary Society in the colony voted in 1843 to join the Free Church of Scotland. Elbourne suggests that the 'disputes over spiritual authority and its relationship to temporal authority were occurring in parallel in Scotland and the Cape Colony, both industrialising countries with an expanding potential electorate in which debates about political citizenship interacted with debates about the relationship of church and state': *The London Missionary Society in Southern Africa,* ed. Gruchy, 136. This seems a less than compelling statement, given the rather uncertain basis upon which the early 19th-century Cape can be defined as an 'industrialising' society. The fundamental issues at stake in the disputes were clearly ecclesiastical, and in the case of the colony, also racial.

incessant conflict between his missionaries, and tired from his long struggle against the abuses of the colonial system, Philip tendered his resignation to the directors in 1843. He was forthright in defending the Reads against the charges of Calderwood and the eastern committee, and expressed his deep sadness at the sight of missionaries of the LMS turning against one another. He pointedly advised the directors to recall that James Read and his son were 'more popular with the natives . . . than those who oppose them', and formed 'the only party among our missionaries in whom the chiefs have confidence'. He warned of dire consequences for the Xhosa should the Reads be dismissed, and expressed frustration at his seemingly diminished influence at Mission House in London. The respect recently given to his opinions by the directors 'has been in the inverse ratio of the opportunities I have had of forming sound conclusions on every subject connected with our missions', he wrote, with a profound sense of bitterness.[21]

The intensely independent Read had bristled at times over conduct by Philip that might have infringed upon his autonomy. He believed that the society's fundamental principle granted the missionaries considerable freedom from the interference of the superintendent. 'Here I am a little independent of the Doctor', he had written from Kat River in 1839, with a considerable sense of pride; 'We have our own plans and we execute them. If the Doctor will give us any assistance we take it, otherwise we get on without it as well as we can.'[22] Yet, for nearly two decades, James Read and John Philip had always seen eye-to-eye on the struggle to secure the rights of indigenous peoples. Both men perceived the importance of the other as the primary advocates of the African cause. 'We could spare him as superintendent', wrote Read upon hearing of Philip's possible resignation, 'but not as a friend of the aborigines and coloured people generally.' Defending Philip's tactics, and his own, Read dismissed those, like Moffat and Calderwood, who would call 'trying to prevent ill treatment, bloodshed and war, meddling with politics'.[23]

The directors ultimately refused Philip's resignation, and despite his sorrow at the abiding conflict between his missionaries, he continued to defend his egalitarian convictions. Both Philip and Read recognized that the logic of Calderwood and the others regarding church government in the mission ultimately stemmed from a greater antipathy towards the African population. This new generation desired 'not to have Native agents or Native churches to have a voice in anything'. Read had expressed his anxieties about the racial attitudes of the new missionaries to Kitchingman as early as 1840: 'Few of the brethren think as we do respecting Native Agency in any way, and I fear the feeling respecting colour is retrograding. With us we are pushing on to raise the people in the scale of society; others are for leaving them behind or pushing them back.'[24] Attempting to explain to the society's directors the source of the dispute between Read and Calderwood, Philip plainly identified their respective attitudes towards race as the heart of the matter:

[21] *Kitchingman Papers*, 194: Philip to board of directors, 26 June 1843.
[22] *Kitchingman Papers*, 206: Read to Kitchingman, 11 Mar. 1839.
[23] *Kitchingman Papers*, 210: Read to Kitchingman, 24 June 1839.
[24] *Kitchingman Papers*, 218: Read to Kitchingman, 2 Dec. 1840.

The parties never can be brought to act together and the only thing we can do with them is to keep them from threatening each other and from open war. They are entirely different men and represent two different classes of missionary. What is esteemed and practiced as a virtue by the one is viewed as a crime in the eyes of the other. You will find the key to this secret in the following passage in Calderwood's letter . . . 'We object to the kind of intercourse which [Read] has with the coloured people'. . . . Both parties would do the coloured people good but in different ways. In order to raise the people James Read would treat them as brethren and to this Mr. Calderwood says 'We object.'[25]

The tone of the passage leaves little doubt as to which approach Philip believed to be the most suitable to the progress of the Khoi and the colony as a whole.[26]

The debates within the LMS over the role and status of missionaries, suggest that missionaries were more than simple agents to the expansion of British culture, values, and power around the globe. In their theological and political convictions, figures such as Read and Philip posed an alternative model of British imperialism, grounded upon the basic rights of religious, economic, and political freedom. During the 1840s, the egalitarian beliefs of Philip and Read were slowly losing ground to the advance of new and more racist attitudes within British society, as well as among the new generation of missionaries. However, their impact upon the political structure of southern Africa can be seen in the liberal Cape constitution of 1853, and the voices of protest against white domination throughout the late 19th and 20th centuries. Their place within the development of British politics during the first half of the 19th century is equally significant. John Philip's most recent biographer has noted that Philip 'refused to have anything to do' with the politics of 'faction fights between Whig and Tory oligarchs' that characterised pre-reform Britain.[27] This may be so, but the statement fails to recognize the important shifts in British politics taking place at the time.

The first decades of the 19th century saw the rise of petition campaigns, and the influence of public opinion in British politics. The movements against slavery and the Test and Corporation Acts, to take two examples, reflected what Peter Jupp has called the public's 'general expectation that Parliament's function was to redress grievances'.[28] The South African missionaries made full use of the press, of the anti-slavery movement, and of their connections to important political figures, to advance their agenda. Contrary to the assertions of their critics, Philip and Read did not feel themselves compromised by their involvement in politics. James Read, jr captured their perspective, reflecting upon his father's career in 1851. 'As regard ourselves, we have tried to do our duty by the people . . . in promoting industry, education and godliness.

[25] SOAS, CWM/LMS, South Africa, 22/1: Philip to directors, 31 Mar. 1846.

[26] Calderwood ultimately left the service of the LMS and took up a position as a government agent in the Xhosa territories. In this capacity he became an influential advisor to successive governors on colonial policy during the late 1840s and 1850s.

[27] Ross, *John Philip*, 79.

[28] P. Jupp, *British Politics on the Eve of Reform: The Duke of Wellington's Administration, 1828–1830* (1998), 445; see also, 216–21.

... When they have been wronged, we have fearlessly, but in constitutional way, sought redress for them.'[29] Thus were Read and Philip both agents of the expansion of British religion, culture and values, and at the same time, vocal critics of British colonial policy. And thus did their careers leave an indelible mark upon the political institutions of Britain and its empire.

[29] *Kitchingman Papers*, 26.

After Emancipation: Thomas Fowell Buxton and Evangelical Politics in the 1830s

RICHARD R. FOLLETT

After the Emancipation Act of 1833 officially abolished slavery in the British empire, it became clear that the anti-slavery coalition was even more tenuous than many had believed. The expectations created by reform, and by the previous measures removing disabilities on dissenters and catholics, sent the various elements within the anti-slavery camp in different directions. This splintering of efforts was especially true of evangelicals in parliament. During the next four years, the anti-slavery leader, Thomas Fowell Buxton, went through a reorientation as he worked to make sense of his priorities under new political conditions. Although involved with many issues of the day, Buxton came to focus on the plight of aboriginal peoples in the British empire and then formulated his proposals to end African slavery. Buxton's shift represents a larger one for evangelicals in England. While they could not all agree on the benefits or morality of poor law reform or the appropriate way to handle the Irish Church question, most could agree that the peoples coming under British rule should have their rights protected, especially if it opened a way for further missionary activity. By 1840, Buxton's efforts provided a set of concepts and an agenda for many people of otherwise diverse political bent. Domestically, the evangelical communities in Britain might disagree on what policy and programmes served their civilisation best; but they all agreed that Britain's growing empire needed to be directed in a way that promoted christianity and commerce, and hence the spread of 'civilisation'.

Keywords: aborigine; African slave trade; anglican; anti-slavery; apprenticeship; Buxton; catholic; dissent; Irish Church; Niger expedition

On 1 June 1840, a most august gathering convened in London at Exeter Hall, the meeting place of much philanthropy and other agitation in the 1830s and 1840s. Howard Temperly has called this the 'inauguration' of the African Civilization Society, although it was, technically, the very public outgrowth of meetings begun the previous summer, when Thomas Fowell Buxton, Dr Stephen Lushington, and other anti-slavery advocates had initiated a new organisation to replace the disbanded Anti-Slavery Society.[1] The new association sought to take the fight against slavery beyond legislative prohibitions on the trade and owning of slaves, and into the African source of supply. The reason for the 1 June meeting was the discussion, advertisement, and endorsement of an expedition to Africa, to the Niger River in particular, for the purpose of establishing a commercial

---

[1] Howard Temperly, *White Dreams, Black Africa: The Antislavery Expedition to the River Niger, 1841–1842* (New Haven, 1991), 1ff.; *Memoirs of Sir Thomas Fowell Buxton, Baronet*, ed. Charles Buxton (Philadelphia, 1849), 381–2.

farm to be run, eventually, by and for Africans, to provide an alternative commercial enterprise to the iniquitous slave trade which still plagued Africa.

The list of attenders on 1 June read like a who's who of philanthropy and social improvement, but also of the political high and mighty. The duke of Norfolk, Viscount Sandon, and Sir Robert Peel sat on the platform, flanked by members of the Church Missionary Society, the British and Foreign Bible Society, the Baptist Missionary Society, and other bodies of both the low, high and dissenting churches. In the crowd could be found the young Mr Gladstone, Sir George Grey, and Lord Nugent. Even Daniel O'Connell joined the meeting, greeted with loud cheers from at least a portion of the attenders. Formally presiding over the whole was the new prince consort, Albert, making his first appearance at a public gathering of this sort since his marriage to Queen Victoria the previous February.[2] Prince Albert's presence, as well as the broad representation of early Victorian religious and social leaders, confirmed the general agreement that Britain should take an active role, not only in ending slavery within its realms, but in every region within its reasonable reach. Most interesting, perhaps, was that the method sought to end the iniquitous trade was trade itself, but this time an exchange of goods and raw materials from Africa, for 'manufactures' from Britain and other parts of Europe, which, Buxton assured the British public in his new book *The African Slave Trade and its Remedy*, the Africans were 'desirous of possessing'.[3]

In one sense, the African Civilization Society would appear merely to illustrate that most middle- and upper-class Britons had become anti-slavery supporters by 1840. But in another sense, the gathering in Exeter Hall was quite odd, because many who attended that June morning had been at odds with one another over numerous political measures through most of the mid and late 1830s. The expectations created by reform, and by the measures removing political disabilities on dissenters and catholics, sent the various elements within the anti-slavery camp in different directions. This splintering of efforts was especially true of evangelicals in parliament. During the four years after emancipation, Buxton could occasionally rally support to focus attention on this or that abuse in the implementation of the apprenticeship which had been a condition of emancipation, or on specific colonial abuses of native peoples, but he found it impossible to maintain a steady pressure group in or out of parliament. But in 1840, after Buxton had been out of parliament for three years, many of his evangelical connections, who had fallen on opposite sides of various reform measures and questions of the church establishment, were able to sweep domestic differences aside to support this new anti-slavery proposal, even though it carried potentially enormous implications for imperial policy and British foreign commitments. This essay explores the controversies and political actions pursued by Thomas Fowell Buxton in the 1830s after slave emancipation. Buxton, interesting as much for his quaker and dissenting connections as for his commitment to the evangelical wing in the Church of England, found himself voting sometimes with and sometimes against other evangelical members of parliament on reforming legislation, even as he came to focus on the plight of aboriginal peoples in the British empire and to formulate his perspective on the next step toward ending African slavery once and for all.

[2] Buxton, *Memoirs*, ed. Buxton, 438–9.

[3] Thomas Fowell Buxton, *The African Slave Trade and its Remedy* (1840), 342.

1. *Reasons for Dissent among Evangelicals*

Although portrayed as a buttress to Conservatism in many accounts of the 19th century, evangelicalism never provided its adherents with a unified political agenda, although occasionally an issue like slavery did provide a common cause uniting otherwise disparate elements of dissenting and anglican political agitation.[4] For a while, it had looked as if a united humanitarian front had been created, which might have long-term implications. But once the goal of abolishing slavery was accomplished, what was left? Judged from the rhetoric and political commitments in the mid and late 1830s, it appeared very little. Michael Watts has noted that one of the first declarations of conflict among evangelicals came in October 1833, when the London congregationalist and anti-slavery activist, Thomas Binney, published a tract proclaiming 'that the Established Church is a great national evil'.[5] Only a few months earlier, in July, John Keble, responding to the whig government's proposal to abolish ten Irish bishoprics, preached his famous sermon on 'national apostasy', in effect giving birth to the Oxford Movement and the effort to return the anglican church to more catholic roots. These events were but starters, for as Watt observes, the 'result was to polarize Christian England to a greater extent than at any time since the Civil War'.[6]

Perhaps the most volatile set of issues grew from the implications of catholic emancipation. Though the evangelicals certainly shared the general British 'aversion to popery as a compendium of all that was foreign to national life', the general tone of toleration had kept virulent anti-catholic attacks to a minimum in the early 19th century.[7] The agitation leading to catholic emancipation in 1829 changed the mood. From such organisations as the Protestant Reformation Society, founded in 1827, to the Protestant Association formed in 1835, came a flow of anti-catholic propaganda and a steady resistance to any government measure that might be seen as aiding the Roman catholic church.[8]

By the mid 1830s, the debate had come to focus on the status of the established church in Ireland. This issue flowed into the debate over having a state church, which quickly roused passions that split evangelical dissenters from evangelical anglicans.[9] The debates over Lord John Russell's proposal for reorganisation of the Irish church tithe and the use of surplus funds for education, which might or might not include Roman catholic doctrine, fuelled major disagreement from 1835 to 1838. For Conservative anglicans, among them an increasing number of evangelicals, the attack on the Irish church was seen as a first action threatening the anglican establishment as a whole. This cry of 'church in danger' appeared in numerous speeches and pamphlets, which we must

---

[4] David Hempton notes that by 1833, 'the whole range of evangelical Nonconformity was mobilized against slavery', in *Methodism and Politics in British Society, 1750–1850* (Stanford, 1984), 209.

[5] Thomas Binney, *An Address Delivered on Laying the First Stone of the New King's Weigh House* (5th edn, 1834), 34, quoted in Michael R. Watts, *The Dissenters; Volume II: The Expansion of Evangelical Nonconformity* (Oxford, 1995), 454.

[6] Watts, *Dissenters*, ii, 455.

[7] David Bebbington, *Evangelicalism in Modern Britain: A History from the 1730s to the 1980s* (1989), 101.

[8] Evangelical anti-catholicism is well explored in John Wolffe, *The Protestant Crusade in Great Britain, 1829–1860* (Oxford, 1991).

[9] See Bebbington, *Evangelicalism*, 97–9.

see not only as presenting a newly perceived 'threat', but also as revealing the loss of the confidence that had been characteristic of evangelical politics in the first three decades of the 19th century.

The question of education had other dimensions that separated evangelicals. In the wake of emancipation, the government took action to assist with the provision of education for the freed slaves by helping to fund the building of school houses. As with all educational measures in the 1830s, this engendered debates about what type of religious instruction would be given, pitting anglican against dissent, and splitting the dissenters as well. Michael Rutz has documented the arguments among dissenters, and particularly among those connected with the predominantly congregationalist London Missionary Society, over whether accepting government funds for school construction or support of teachers would help or hurt their cause.[10] This colonial debate was nearly drowned out by the arguments over the annual government grants for education that began with the Factory Act in 1833. David Hempton has shown how incredibly divisive the discussions over the provisions of these grants became for methodists, with the added dimension of anti-catholicism becoming increasingly intrusive as the decade wore on and the grant was enlarged.[11]

Finally, the late 1820s and 1830s saw an increase in the variety of theological approaches within evangelical protestantism. In this period began a revival of calvinism, an impact of romanticism in such periodicals as the *Record*, a new millenarian concern, with the modern 'birth' of multiple varieties of premillennialism, and a reaction to some liberal questions on the inspiration of scripture with a new biblical literalism. It is also the period in which high church concerns break forth in general, and in the Oxford Movement in particular, a movement which David Bebbington and others have argued found grounding among those first nurtured within the evangelical wing of the Church of England.[12]

2. *Buxton's Issues in the 1830s*

So in the midst of all this, what was Buxton doing? Buxton hated to lose allies, or to see them turn on one another, but he was himself the target of sectarian attacks, especially as he, a member of the Church of England, supported many of the proposals attacked as 'liberal monstrosities' by evangelical defenders of the established church. With regard to the new theological trends, Buxton held to the very moderate calvinism he had learned from Josiah Pratt when he had first moved to London, but always with an empathetic foot in the quaker connections of his family, and a hand reaching out toward evangelical dissenters in general.

As might be expected, the most pressing activity for Buxton was monitoring the implementation of emancipation. From numerous correspondents he learned of the

---

[10] Michael Rutz, 'The British Zion: Evangelization and the Politics of Dissent in Britain and the Empire', Washington University PhD, 2002, pp. 137–9.

[11] Hempton, *Methodism*, 151–64.

[12] Bebbington, *Evangelicalism*, 95–7; see also Frank Turner, *John Henry Newman: The Challenge to Evangelical Religion* (New Haven, 2002).

regulations adopted in the West Indies, of the efforts to provide education to former slaves, and of those persecuted for their anti-slavery views. Sometimes Buxton was moved to assist personally, as when he sought help from Lord Brougham for a clergyman forced from his living in the West Indies.[13] Buxton disliked the seven-year apprenticeship attached to the Emancipation Act, but had recognized that it, like compensation to the slave owners, had been a necessary political condition. But he did investigate abuses, which led to a formal house of commons committee of inquiry in March 1836.[14] The committee findings were somewhat ambivalent, but it did initiate measures to curb the most blatant abuses, and clarified that at the end of the apprenticeship liberated slaves would enjoy an 'unqualified freedom', and would be 'subject to no other restrictions than those imposed on white labourers at home'.[15] Eventually, in May 1838, a measure passed the Commons which would have abolished the apprenticeship; after this the planters agreed, voluntarily, to end the system on 1 August that year, three years early. Buxton had lost his parliamentary seat in the 1837 election, but was present as an observer during the vote, and made such a ruckus in his joy for its passage that he was forced to leave the gallery.[16]

3. Growing Concern for Aboriginals

But it was not only the former slaves that disturbed Buxton's conscience. Increasingly he heard reports of white settlers in the British colonies abusing indigenous peoples and taking away their cattle or land and curtailing their traditional ways of life. In December 1833, he wrote to the southern African colonist, Thomas Pringle, regarding reports from the Cape Colony of the 'commando system', which the colonists used to attack natives for minor wrongs, despoiling them of cattle or property far in excess of the colonists' original claims.[17] He sought clarification and evidence from Pringle and from the dissenting minister, John Philip, in Cape Town. Buxton argued for a policy which recognized the rights of the natives to their lands, which provided for protection and promotion of missionary work, and which also granted compensation for wrongs inflicted.[18] On 1 July 1834, Buxton moved an address to the king regarding these subjects, which was seconded by Colonial Secretary Spring Rice. This effort was tied directly to the formation of the Aborigines Protection Society and an aborigines' committee in the house of commons. One may well bemoan the inconsistent application of these early efforts, but one must also grant that Buxton and his allies did try to curb

[13] University College Library, London, Brougham Papers, 22,329: Buxton to Lord Henry Brougham, 16 Aug. 1834; see also Buxton, *Memoirs*, ed. Buxton, 296ff.

[14] Rhodes House, Oxford, Buxton Papers, MS Brit. Emp. s. 444, 12, ff. 113–17: T.F. Buxton to Thomas Clarkson, 25 Sept. 1833.

[15] Buxton, *Memoirs*, ed. Buxton, 325–6, from a letter to Zachary Macaulay, 6 Sept. 1836.

[16] Oliver Barclay, *Thomas Fowell Buxton and the Liberation of the Slaves* (York, 2001), 105.

[17] Rhodes House, Buxton Papers, 12, ff. 145, a–d: Buxton to [Thomas] Pringle, 5 Dec. 1833; see also Rutz, 'British Zion', ch. 6.

[18] Rhodes House, Buxton Papers, 12, ff. 148–51: Buxton to John Pringle, 17 Jan. 1834.

oppression of colonial natives, with some temporary success at least.[19] Because of their efforts, and the willing aid of Lord Glenelg, secretary for war and the colonies, land taken from the Xhosa people of southern Africa in 1835 was returned to them before the Queen Adelaide Province could be flooded by white settlers.[20] The whig minister, Lord Glenelg, from a strongly evangelical family with long anti-slavery and humanitarian connections, was a natural ally for Buxton. He would not always have such friends in office, but the measures brought forth began to shape a policy, however imperfectly.

4. *The Irish Church*

In curtailing apprenticeship or curbing colonial abuses, Buxton had considerable support from other evangelicals in parliament, but on one major issue he found himself at odds with most anglican evangelicals and with many in dissent. This was the contentious issue of the Irish church. Buxton, who had attended Trinity College, Dublin, well understood the relationship of the established church to the majority of the population in Ireland.[21] The Irish Church Temporalities Act in 1833 had eliminated ten redundant bishoprics and several parish positions. In theory this should have freed considerable 'surplus resources', and therein lay the bigger controversy: what to do with them? The measure in 1833 passed with no 'appropriation clause' to direct the money to new uses. In 1834, Lord John Russell revived the matter, and continued to pursue it through 1835 and 1836 in the context of church tithe reform in general. By this time, Buxton, after much study and soul-searching, had decided to speak in favour of Russell's bill, which would distribute the extra resources into education for the general population of Ireland. His position as a prominent evangelical, and a member of the Church of England, attracted attention and much loathing by many in the established church.[22] Nor did his stand do much to endear him to evangelical dissenters, as they were also split on the issue. In June 1836, he defended the justice of Russell's proposal. The bill would have shifted tithe costs from renters to land owners, would redistribute salaries more equitably, and would provide for basic education for many in Ireland. Speaking directly to the cries of those reactionaries who feared for the church because of government interference, Buxton asked, 'where is the wickedness of all this, and where lies the danger?'. While he believed the catholic church would limit students' Bible reading, he argued that still the education would

[19] Andrew Porter calls the aborigines' committee 'a milestone in revealing the adaptation of the missionary movement to the world of expanding British commerce', but his discussion goes even further to show its high hopes and, perhaps, impossible ambitions for disciplining an expanding empire from the metropolis. Andrew Porter, *Religion Versus Empire?: British Protestant Missionaries and Overseas Expansion, 1700–1914* (Manchester, 2004), 146ff.

[20] Buxton, *Memoirs*, ed. Buxton, 312–13; see also Christopher Saunders and Iain R. Smith, 'Southern Africa, 1795–1900', in *The Oxford History of the British Empire, III: The Nineteenth Century*, ed. Andrew Porter (Oxford, 1999), 597–623.

[21] Only 7% of the Irish population were members of the established church, but all were compelled to pay for its support through tithes. Statistic from Eric J. Evans, *The Forging of the Modern State: Early Industrial Britain, 1783–1870* (3rd edn, 2001), 299.

[22] Buxton, *Memoirs*, ed. Buxton, 319.

teach 'the Catholic to read – it gives him a portion of Scripture to read. I have better faith in the truth of my religion, than to dread that instruction can damage it; and this is good, old, sound, Protestant doctrine.'[23]

Buxton may have known in 1836, as others have argued for Russell and the cabinet, that the appropriation would never make it through the house of lords.[24] But this made his support of the Irish church reform all the more a matter of conscience than of politics. He received 'censure' for his support of the bill, and it really gained him nothing with his constituency in Weymouth.[25] Indeed, his stance caused controversy within his own household, as his daughter Priscilla, who had married the Scottish MP, Andrew Johnston, in 1834, took great pains to explain to her brothers the difference between her husband's stance (Johnston was firmly against the measure) and their father's, though she fully acknowledged Buxton's long deliberation and prayer over the matter.[26]

5. *Political Defeat and Return to Slave Trade Issues*

This reputation for careful investigation may well have softened the perception that Buxton was betraying the protestant and evangelical cause, but the issue tied him more closely to the whigs than had other matters. And it was this connection, more than the Irish church question alone, which led to his loss in the election in July 1837. The 'other' whig candidate for Weymouth decided not to run, and while Buxton did not normally identify himself as a party man, he knew he was to some extent so connected in the minds of his constituents. Buxton had never been one to pursue politics for politics sake, having entered the house of commons to pursue law reforms and having stayed to work for abolition of slavery.[27] His weariness with the process showed clearly in 1835, after the first round of clerical disapproval: 'I hope to bring forward the Slave Trade question next Tuesday. I have an abundance of facts, but the House of Commons "careth for none of these things", and I care very little for any political things, these excepted.'[28] In May 1837, Buxton had written to a colleague that he would find great satisfaction on retirement, if only the aborigines, apprenticeship, foreign slave trade and Indian slavery issues could be settled, or brought to a point where they soon would be.[29] Indeed, he was most concerned to complete the aborigines' committee report in spring 1837, before another parliamentary session ended.[30] Thus, when he learned he would likely lose in the late July election, he could write without duplicity, 'that I am confident I shall be very thankful if I am turned out'.[31] After the event, many of the electors in Weymouth

[23] Quoted in Buxton, *Memoirs*, ed. Buxton, 332–3.

[24] Ian Newbould, *Whiggery and Reform, 1830–41* (Stanford, 1990), 286ff.

[25] Rhodes House, Buxton Papers, 15, f. 223: Priscilla Johnston to Anna Gurney, 15 Mar. 1837.

[26] Rhodes House, Buxton Papers, 13, ff. 418–20, 430–1, 423–4: Priscilla Johnston to her brothers, 28 Mar. 1835, and again on 4 Apr. 1835, and to Sarah Buxton, on 2 Apr. 1835.

[27] On Buxton's reasons for entering politics, see Richard R. Follett, *Evangelicalism, Penal Theory and the Politics of Criminal Law Reform in England, 1808–30* (New York, 2001), 99–105.

[28] Rhodes House, Buxton Papers, 14, f. 30: Buxton to Anna Gurney, 6 May 1838.

[29] Rhodes House, Buxton Papers, 15, ff. 276–81: Buxton to John Jeremie, 8 May 1837.

[30] Buxton, *Memoirs*, ed. Buxton, 354.

[31] Quoted in Buxton, *Memoirs*, ed. Buxton, 357.

expressed their regret, and to some degree their embarrassment, that he had not been re-elected. A collection was taken, and several gifts were given to him as tokens of thanks for his time of service. Over 20 other seats were offered to him, but he would have none of them.[32] Ill health had plagued him while parliament was in session; now was the opportunity to rest and recuperate completely.[33]

6. *The 'Solution' and its Promotion*

Buxton's 'retirement', however, was short-lived. Soon he became restless and turned again to matters of the slave trade. His absence from parliament only made it easier for him to sit in the colonial office and gather new information or verify facts sent to him by missionaries and empathetic officials in Africa and the West Indies. By the winter of 1837–8, he was hard at work putting together his evidence to prove that the slave trade in Africa still caused great evil, and that Africa contained enough capabilities and resources to make it a region 'peaceful, flourishing, and productive, by the force of legitimate commerce'.[34] In this pursuit, Buxton moved from insisting primarily on protecting the natives in British colonies, to seeking new avenues to bring positive good and eliminate the attractiveness of the slave trade. Andrew Porter has argued persuasively that it was the missionary testimony before the aborigines' committee that served as a turning point in Buxton's views.[35] Not only had they all espoused the importance of just commercial relations as a key factor in promoting christianity, they had testified to the benefit of legitimate trade in itself. The message of commerce and christianity moving forward hand-in-hand was ready for full proclamation.

Buxton had frequently inquired about British intervention in the slave trade. He pressed his own government to use diplomatic pressure to get foreign governments to abide by their commitments to end the slave trade. The foreign secretary, Lord Palmerston, listened to Buxton politely, but affirmed that while he would continue to work for strong treaties, he felt 'the only real Instrument of Prevention is the British Cruiser'.[36] Buxton was not against the use of force to interdict the slave trade,[37] but he wanted something more than a stick with which to attack the problem. The goal was to find a way of turning slave traders toward another, more profitable trade, one less wasteful of human resources, literally.

[32] Buxton, *Memoirs*, ed. Buxton, 360. Among the offered seats were Southampton, Nottingham, Middlesex, Norwich and Cambridge; from a handwritten insert in Rhodes House, Buxton Papers, 3, between pages 462 and 463.

[33] Buxton had not cultivated a 'successor' to lead anti-slavery in parliament, but a letter in Sept. 1837 suggests he hoped the place might one day be filled by William E. Gladstone. BL, Add. MS 44355, f. 252: Buxton to W.E. Gladstone, 16 Sept. 1837.

[34] Buxton, *Memoirs*, ed. Buxton, 366.

[35] Andrew Porter, ' "Commerce and Christianity": The Rise and Fall of a Nineteenth-Century Missionary Slogan', *HJ*, xxviii (1985), 613–15.

[36] Friends House Library, Temp. MS 434, 1/130: Lord Palmerston to T.F. Buxton, 14 Apr. 1838.

[37] A point that would put him in conflict with the more arduous anti-slavery quakers and other members of the Agency Society led by Joseph Sturge; see Temperly, *White Dreams*, 33–6.

Buxton began with a long and published letter to Lord Melbourne in 1838, detailing the 'failure' of the existing efforts, and outlining what should be done next.[38] Melbourne's administration asked Buxton to produce a fuller book to persuade the British public. He had an awkward task. To convince people that action must be taken, Buxton had on the one hand to depict Africa as a place of darkness, danger, and degeneracy, and on the other to show that not only could it and its inhabitants be redeemed, but that it had the resources to prosper.[39] *The African Slave Trade and its Remedy* appeared in 1840. The first part contained his initial appeal to the government. In the latter part, Buxton described, in decidedly optimistic terms, the resources of Africa that would contribute to trade with Europe: gold, iron, copper, and especially vast regions of fertile soil, capable of producing rice, wheat, hemp, indigo, coffee, and above all, 'sugar-cane and cotton'.[40] He argued that with support from the British government, and appropriate treaties with the natives to relinquish the slave trade in exchange for arrangements to trade 'legitimate' goods with the British, commerce could be established along the Niger River and private enterprise would thrive. Missionaries would, of course, settle with the traders and agriculturalists, so that christianity would go hand-in-hand with legitimate commerce.[41]

Buxton did not conceive his proposal as one of founding a new colony as such. The plan was to be a means of getting the Africans themselves into the commercial game – white control was supposed, in Buxton's mind at least, to be temporary, a means of education and example. The treaties he called for were to be freely entered; the threat of force reserved only for defence, and never for persuasion.[42] If Buxton did not conceive of himself as an imperialist, he did believe he was pressing forward the missionary cause, but in his mind that was a different matter, as in his experience it had always been the missionaries who defended the indigenous peoples and tried to help them improve their conditions.[43]

These were hopeful plans, but Buxton left nothing to chance that he could influence. He had written to many of his allies and had employed his long-time friend, Dr Stephen Lushington, to assist him as well. A small group began gathering in April 1839, and by the summer they were ready to take more formal steps of organisation.[44] At a meeting on 23 July, those attending included the bishop of London, Lord Ashley, Sir Robert Inglis, Sir Thomas Acland, and others who, in Buxton's words, represented the 'epitome of the state. Whig, Tory, and Radical; Dissenter, Low Church, High Church, tip-top High

---

[38] A 215 page 'letter' published as *Letter on the Slave Trade to the Lord Viscount Melbourne and the Other Members of Her Majesty's Cabinet Council* (1838).

[39] Temperly, *White Dreams*, 12–13. Thus, in the very effort to help the Africans, Buxton was guilty of perpetuating a very misleading stereotype and building on the myth of the 'darkness' of Africa, as traced by Patrick Brantlinger in 'Victorians and Africans: The Genealogy of the Myth of the Dark Continent', in *Race, Writing, and Difference*, ed. Henry Louis Gates (Chicago, 1986). Buxton might not have seen any contradictions in what he wrote – in part because the *African Slave Trade* was geared to sway an uncertain audience, but also because he really believed much of the continent to be 'dark', at least in a spiritual sense.

[40] Buxton, *Memoirs*, ed. Buxton, 370–3.

[41] Buxton, *Memoirs*, ed. Buxton, 380.

[42] The accounts of the expedition bear out that this goal was mostly followed on the British side, at least in principle. How the natives really perceived the British steamships and their odd crews and weapons might not have left quite an 'equal' feeling in their breasts. See Temperly, *White Dreams*, 88ff.

[43] Porter, *Religion Versus Empire?*, 136ff.

[44] Rhodes House, Buxton Papers, 18, ff. 156, r–u: Stephen Lushington to Buxton, 21 July 1839.

Church, or Oxfordism, all united.'[45] Here it was – the odd gathering of disparate forces for a common goal. While the most vitriolic in any given party had not been invited, many of the attenders *had* opposed one another over educational issues or Irish church matters at some time in the past seven years, sometimes in the previous few months. A company was not founded, but the Society for the Suppression of the Slave Trade and the Civilization of Africa (the African Civilization Society for short) was. During the coming months, each participant would agitate and assist where he could, and the government would make plans and preparations, so that when the large public meeting was held in June 1840, it was more an announcement and a celebration than an organisational meeting.

Most of those who mattered to the process liked the Niger expedition proposal, including many tories.[46] In its conception it addressed many points of concern and hope. On the side of political realism, Palmerston had been persuaded, because the securing of the island of Fernando Po and obtaining a lasting influence along the Niger served British national interest, especially in light of recent efforts by the French in northern Africa. Although the commercial case was still speculative, merchants got on board in the hopes that it might open new opportunities; the Manchester Chamber of Commerce said it would support any scheme 'to free them from their almost total dependence on American cotton'.[47] Missionary organisations all applauded. For the anti-slavery advocates, the plans pressed beyond the British policy of search and seizure, and promoted a relatively peaceful set of opportunities. For the whigs, who planned it, the expedition provided a chance to satisfy the various political groups who had made the whig government possible; for the tories who succeeded them in August 1841, right about the time of the expedition's ascent up the Niger, their support confirmed their anti-slavery credentials, but they could not be held responsible if things went wrong, since they had been little involved in the preparations. For all, it proved that it was easier to dream of creating civilization in Africa than in compromising over the content of legislation in Britain.

The grand experiment of the Niger expedition failed in its primary objective of establishing a commercial plantation and trading post in the interior of the Niger River basin. Two-thirds of those on the three steamships fell ill with malaria, and 41 died within weeks of entering the Niger River. But if the model farm had to be abandoned, the confluence of motivations for its founding remained and continued to give rise to 'moral imperatives requiring action'.[48] The Niger expedition may have been the high water-mark of 'humanitarian' influence on British colonial policy and official government actions, but this kind of approach to imperial expansion, this hope for a 'just' commerce and christian influence in a place still plagued by slavery and pagan superstition, activated

[45] Quoted in Buxton, *Memoirs,* ed. Buxton, 382.

[46] One significant exception: *The Times* and its editor John Walter were hostile to the project all the way through. Temperly, *White Dreams*, 60–1.

[47] Temperly, *White Dreams*, 37. Buxton thought that the commercial argument was the most compelling and had complained that the benevolent side of the proposal had been overemphasized. Rhodes House, Buxton Papers, 18, ff. 167–8: Buxton to Trew, 26 July 1839.

[48] Howard Temperley, 'Anti-Slavery as a Form of Cultural Imperialism', in *Anti-Slavery, Religion, and Reform: Essays in Memory of Roger Anstey,* ed. Christine Bolt and Seymour Drescher (Folkestone, 1980), 335.

many to support future efforts and fuelled the fascination of those like David Living-stone, who had likely observed the steamships' departure at the expedition's start.[49]

Buxton's interests grew naturally from those he had pursued throughout his parliamentary career, but in many ways his focus on the problems and opportunities that British colonialism created for non-European peoples, reflected a larger shift for evangelicals in Britain. While they could not all agree on the benefits or morality of poor law reform or the appropriate way to handle the Irish church question, most could agree that the 'heathen' and 'primitive' peoples coming under British rule deserved to have their rights protected, and all the more if doing so would open a way for the further spread of the gospel. It did not work out as planned. But combining the hope of ending the slave trade with opening new commercial frontiers, Buxton's speculations in *The African Slave Trade and its Remedy* provided a set of concepts and an agenda to which many ardent believers of otherwise diverse political bent could agree. Domestically, the evangelical communities in Britain might disagree on what policy and programmes served their civilization best; but they all agreed that Britain's growing empire needed to be directed in a way that promoted christianity and commerce, and hence the spread of that 'civilization'.

[49] The connection with later efforts is explored briefly by Andrew Walls in 'The Legacy of Thomas Fowell Buxton', *International Bulletin of Missionary Research*, xv (1991), 76ff. For a fuller discussion of the context and assessment of the impact, see Alan Lester, 'Humanitarians and White Settlers in the Nineteenth Century', in *Missions and Empire*, ed. Norman Etherington (Oxford, 2005), 64–85.

A Provincial Minister in Politics: Henry W. Crosskey*

R.K. WEBB

Henry W. Crosskey (1826–93), a late Victorian unitarian minister who served in Derby, Glasgow and Birmingham, is now best remembered for his involvement in Liberal politics and policy, especially education, as both an advocate and as a member of the Birmingham School Board. An eloquent preacher, he was also an important geologist, recognized both for his original research and for popularising the science and its impact on theology, and a revealing figure in the evolution of English unitarian thought. From his student days at Manchester College, Crosskey was a follower of his teacher, James Martineau, but, unlike Martineau, he advocated an active role for government, particularly local government, in promoting social well-being. In the political crises of 1885–6, though differing from Gladstone on religious education, disestablishment, and home rule for Ireland, he was unable to follow Joseph Chamberlain, a member of his congregation, into alliance with the Conservative Party. His scientific convictions led to his emergence in later life as an admirer of the broad piety of the early unitarian theologian and scientist, Joseph Priestley, whose followers had warred with Martineau's disciples in the bitter mid century struggle between 'Old' and 'New' unitarianism, thus serving as a bridge between the two schools of interpretation. He is also an important reminder of the expanding demands, internal and external, of an urban pastorate in the later 19th century.

Keywords: Birmingham; Henry W. Crosskey; education; geology; Glasgow; James Martineau; Joseph Priestley; religion and politics; religion and science; unitarianism

Henry Crosskey's working career took place in three important industrial towns: Derby in 1848–52, Glasgow in 1852–69, and Birmingham, at the Church of the Messiah – his best-known ministry – from 1869 to his death in 1893. After his unitarianism, his career has been most often defined by his political and social involvement, particularly in Birmingham. This essay is an effort at (as the literary scholars say – or used to say) unpacking that heavily-freighted description.

Crosskey's origins were also provincial, but of a very different kind: he was born in Lewes, in Sussex, on 7 December 1826. Lewes was an ancient market town just beginning to turn satellite, as the nearby shipping and fishing port of Brighton, benefiting from royal patronage and fashion, became the main commercial hub of the region. Crosskey's father, William, from old Sussex yeoman stock, was a partner in the drapery and outfitting firm of Browne and Crosskey, sufficiently prosperous to afford him a handsome house in Castlegate, Lewes; at his death in 1874, he left personal wealth,

* For advice and criticism, the author wishes to thank, and to absolve from any remaining errors, Sandra Herbert, Linda Lear, Peter Marsh, Joyce Meakin, and David Wykes.

as against landed property, valued at under £12,000, the equivalent in 2004 (using the retail price index) of over £721,000.[1]

William Crosskey belonged to the unitarian congregation in Westgate, Lewes; his wife by a second marriage and Henry Crosskey's mother, the former Elizabeth Rowland, came from the congregation at Horsham, a general baptist foundation of 1648. The general baptists had been the principal carriers of heterodoxy in south-eastern England – or a part of them, known as the Old Connexion, which remained after the much larger, evangelical, New Connexion broke away in 1770. Some characteristics of the Old Connexion's origins as a 'gathered church' – rural orientation, congregationally-imposed discipline, and reliance on an unpaid (or poorly paid) ministry – were still evident in the early 19th century. But over the next century and a half, the heterodox remnant drew closer to mainstream unitarians, formally joining them as a body in 1916; the general baptist congregation in Eastport Lane, Lewes, had merged with the Westgate congregation much earlier, in 1826. Though the general baptist name continued as did to some degree the tradition, co-operation had grown closer and ministers moved easily between the two churches. The Westgate congregation maintained a close relationship with the small general baptist congregation at nearby Ditchling, where Henry Crosskey occasionally visited and preached, and William Crosskey was buried.

In the mid 17th century, the Lewes congregation, like many others, had included both presbyterians and congregationalists (or independents). But when the unifying force of persecution lessened, the Lewes presbyterians withdrew to a private house in Westgate, eventually altered to suit its new purpose. The sorting out of presbyterians and congregationalists tended to follow the fault lines, not only of theological and ecclesiastical differences, but of wealth, social position, and education, and presbyterians moved easily into the national leadership of dissent, not contested until the early 19th century. Even then, as successors to the presbyterians, unitarians claimed higher social prestige, until the weight of sheer numbers in evangelically-inclined denominations, coupled with losses to the Church of England and growing disaffection from religion, gradually lessened unitarian importance.[2]

Henry Crosskey, one of five children, four of them boys, studied with the minister at Lewes, C.P. Valentine, then with a Mr Button in the town, and finally with John Fullagar, minister at Chichester. Crosskey later regretted his lack of rigorous schooling, but he admired both Valentine and Fullagar, and gained much from days spent on Valentine's farm and from his desultory reading. The examples of Valentine and Fullagar underlay his choice of the unitarian ministry over his father's preference that he become a chemist or

[1] Richard Acland Armstrong, *Henry William Crosskey . . . His Life and Work* (Birmingham, 1895), draws on Crosskey's own manuscript account, which I have not been able to trace. The informative entry in the *Oxford Dictionary of National Biography* [ODNB] is by Albert R. Vogeler. Colin E. Brent, *A Short Economic and Social History of Brighton, Lewes . . . 1500–1900* (Brighton, 1976). A photograph of the shop at 214 High Street, c.1880, is reproduced in Colin Brent and William Rector, *Victorian Lewes* (1980). Present-day equivalents of 19th-century sterling are found at the website, http://www.eh.net/hmit, where the differences in various indexes are also explained; the RPI is the lowest scale, others rising in this instance to more than £11m.

[2] For unitarianism generally, R.K. Webb, 'The Background: English Unitarianism in the Nineteenth Century', in *Unitarian to the Core: Unitarian College Manchester, 1854–2004,* ed. Leonard Smith (Manchester, 2004), 1–29. On Lewes dissenters, see Jeremy Goring, *Burn, Holy Fire!* (Cambridge, 2003).

Button's urging that he read for the bar.[3] In the autumn of 1843, he entered Manchester New College for the five-year ministerial course.

1

Founded at Manchester in 1786 as one of the dissenting academies for educating young men excluded by religious tests from Oxford and Cambridge, Manchester College migrated to York in 1803, where the minister, Charles Wellbeloved, had been named principal. With Wellbeloved's retirement in 1840, the college returned to Manchester, remaining there until its removal to London in 1853. The transition of the college in the 1840s and 1850s, coinciding with a profound shift in the nature of English unitarianism, determined that Crosskey would be an adherent of the 'New' unitarianism as against the 'Old'.

In the early 19th century, unitarianism had emerged as a denomination, as against an anti-trinitarian tendency found from the mid 18th century in a number of religious groupings, including anglican latitudinarians. Unitarians maintained that Jesus was human, not divine; rejected the propitiatory sacrifice of the cross and orthodox views of atonement; and, increasingly, believed in universal salvation as against calvinist election. By the early 19th century a distinctive philosophical outlook was added, drawn from David Hartley (1705–57), idiosyncratic anglican, physician, and innovative psychologist, and Joseph Priestley (1733–1804), unitarian minister, pioneering chemist, radical political theorist, and untiring controversialist. Priestley's centrality in unitarian history was hallowed in the Birmingham riots of 1791, when his chapel was destroyed, with his house, library, and laboratory, leading to his emigration to the United States in 1794. Hartley's place was assured by Priestley's adoption of the psychological and theological insights of Hartley's *Observations on Man: His Frame, his Duties, and his Expectations* (1749), a book Priestley insisted was second in importance only to the Bible. Called necessarianism, this philosophical amalgam emphasized the strictly causal dependence of action on prior motives; although every outcome was thus psychologically determined, necessarians differentiated themselves from fatalism or predestination by insisting that motives could be changed by circumstances and education, and that in time all human beings could attain perfection. Dependent on the Bible as the authoritative revelation of God's will and of Jesus's benevolent mission, necessarians also displayed a profound dependence on natural law and scientific methods. Manchester College, York was a forcing house for this system.[4]

Hartley's arguments affected many well-placed individuals besides Priestley, notably a group of philosophers and writers associated with Cambridge University. The most prominent of them was Samuel Taylor Coleridge, who also soon came to reject the system as his emerging romantic views came into conflict with necessarian positivism. A similar outlook began to shape younger unitarians by the 1830s, along with advances in

---

[3] For Crosskey's own account of his education, see Armstrong, *Crosskey*, 15–20.

[4] The most recent biography of Priestley is by Robert E. Schofield, *The Enlightenment of Joseph Priestley* and *The Enlightened Priestley* (University Park, PA, 1997, 2004); see also Webb, 'The Background', cited above. An indispensable unifying perspective on Hartley has been introduced by Richard C. Allen, *David Hartley on Human Nature* (Albany, NY, 1999).

biblical criticism, German-inspired or home-grown, to which Priestley and his followers had made their own adventurous contributions. By the 1840s, this new outlook was reinforced by the impact of the eloquent sermons of the American unitarian, William Ellery Channing. Thus the return of the college to Manchester marked an epoch.

Among Crosskey's teachers was the eminent scholar, John Kenrick, who had moved with the college from York and whose pathbreaking criticism of the Old Testament as historical testimony, *An Essay on Primaeval History*, was published in 1846, halfway through Crosskey's residence. Others included the radical classicist, Francis W. Newman, brother of John Henry Newman, and the Manchester minister, William Gaskell, an irenic and admired adherent of the old school and husband of the novelist, Elizabeth Gaskell. The main forces for doctrinal change were John James Tayler, minister at Upper Brook Street, Manchester, who taught ecclesiastical history, and James Martineau, from Paradise Street (later Hope Street), Liverpool, who taught philosophy; both moved with the college to London in 1853, with Tayler as principal. In the early 1830s, Tayler had emerged from a breakdown deeply distrustful of traditional biblical or scientific evidences, and certain that moral truths arose from within the soul. Martineau, who shared that belief in the source of religious emotion, was a gradualist in acknowledging doubts about the Bible and miracles. But as a controversialist, he was fiercer in speech than in print and fiercer in print than in settled conviction, ensuring that his students, with the natural iconoclastic delight of the young, would become the first generation of his disciples.

2

Derby, like Lewes, was a town in transition, from an economy based on silk, cotton, and knitting of stockings to one based on railways and engineering. The signature of the great innovator in the hosiery trade, Jedediah Strutt, appears for the first time on the settling of chapel accounts in 1776, and the Strutt family remained benefactors even after 1788, when they opened a chapel for workers in their model town of Belper. For example, they continued to own the organ at Derby until repairs proved necessary at the end of 1841, when (in a sound business decision?) they gave it to the congregation.[5] A well-governed congregation, Friar Gate left Crosskey free to hone his pulpit and pastoral skills, and he quickly demonstrated broader commitments. In 1850, he proposed that the congregation reorganise itself as an association to serve the welfare of the poor through charitable activity, day and Sunday schools, and a domestic mission. The idea of congregational reorganisation for benevolent purposes had been pioneered in England by Martineau's close friend, John Hamilton Thom at Renshaw Street, Liverpool. Domestic missions, for non-proselytising visiting to relieve and encourage the poor and to investigate social conditions, were inspired by the American minister, Joseph Tuckerman; English unitarians had made them a cause since the early 1830s. But Crosskey also took on national political questions, notably in opposing Lord John Russell's politically calculated effort to halt the creation of Roman catholic bishoprics in England, and in his

---

[5] This account based on two account and minute books, 1697–1819 and 1819–72, in the Derbyshire RO.

early support of national, state–supported, non–sectarian education.[6] Looking back in 1852, Crosskey summed up his Derby ministry in two major themes – doing 'some little towards giving the ignorant . . . a chance of growing in wisdom and integrity'; and 'protesting earnestly against sectarian intolerance'.[7]

This reflection resulted from his acceptance of the pulpit at Glasgow. He had also been invited to move, at a stipend of £300, nearly twice Glasgow's offer, to George's Meeting, Exeter, which, after playing a key role in the 18th-century emergence of rational dissent, had retained its eminence among unitarians. In both towns, to be sure, unitarianism faced serious sectarian disadvantage: in Exeter, the dominant anglican culture of a cathedral city, in Glasgow, the presence of the Church of Scotland, dramatically challenged by the aggressive free church formed in the Great Disruption of 1843. Yet unitarianism was falling away with the declining economy of south-west England, while a great port – with an economy changing from textiles to shipping, shipbuilding, and tobacco and with growing social problems – must have seemed to offer wider vistas for someone with Crosskey's commitments. Early in 1852, he married; his seven children were all born in Glasgow.

3

In 1854, in Chapman's *Library for the People*, Crosskey published *A Defence of Religion*, arguing the case against free-thinkers, which he dedicated to the famous secularist, George Jacob Holyoake, 'a man who, notwithstanding his inability to share the theist's faith, must permit a theist to regard his brave sincerity, and reverence for truth and justice, as acceptable worship at the altar of the Holy of Holies'. With this youthful flourish, Crosskey came up against the history of his congregation and a developing quarrel within unitarianism. That year, a deputation from Glasgow unsuccessfully visited London to raise funds for a new chapel. The emissaries blamed their failure on accusations circulating in London that the Glasgow congregation and its minister sympathised with Holyoake's views, that the Bible had been abandoned, and that Sunday sermons had been perverted into mere literary discourses, rumours recalling an awkward crisis ten years earlier, when a Glasgow minister had turned free-thinker. The facts were that on some Sunday evenings, Crosskey had lectured on religious aspects of literature and the bearing of modern biblical criticism on the scriptures, commonplace subjects later in the century. But this brought a stern protest from a former minister, James Yates. A son of an eminent, wealthy Liverpool minister, John Yates, James Yates had served at Glasgow in 1811–16, where he wrote an influential defence of unitarianism and was a co-founder of the Scottish Unitarian Association. He later preached in Birmingham and briefly in London, held some denominational posts, served as an administrator of the British Association for the Advancement of Science, and then retired into scholarly life. Dead-set against the new school of Tayler and Martineau, he had sympathisers in the Glasgow congregation, among them Henry Hilliard, who, in writing to Yates about his unhappiness with a property decision made by his fellow-trustees, had said that he welcomed

[6] Amstrong, *Crosskey*, 33–55.
[7] Derbyshire RO, account and minute book, 1819–72: 18 July 1852.

the rebuff of the London mission. But in the end, like the deputation, the Glasgow congregation overwhelmingly supported their minister, and the new chapel in St Vincent Street – its interior a unique variation on classical themes at a time when most new chapels were being built in the gothic style – was opened in April 1856.[8]

In the next dozen years, Crosskey continued his energetic involvement in congregational life and perfected a pulpit style that combined emotional appeal with persuasive argument, more accessible though no less affecting than the complex, self-conscious rhetoric of Thom and Martineau. Following common practice, morning services were 'devotional and practical', while controversial questions were reserved for Sunday evenings. Again, Crosskey became deeply involved in political questions, advocating extension of the suffrage, not only more widely among men but to women, and he publicly welcomed the American abolitionist, William Lloyd Garrison, and the Italian hero, General Garibaldi, to Glasgow. His abiding concern with education was reflected in his work with the Glasgow Public School Association, dedicated to confining rate-supported education to secular schools, and leaving doctrinal teaching to ministers of the different denominations.[9]

Another broad concern surfaced in Crosskey's Glasgow years: intense involvement with geology. By the 1830s, geology was replacing chemistry as the science of the moment, helped on by an immense increase in collecting, the advance of geological theorising, and arresting controversies that engaged even the casual interest of the public: the antiquity of the earth, with its implications for the historicity of the biblical flood, and startling paleontological discoveries, in the revelation, not only of vast numbers of fossils, but also of the apparent extinction of old species and the possible ongoing creation of new.[10] While geology might seem a natural enthusiasm for someone who, as a boy, had roamed the chalk hills above Lewes, Crosskey was encouraged in this new interest by his wife, the former Hannah Aspden, who in earlier years had taken many fossil-hunting walks in the Isle of Wight and who frequently joined him on his expeditions in Britain and Europe, some of the latter certainly tied to a new enthusiasm for alpinism. His interests lay chiefly in the sub-field of glaciology, given prominence by the Swiss-American zoologist and geologist, Louis Agassiz, whose hypothesis explaining the distribution and characteristics of rocks and fossils by the action of advancing and retreating glaciers had gained increasing acceptance by the 1850s. Crosskey collected and classified (he presented collections to both the University of Glasgow and Mason College, later incorporated in the University of Birmingham), and he published papers in both the proceedings of local geological and philosophical societies and in national publications such as the *Geological Magazine* and the *Quarterly Journal of the Geological Society*. He was active in those societies and in the influential British Association for the Advancement of Science, where he served from 1873 to his death, as secretary of a committee on the origin, distribution, composition, and preservation of 'erratic blocks',

[8] On Crosskey's book, the deputation's report, and its reception, Armstrong, *Crosskey*, ch. 3; the Hilliard-Yates correspondence is discussed in the trustees' minutes, 14 July 1854, Mitchell Library, Glasgow, GB243/TD978/4. Excerpts from Yates's letter and Crosskey's reply appear in Armstrong, *Crosskey*, 82–7; for the hostile report of the London District Unitarian Society and subsequent correspondence, see *Inquirer*, 2–30 Dec. 1854.

[9] Armstrong, *Crosskey*, 104–34.

[10] A recent way into the vast literature on the subject is provided by the text and extensive references in Sandra Herbert, *Charles Darwin, Geologist* (Ithaca, NY, 2005).

unique boulders scattered throughout England, Wales, and Ireland. Finally, in the best and broadest sense, he was a populariser of geology and science and of their bearings on theology and religion.[11]

4

A widening denominational reputation, reinforced by a recommendation from James Martineau, brought Crosskey to the attention of the historic congregation at the Church of the Messiah, Birmingham – as New Meeting, it had been Priestley's pulpit and the object of the rioters' rage in 1791 – and an offer was made early in 1869. A long ministry may bring striking change at its end, and so it was in Birmingham. When he retired in 1868, Samuel Bache had been minister since 1832. By mid century he had emerged as a leading champion of the old school, defending the gospel miracles and the messiahship, the latter point reinforced in 1862, when he persuaded his congregation, on moving into its new gothic building, to rename itself the Church of the Messiah. Less auspiciously, in 1866 he stood with James Yates as one of three supporters of a resolution limiting membership of the British and Foreign Unitarian Association to those who accepted the theological views of its founders in 1825. But the vestry minute books for 1868–9 give no indication that the prospect of generational change was even noted. It may be that members of the deputation that carried the formal invitation to Glasgow – Joseph and Arthur Chamberlain, J. Arthur and William Kenrick, Follett Osler, and Dr William Russell, their names echoing the history of the congregation and of wider Birmingham society – discussed the doctrinal shift among themselves. But it seems more probable that, with a civic revolution in the making, they had simply abandoned the theological concerns of an earlier generation to concentrate on a proven political and social record. Worried that a contested election might compromise his leadership, Crosskey agreed to candidacy when he was assured that his name alone would be put forward, and only when he was told that the 11 votes by which the decision in a large congregational meeting fell short of unanimity came mostly from one relatively inactive family, did he signal his acceptance.[12] He quickly justified the confidence placed in him.

Crosskey is less known now for his advocacy of the 'civic gospel' in Birmingham than are two other ministers: George Dawson at the non-denominational Church of the Saviour, and R.W. Dale, the most celebrated congregational minister of his time. Yet, as one observer put it, though Crosskey was not the equal 'in force of character and

[11] On Crosskey, Charles Lapworth, 'Scientific Researches and Publications' in Armstrong, *Crosskey*, ch. 10. Lapworth, professor of geology in Mason College, had worked in both Scotland and the midlands: *Dictionary of Scientific Biography* (18 vols, New York, 1970–90). The authoritative *Catalogue of Scientific Papers, 1800–1900* compiled by the Royal Society of London, (19 vols, 1867–1925), ii, vii, ix, xiv, lists Crosskey as sole author of 14 articles and as a collaborator in five. Twenty catalogues of erratic blocks, compiled by Crosskey for the British Association committee, appear yearly in the Association's *Reports*, 1873–92. In addition to sermons touching on science (e.g., on pending local meetings of the British Association), the best instance of his popularising is *The Method of Creation: A Comparison of the Book of Nature with the Book of Genesis* (2nd edn, 1889), published by the Sunday School Association.

[12] This reconstruction is based on letters in 1868–9 from Crosskey to John Gordon, minister at Coventry, John Rylands University of Manchester Library, Unitarian College MS B1[11], an archive that demonstrates the immense respect accorded Gordon by unitarian ministers on all sides of mid century disputes.

picturesqueness of personality' of Dawson, 'a prophet pure and simple', or Dale, the consummate platform orator, he far surpassed them in breadth of accomplishment, 'at once a devoted pastor, an educational pioneer, a successful scientific discoverer, an accepted leader in social and political reform'.[13] He joined the Liberal Association as soon as he settled in Birmingham and was closely involved in all its activities, from elections to advocacy of sanitary reform, 'gas-and-water' socialism, the creation of parks and playing fields, and broadened missions for libraries and art institutions. Birmingham may have differed in social structure from the factory towns to the north, but it had town problems in plenty, housing, sanitation, and education chief among them.

As before, schools were Crosskey's main concern. From his arrival, he was active in the forming and expansion of the National Education League; as a member of its committee, he agitated steadily for establishing secular national schools; he opposed the relevant provisions of the Education Act of 1870 and wrote a succession of pamphlets on education published by the National Liberal Federation. He was elected as a representative of the town council on the Birmingham School Board in 1876, serving as chairman of the school management committee from 1881 to his resignation in 1892. He was a governor, again representing the council, of King Edward's School; a reformer of technical education; and a leading advocate of the creation of a university in Birmingham.

The sweeping changes in the political landscape in 1885-6, precipitated by the Irish Home Rule Bill and Chamberlain's subsequent break with the Liberal Party, challenged both the Church of the Messiah and its pastor. Though Crosskey differed deeply from Gladstone on the place of religion in national education, disestablishment, and home rule, he could not follow Chamberlain into alliance with the Conservatives.[14] Unfortunately, the effects of these events on the congregation are unclear, as the vestry minute book for these years is missing from an otherwise remarkably full run, but when L.P. Jacks succeeded Crosskey in 1894, he felt it necessary to make clear that he was a strict Gladstonian and a home ruler. The deputation replied that not all of them agreed with Chamberlain, who in any event, although he handsomely supported the congregation, rarely attended; it was a situation where discretion was all.[15]

The drive behind Crosskey's public activities, apart from education, was greatly reduced in the last seven years of his life. Some of his energy was dimmed by the death, in 1886, of his third son, Lionel, a Cambridge graduate, newly married and beginning a promising career as a barrister in London; and from 1890 Crosskey was battling with heart failure. The congregation appointed two assistant ministers in succession, and Crosskey took extended leave in 1892 to journey to Italy. But his health was not to be recaptured, and he died as he was putting the finishing touches to a sermon early on a Sunday morning, on 1 October 1893.

[13] In an anonymous review of Armstrong's biography in *The Speaker*, 10 Aug. 1895, pp. 158–9; the *Inquirer*, 7 Oct. 1893, where it is reprinted, insisted on good authority that the writer was not unitarian. For Dale's own extended judgment, see Armstrong, *Crosskey*, 247–58. Crosskey's summary of his public activities is transcribed on pp. 259–73, and ch. 13, on his educational work, is by his Birmingham School Board associate (an anglican), the Rev. E.F.M. MacCarthy.

[14] Some of his views on Ireland are outlined in a letter to Chamberlain: University of Birmingham Library, Chamberlain MSS, JC8/5/3/14: 22 Apr. 1886.

[15] Lawrence P. Jacks, *The Confession of an Octogenarian* (1942), 148–9. Central Reference Library, Birmingham, Church of the Messiah records UC2.

5

The demands of Crosskey's multifold activities may have played a part in his worsening health. But political work, however extensive and broadly defined, was only part of what he did. There have always been ministers, unitarian and otherwise, for whom politics has been a principal preoccupation, like William Shepherd, at Gateacre outside Liverpool, at the turn of the century, or the early Victorian reformer, journalist, organiser, and MP, W.J. Fox. Many 19th-century unitarian ministers engaged in local and national politics as journalists. Others added yet more demands on time and energy, the best example surely being Charles Beard, at Renshaw Street, Liverpool, who was not only a regular leader-writer for the *Liverpool Daily Post*, but editor of the *Theological Review*, and a serious historical scholar.

Still, Crosskey stands as a warning against a foreshortening characteristic of our somewhat forgetful age. It is easy to read contemporary preoccupations with politics and policy back into the Victorian period and to neglect the over-riding priorities of religion, as both structural and interior commitment. Crosskey repeatedly traced the roots of his campaigns for civic betterment, especially in education, to christian ideals and obligations to the less advantaged. But even more likely to be forgotten these days are the unavoidable demands of leading a large congregation. Preaching (and writing) two or three sermons and lectures a week and seeing a flock through successive stages of their lives were more or less constants in any age. But other tasks markedly increased in the course of the century. In 1800, a unitarian minister could still conform (or pretend to conform) to the old presbyterian ideal of the learned minister, isolated from the business of his congregation and feeling only limited personal obligations to them. As the century progressed, ministers became increasingly involved in congregational business, and members' expectations grew with more extended participation in chapel affairs, especially as women became active, at first in their own groups and then more generally. Teas, *conversazioni*, fêtes, and bazaars multiplied. The growing attractions of town life led congregations to offer young people alternatives such as reading groups and mutual improvement societies and to look favourably on picnics, excursions, and even dances – activities that might also help to maintain the loyalty of a new generation. The minister was closely involved with almost all of them. While numbers of congregationally-supported day schools declined with national education, Sunday schools remained a central demand on a minister's time and attention; so did widening charitable needs. And, with greater ease of transportation reinforcing an inbuilt tendency to expand, denominational organisations grew, locally, regionally, and nationally. Imperial Britain was oddly echoed in an imperial ministry.

By the late 1880s, Crosskey was taking a larger role in denominational work. He enthusiastically supported the National Conference, a new Martineau-inspired umbrella organisation of religious liberals, meeting triennially, to counterbalance the British and Foreign Unitarian Association (BFUA), the very name of which affronted Martineau's conviction that unitarianism was, theologically, a mere stopping-place in the evolution of a grander religious vision. But Crosskey was also involved in the BFUA, as president in the late 1880s, and giving the presidential address in 1890. R.W. Dale maintained that Crosskey was little interested in theology and philosophy. That is true enough of philosophy, but the overwhelming burden of Crosskey's geological publications addressed to a wider audience was, as the title of an early lecture has it, *The Influence of Science upon Theology* (1863). The absolute authority of science left little leeway for much traditional theology, but it also offered certainties that could underlie broader affirmations.

From the first, Crosskey had departed from Martineau's political assumptions, emphasizing the potential of government, from which Martineau had recoiled to encourage individual interaction and example. Martineau had also been skeptical in his college lectures in the sixties of the argument from design, although in his revision and expansion of those lectures in the 1880s, he returned to a grander view of nature and of the power of the creator. Much earlier, Crosskey, as a scientist, had emphasized that expanded view of the creator.[16] Here, then, was a link that connected him, across the doubts of James Martineau, to the Priestleyans. But there was an even more striking link. On 1 August 1874, not without evangelical protest, Birmingham dedicated a statue of Priestley. The next day Crosskey delivered a perceptive, and I think beautiful, sermon on his predecessor. He is particularly insightful about Priestley's deep religious sense, notably emphasizing his *Discourse on Habitual Devotion* (1786), 'one of the most thoroughly religious discourses in the English language [which expresses] the simple and childlike, yet thoughtful and profound piety of his soul'; 'fervour of devotion' is simply not available to all minds, he argued, but devoutness can flourish without that emotional impulse. In 1775, Priestley's friend, the poet Anna Laetitia Barbauld, had published a book suggesting (as many evangelicals were also to do) that the dominant religion of her time lacked warmth and emotion. When she asked his opinion, Priestley rejected the implication of fashion in her view of 'devotional taste', emphasizing instead the centrality of devotion: in that sense, his, too, was a religion of the heart.[17] Crosskey had certainly been influenced by the deep religious and devotional elements in Martineau; that he also discerned them in Priestley (as indeed Martineau had done in early essays) may be even more significant.

In the last year of his life, Crosskey undertook two projects. One was the manuscript memoir, central to Armstrong's account. The other was an epitome of his published and unpublished sermons, a collection of aphorisms and brief musings that, he said wryly, 'may yet not be quite so unheeded as long sermons themselves often are'. He called it *A Handbook of Rational Piety*. His principal concerns in the book, addressing those who had abandoned or doubted faith, were the divine origins of this world and of man, the supremacy of divine law in nature and in human affairs, and the injunction to piety or righteousness. He emphasized God or the creator – the term he is more likely to use in argumentative passages – rather than Jesus or the Christ, in keeping with the deep explanatory role of science. Here is another reversion to the balance of the Priestleyan generations from the anti-positivist, deeply personal, and rather more christo-centric outlook of the new school. But that is not all. The religious world, Crosskey insisted, does

[16] Crosskey's repeated references to the creator would have confirmed Harriet Martineau in her regret that Charles Darwin, in *The Origin of Species*, had gone 'out of his way two or three times [I think not more] to speak of "the Creator" in the popular sense of the First Cause', giving occasion 'for people to ride off from the argument in a way which need not have been granted to them': Harriet Martineau to Fanny Wedgwood, 13 Mar. 1860, in *Harriet Martineau's Letters to Fanny Wedgwood*, ed. Elisabeth Sanders Arbuckle (Stanford, 1983), 189.

[17] R.K. Webb, 'Rational Piety', in *Enlightenment and Religion: Rational Dissent in Eighteenth-Century Britain*, ed. Knud Haakonssen (Cambridge, 1996), esp. 298–301; the chapter – written, alas, without knowledge of Crosskey's last book – offers a wider context for unitarian devotion.

not stand apart from the ordinary world, the world of books, pictures, and music, the world in which business and the work of town and county councils, school boards and parliament, not the churches, are the dominant authorities, a world where the practically useful and the divinely good are identical. Priestley, with reason, had distrusted the state; Crosskey was deeply involved in its recreation. But both men insisted that piety must infuse everything in life, individual or public.

If I am right, Crosskey was a herald of 20th-century unitarianism, not only in emphasizing public service and practical obligations, but in the dimming of the doctrinal quarrels that had bitterly divided unitarians in his youth. In the historical amalgam of unitarian thought since 1900, the two heroic figures of Priestley and Martineau, martyr and saint, stand above all the rest. There is today, inevitably, some unawareness or incomprehension of how differently their thought was based and even more of the gulf that separated their disciples. But that is a usual phenomenon. Historians make distinctions, heeded or not, but they should note their blurring as well.

The Archbishop of Canterbury, the Episcopal Bench, and the Passage of the 1911 Parliament Act

DEREK W. BLAKELEY

The passage of the 1911 Parliament Bill ended the power of the British house of lords to veto any legislation passed by the house of commons. Henceforth, it could only delay the passage of a measure. The bill was carried by a mere 17 votes and friction between Unionists who took up die-hard opposition, advised abstention, or actively sought to aid passage was bitter. The role which the archbishop of Canterbury played in canvassing the episcopal bench and helping to ensure final passage of the bill has not attracted much attention. Prior to the debate, the archbishop advised abstention but did not dissuade others from encouraging bishops to support the bill to help ensure passage. Before the vote, therefore, 'die-hards' opposing any concession to the government, 'hedgers' advising Unionist abstention in the vote, and 'rats', Unionists willing to vote for the bill to ensure passage despite personal reservations, attempted to sound out and pressure the bishops in their direction. At the debate, the archbishop changed his mind and decided he must support the bill in order to avoid a greater crisis, and 12 other bishops joined him in the government lobby, helping to create the final majority of 17 by which the measure passed. Consideration of the role of the bishops adds to the understanding of the mechanics by which the bill passed, amidst considerable intrigue, pressure and acrimony, as well as further illuminating the extent and intensity of the divisions within the Unionist party at this critical moment.

Keywords: 1911 Parliament Bill; house of lords; archbishop of Canterbury; Randall T. Davidson; die-hards; Lord Curzon of Kedleston; Lord Lansdowne; Lord Stamfordham; Lord Salisbury; Unionist Party

Throughout the late Victorian and Edwardian era, the potential for a constitutional crisis surrounding the position of the house of lords loomed as a spectre over the political stage. Using their majority in the upper House, the Unionists blocked Mr Gladstone's Second Home Rule Bill in 1893 and threatened to use it to reject other 'revolutionary' legislation.[1] After retreating to the background during the Conservative ministries of Salisbury and Balfour, the Lords returned to the forefront of the political fray when the Liberals returned to power in 1906. Thereafter, they blocked a number of key ministerial bills culminating with the rejection in 1909 of the 'People's Budget' – David Lloyd George's radical programme of increased taxes, notably a 'supertax' on the highest incomes, to pay for the rising costs of new social programmes and rising defence

---

[1] Corinne Comstock Weston, *The House of Lords and Ideological Politics: Lord Salisbury's Referendal Theory and the Conservative Party, 1846–1922* (Phildadephia, 1995) is the best study of the political philosophy that the Unionists employed to justify their rejection of Liberal legislation.

expenditures. The rejection of the budget – overturning a centuries-old understanding that the Lords was not to touch money bills – initiated a political crisis, the dissolution of parliament, and an election in January 1910 on the issue, which the Liberals narrowly won.[2]

Subsequently, the budget was reintroduced and passed in the new parliament, but the question of the powers of the house of lords was now squarely at the centre of British politics. A second narrow Liberal victory in the December 1910 election failed to convince the Unionists to accept any modification of the existing powers of the upper chamber, thus, in the spring of 1911, the Liberal government introduced the Parliament Bill which would strip the Lords of its absolute veto and replace it with a suspensory one. Henceforth, any bill passed by the Commons in three successive sessions would automatically become law, regardless of any objections held by the Lords. Approved by the Commons in the spring of 1911, it was sent to the upper House where amendments were proffered. These were subsequently rejected by the government majority in the Commons and the bill was returned to the Lords in late July. The stage was now set for an epic clash regarding the proper form of the English constitution, but one, as we shall see, that was marked by both political calculation and intense personal emotion. In early August, the bill passed the house of lords by the thinnest of margins, following acrimony that stretched both across the party aisle and within the Unionist Party.

Given the significance of the bill and the narrowness of the final vote – a majority of only 17 – the circumstances surrounding the passage of the Parliament Bill have naturally attracted a great deal of historical attention, but the involvement of Randall Davidson, archbishop of Canterbury, and the episcopal bench in its passage has been generally underestimated. Of the 24 bishops and two archbishops with seats in the house of lords, 13 voted with the government in the final division on 10 August, and only two sided with the 'die-hards' in stalwart opposition to the bill. Since the Unionist 'rats', who voted with the government to avoid a large creation of peers, rather than the bishops, provided the decisive margin, historical attention has naturally turned toward them. But in the days preceding the division the majority was, of course, unknown and the votes of the lords spiritual, were keenly sought by 'rats', 'hedgers' (those peers hoping that the measure would pass while most Unionists abstained from the vote) and 'ditchers' (those Unionists who pledged to oppose the Bill 'to the last ditch'). Without the 13 votes of the bishops the ultimate government majority (131 to 114) would have been excruciatingly thin. The examination of the role which the bishops, and especially the archbishop of Canterbury, could still play in the house of lords, even in an admittedly exceptional case, is in itself valuable, and the case further demonstrates the intensity of the struggle over the Parliament Bill.

Key to understanding the involvement of the bishops in such a constitutional issue was the position of the archbishop of Canterbury. Davidson envisioned the role of the primate of the Church of England, and indeed the episcopacy as a whole, as national

---

[2] Peter Rowland, *The Last Liberal Governments* (2 vols, New York, 1969–72), and Bruce Murray, *The People's Budget 1909/10: Lloyd George and Liberal Politics* (Oxford, 1980) provide the best narratives of the events leading up to the introduction and rejection of the 1909 budget. Neal Blewett, *The Peers, the Parties and the People: The British General Elections of 1910* (Toronto, 1972) chronicles and explains the events of the dual 1910 elections. For a summary, see Lord Longford, *A History of the House of Lords* (1988), 136–52.

rather than merely ecclesiastical.[3] But he was equally clear that in addressing political questions, the bishops served: 'the interests both of Church and Nation by abstaining from identifying [themselves] vociferously with one side or the other in an acute political conflict wherein Church questions occupy really a subordinate place'.[4]

Within these limits, however, Davidson was 'prepared to take an active part in national politics and he was in a position to do so. He had been near the centre of the political world throughout his career and had made many influential friends. Later he admitted that: 'There has hardly been a member of a cabinet on either side whom I have not known more or less, and some . . . were very old friends.'[5] Such associations, and particularly Davidson's long friendship with Sir Arthur Bigge, King George V's private secretary, were vital to Davidson's acquiring the trusted position he held within the political elite. This acceptance, indeed welcome, in the debating chamber and at the conference table had been evident in the leading role Davidson played in trying to find an acceptable compromise to the education question after 1905 and in his membership of Lord Rosebery's committee on the reform of the house of lords.

It was in the role of confidential advisor and intermediary that Davidson first entered the constitutional conflict after the defeat of the 1909 budget. In January 1910, the archbishop wrote to Lord Knollys, the king's private secretary, suggesting that, without having any desire to interfere, 'an hour might very easily come in the near future when it might be useful to have somebody at hand who knows the political leaders intimately and who yet stands quite outside political strifes and parties . . . I am wholly available at a few hours notice if any such necessity or even probable advantage should occur.'[6] This offer was to be taken up on many occasions in the coming months.

In April 1910, at Knollys's suggestion, Davidson convened Balfour, Esher and Knollys at Lambeth palace to discuss the question of the king giving guarantees to the government, and the prospect of Balfour undertaking to form a ministry if the king refused a premature Liberal request for a creation. Davidson does not appear to have taken an active part in the discussion, but the fact that it took place under his aegis – after all, the other three participants were hardly in need of introductions – was indicative of his perceived disinterestedness, and the need for such a conversation to take place in a non-partisan atmosphere.[7] Later in the year, after the second general election, and with still no certainty that the crisis could be resolved without the resignation of the Liberal government, Sir Arthur Bigge again contemplated the intervention of the archbishop as a 'negotiator' should an impasse be reached.[8] That Davidson was considered in such a way reiterated the trust politicians had in him and allowed him to be a useful conduit of information.

[3] G.K.A. Bell, *Randall Davidson, Archbishop of Canterbury* (2 vols, 1935), i, 317–18; J.G. Lockhart, *Cosmo Gordon Lang* (1949), 232.

[4] Davidson to Lord Salisbury, 12 Jan. 1910, quoted in Bell, *Randall Davidson*, i, 604.

[5] Lambeth Palace Library, Davidson Papers, 12, f. 313: 'Autobiographical Memorandum, Easter week, 1913'.

[6] Lambeth Palace Library, Davidson Papers, 5, f. 106: Davidson to Knollys, 24 Jan. 1910.

[7] Lambeth Palace Library, Davidson Papers, 12, ff. 128–31: memorandum of interview with Lord Knollys, 23 Apr. 1910; 12, ff. 134–41: 'memorandum of a conference at Lambeth, 27th Apr. 1910', by Lord Esher; R. Jenkins, *Mr. Balfour's Poodle* (1954), 177.

[8] TNA (PRO), Midleton Papers, PRO 30/67/24, ff. 1251–3, ff. 1255–6: 'memo. of conversation with Sir A. Bigge. Dec. 27, 1910', by Lord Midleton, confidential; Bigge to Midleton, 29 Dec. 1910.

Davidson's principal advisory role, however, was as a source of counsel or information to the king and his private secretaries, on the king's position, and later, as the vote approached, on the prospects for the Parliament Bill's passage. On three occasions in 1911, Davidson submitted memoranda to Bigge or Knollys regarding the position of the king and the question of guarantees, a matter to which he had first given thought privately a year before.[9] The advice was freely proffered, but in each case Davidson carefully pointed out that it had been solicited and offered that if his view should be 'stale or commonplace or without value, you can quite easily commit it to the waste-paper basket'.[10] Davidson believed that the king had every right to withhold a guarantee of the creation of peers to pass the Parliament Bill until the crucial moment had arrived when the measure was before the house of lords.[11] The king had no duty to pronounce on a hypothetical case, though, of course, he would have to submit to a creation if there was no viable alternative government. Even so, Davidson felt that the king had a clear right to have the circumstances of the transaction carefully put on record.[12] This was especially true after the revelation of the guarantees the king had given to the prime minister in November 1910. Although Davidson did not entirely exonerate the king from blame in submitting to the hypothetical guarantees, Davidson thought it essential that it be known that the king had only done so under pressure and with reluctance.[13]

The king and his private secretaries agreed with Davidson's view that King George had not been well served in the matter of obtaining the guarantees, and asked for the archbishop's assistance in communicating the king's position more widely. First, Stamfordham 'wished to know if [Davidson] could do anything to get Arthur Balfour to speak more strongly as to the responsibility being Asquith's and not the King's'. Neither the king nor his secretaries could directly approach Balfour on such a matter, so they turned to Davidson.[14] Later, the archbishop was asked to suggest a statement that the Liberals might make to clarify the circumstances of the king's agreement.[15] Davidson drafted one and Asquith agreed to make such a statement but it was never done, and the king and his advisers subsequently agreed that it was best not to reopen the question.[16]

The extent of Davidson's intimacy and trust with the king, Knollys, and Stamfordham was such that all three discussed with him the friction which developed between the two private secretaries during the crisis. The wisdom of Knollys's advice over the November guarantees and his conception of the limits to the king's contacts with the opposition

[9] Davidson wrote a memorandum of his own thoughts on the subject in the spring of 1910, see Bell, *Randall Davidson*, i, 606–7, and submitted memoranda to the king's secretaries on 11 Jan., 13 Apr. and 24 July 1911: Bell, *Randall Davidson*, i, 621–3; Lambeth Palace Library, Davidson Papers, 12, ff. 184–9, 199–200.

[10] Lambeth Palace Library, Davidson Papers, 12, f. 105: Davidson to Bigge, 11 Jan. 1911 [letter misdated as 11 Jan. 1910].

[11] Bell, *Randall Davidson*, i, 623.

[12] This point was the subject of Davidson's two memoranda of Apr. and July 1911 (see n. 9 above).

[13] Lambeth Palace Library, Davidson Papers, 12, ff. 255–6: Davidson to Knollys, 8 Aug. 1911.

[14] Davidson's memorandum of the events of July and Aug. 1911; Lambeth Palace Library, Davidson Papers, 12, f. 219: 28 July. In this instance, Davidson did not feel he could approach Balfour on the matter, as the Unionist leader had never consulted with him on the question.

[15] Lambeth Palace Library, Davidson Papers, 12, f. 258: Davidson Journal, Aug. 1911; Davidson Papers, 12, ff. 255–6: Davidson to Knollys, 8 Aug. 1911.

[16] Lambeth Palace Library, Davidson Papers, 12, ff. 266–8, 270: Knollys to Davidson, 17 Aug. 1911; Davidson to Knollys, 22 Aug. 1911.

were doubted by Stamfordham, and led to contemplation of resignation by the latter. Davidson had broad sympathy with his friend Stamfordham's grievances, but that all three confided in him is notable.[17]

If knowledge of the nature of Davidson's advice to the king remained within a very limited circle, his position as an informal advisor to the crown was more widely known and he proved to be a useful channel of communication between the king and politicians throughout July and August 1911. By the nature of Davidson's own sympathies and the circumstances of the clash, the archbishop largely served to transmit information between the official Unionist opposition and the king's secretaries. As a single example of how easily this could pass, on 20 June Lansdowne informed Davidson of the amendments in which the Unionists intended to persist. Immediately from this interview, the archbishop was summoned to see the king, to whom he related the outlines of his talk with Lansdowne and the Unionist leader's assertion that there could be 'no expectation of the Peers passing tamely the Parliament Bill'. The king replied to this transmitted message with the hope that the opposition would give way after forcing a declaration of the intent to create peers, satisfying themselves with the assurance that they would amend the act when they returned to power.[18] There is not time nor need to relate all of Davidson's many meetings with politicians of all shades during the weeks before the final debate, but he was clearly within the circle of well-informed persons.

It was, however, as leader of the episcopal bench that the archbishop had the most direct impact. As the final division neared and the Unionist opposition split on whether to persevere in their amendments or not, every individual vote was courted by all the competing factions, and the bishops were no exception. A few bishops were approached independently, but most of the attention fell upon their acknowledged political leader. Although Davidson repeatedly refused to 'whip' the episcopal bench in any direction, it was generally believed that the greater part of the bench would follow his lead. Thus on a single day (1 August), Davidson could meet with such a diverse lot as Lord Crewe from the Liberals, Lord Salisbury from the die-hards, Lords Cromer, St Aldwyn and Camperdown representing the 'conscience men', Lord Curzon identifying with Lord Lansdowne's leadership, and Lord Stamfordham from the king – all seeking information on the intentions of the bishops. Additionally, on that day the archbishop saw two of his colleagues on the episcopal bench and discussed the situation with them.[19]

Most of the attention directed toward the episcopal bench concentrated on the question of whether the bulk of the bishops would follow Lansdowne's official advice and abstain from the vote, or whether they would join the group of Unionist peers which Lord Cromer and others were organising and which was prepared to vote, if necessary, for the bill and against their convictions in order to prevent the mass creation threatened by the government. Due to their unique position in the house of lords, holding seats as representatives of the established church rather than as individuals and generally without strong party affinities, the bishops were potentially more amenable than other groups to an appeal to protect the king from the indignity of a mass creation

[17] Lambeth Palace Library, Davidson Papers, 12, ff. 201, 204–5, 208, 262: Davidson Journal, 22, 23, 25, 26 July and 14 Aug. 1911.

[18] Lambeth Palace Library, Davidson Papers, 12, ff. 190–5: Davidson Journal, 20 June 1911.

[19] Lambeth Palace Library, Davidson Papers, 12, ff. 222, 231–2, 239–42: Davidson Journal, 1 Aug. 1911.

and the country from continuing constitutional division. Such a role accorded naturally with Davidson's own conception of the episcopacy's national role and political independence.[20]

The Liberals had some interest in the intentions of the bishops and Crewe enquired about them on 1 August.[21] However, only three of the bishops supported the bill on its merits,[22] and Davidson felt that Crewe left their interview disappointed that the archbishop could not make any further commitment towards supporting the bill.[23] This being so, there was little that the Liberal lord could do but warn that every peer who abstained would have to share responsibility for a creation if the bill was defeated.[24]

The Unionists, upon whom the onus for passage or defeat would ultimately fall, were more persistent in seeking to determine and influence the intentions of the bishops. Lord Curzon spearheaded the attempt to ensure that the bishops would at least follow Lansdowne's lead and abstain. Significantly, he sought, as well, to learn if any bishops would be prepared to vote, if necessary, with the government to ensure passage. Feeling it improper to approach the bishops directly, Curzon asked Davidson if he would be willing to ascertain their intentions.[25] This the archbishop did on 27 July, and the replies to this approach provided the first hard information on the intentions of the episcopal bench. Of the 26 bishops, 23 responded; three intended to vote with the government on the merits of the bill, 14 intended to follow the lead of Lord Lansdowne, and six stated they would vote for the bill if doing so would prevent a creation.[26] The bishops generally had little enthusiasm for the bill. Yet, even a staunch Conservative such as John Wordsworth, bishop of Salisbury – who initiated a spate of letters to *The Times*, after he wrote articulating his belief that the creation of peers with the express purpose of ensuring passage of legislation by way of their votes was as immoral as the purchase of votes –

[20] In 1911, *Dod's Parliamentary Companion* listed two bishops as Liberals, five as Liberal Unionists and four as Conservatives. In 1906, the same figures had been three, five and four, but in 1901, before the reopening of the education issue, the same reference had not given partisan affiliations to any of the 26 bishops with seats in the house of lords. See Appendix.

[21] Lambeth Palace Library, Davidson Papers, 12, f. 222: Davidson Journal, 1 Aug. 1911.

[22] The bishops of Chester, Birmingham, and Hereford. Oddly, the bishop of Chester (Francis Jayne) was considered a Conservative by both *Dod's* and the *Constitutional Yearbook*. Percival, the bishop of Hereford, was an acknowledged Liberal, and Charles Gore, bishop of Birmingham, was sympathetic to democratic measures though not adhering to any particular party. G.L. Prestige, *The Life of Charles Gore* (1935), 274. See Appendix.

[23] Lambeth Palace Library, Davidson Papers, 12, ff. 230–1: Davidson Journal, 1 Aug. 1911.

[24] Lambeth Palace Library, Davidson Papers, 12, f. 222: Davidson Journal, 1 Aug. 1911; 12, ff. 243–4: Crewe to Davidson, 2 Aug. 1911.

[25] Lambeth Palace Library, Davidson Papers, 12, ff. 211–14: Curzon to Davidson, 26 July 1911.

[26] The replies of 20 bishops sent to Curzon are in Lambeth Palace Library, Davidson Papers, 12, ff. 271–301. The intentions of two others are suggested in Davidson's circular letter to the bishops on 27 July 1911 (BL, India Office Library, Curzon Papers, MS Eur. F/112/89/34) and Davidson reported the intention of the bishop of Chester to Curzon in a letter of 28 July 1911 (F/112/89/41). The only complication to tallying the responses of the bishops to Davidson's circular is that at the time it was distributed, Lansdowne had not yet made it clear that following his lead would not involve voting for the bill, but only abstaining from the vote. Thus, some bishops who replied that they intended to follow Lansdowne may have been willing to vote for the bill if necessary to secure its passage, and had misinterpreted Lansdowne's position. Certainly, Curzon thought that as many as nine or ten might be willing to do so, and hoped that Davidson might be able to confirm their intention. In the Appendix, only the six bishops who positively expressed their willingness to vote with the government if necessary (and not merely their intention to follow Lansdowne's lead) are listed as being willing to enter the government's lobby. BL, India Office Library, Curzon Papers, F/112/89/223–30: Curzon to Davidson, nd [c.28–29 July 1911].

recognized the political realities and committed himself to abstention. Already ill, the bishop would not be present for the vote and would die on 16 August. Even so, he felt that acceding to the bill was the lesser of two evils.[27]

It was over the question of how many bishops would vote for the bill in order to prevent a creation that the real struggle occurred, and the concerted efforts which were made to influence them are absent from earlier accounts of the crisis.[28] The king was eager that the bishops should vote with the government in order to save the bill.[29] Cromer and his supporters hoped that sufficient bishops would join their cause to ensure their object.[30] In reply to both, Davidson stuck to his refusal to 'whip' the bishops in any direction, although he was willing to permit others' efforts and provide them with general information on the number of bishops willing to act in the desired way.[31] If Davidson was hesitant to provide a lead to the episcopal bench in joining with Cromer's party, other of its members were less restrained. George Kennion, bishop of Bath and Wells, took it upon himself to circularise a notice of a meeting of Cromer's party on 4 August, requesting that those willing to vote for the bill advise Lord Bath of that intention.[32] A few days earlier, the bishop of Southwell made the case more explicitly in a letter to *The Times*, announcing his willingness to 'stoop to conquer' and vote for the bill, in order 'to chivalrously screen the Throne from the disasters which the Government would inflict by the usage of the power which they have gained', and that it was only by the similar action of other Unionists that this could be achieved.[33] None of these activities went unnoticed by those counting heads for the various factions.[34]

Among the closest of these observers were the leaders and whips of the die-hards. They were also the ones most shocked at the prospect of the bishops voting for the bill. In their astonishment they tended toward over-reaction. Upon the first, exaggerated hints of the bishops voting for the bill as a bloc, Lord Salisbury wrote to the archbishop of his surprise and the hope that the bishops would remain outside party conflict and warning of what passage of the bill would mean for the church, especially in terms of Welsh disestablishment.[35] This preliminary warning, however, had no effect on at least two

[27] 'The Morality of Special Creations', *The Times*, 3 Aug. 1911, p. 5a; Lambeth Palace Library, Davidson Papers, 12, ff. 297–8: bishop of Salisbury to Curzon, 28 July 1911. The bishop's letter began a debate in the letters column of *The Times* which continued for the next week, as various readers, including the prominent lawyer and future cabinet minister, Sir George Cave, contributed their perspectives on whether or not such new creations were inherently corrupt.

[28] Jenkins, *Mr. Balfour's Poodle*, remains the best general account; D. Southern, 'Lord Newton, the Conservative Peers and the Parliament Act of 1911', *EHR*, xcvi (1981), 834–40, and P. Kelvin and C.C. Weston, 'The "Judas Group" and the Parliament Bill of 1911', *EHR*, xcix (1984), 551–63, both closely examine the formation of the group of Unionists who voted with the government to avoid a mass creation, but do not mention the bishops.

[29] Lambeth Palace Library, Davidson Papers, 12, f. 219: Davidson Journal, 28 July 1911.

[30] Lambeth Palace Library, Davidson Papers, 12, f. 245: Cromer to Davidson, 2 Aug. 1911.

[31] Lambeth Palace Library, Davidson Papers, 12, ff. 219, 239: Davidson Memorandum, 28 July, 1 Aug. 1911.

[32] Lambeth Palace Library, Davidson Papers, 12, f. 250: circular letter to the bishops from G. Kennion, bishop of Bath and Wells, 2 Aug. 1911.

[33] 'Stooping to Conquer', letter from Edwyn Hoskyns, bishop of Southwell, *The Times*, 29 July 1911, p. 10a.

[34] TNA (PRO), Cromer Papers, FO 633/34, ff. 39–40: Lansdowne to Cromer, 30 July 1911; BL, India Office Library, Curzon Papers, F/112/89/62–4: Cromer to Curzon, 2 Aug. 1911; *The Crawford Papers*, ed. John Vincent (Manchester, 1984), 202, 212: 26 July, 5 Aug. 1911; Bodl., Selborne Papers, 74, ff. 170–1: Lovat to Selborne, 4 Aug. 1911.

[35] Bell, *Randall Davidson*, i, 627–8: Salisbury to Davidson, 1 Aug. 1911.

bishops who heard of it and continued in their intention to vote to ensure passage.[36] As the climax neared, the approach of the die-hards became more blunt. Selborne wrote to Salisbury on 4 August that the Liberals were relying 'for their majority on a very few Unionist Peers, on cross bench Peers . . . but above all *on the Bishops*. . . . Can we do anything more to put that straight? Can we *frighten* them?'[37]

Salisbury replied more temperately that regarding the bishops, his brother, Lord Robert Cecil, had written to three bishops and he had written himself to Winchester and Canterbury, but that as the latter was 'vastly the most important as he leads others', Selborne might write to him also.[38] This was the 'Hotel Cecil' – or, perhaps, the 'Church Cecil' – in full force, and the die-hard effort to sway the bishops was left in their hands. Selborne, indeed wrote to Davidson:

> I hear on every side that the Government are reckoning to obtain their majority . . . from the Bench of Bishops. I never should have tried to draw the Bishops into the quarrel on our side . . . but I never thought that they would come forward to help the professed enemies of the Church against those who are her most loyal and devoted sons . . . nothing will persuade me either that the Bishops as a body can approve of the Parliament Bill or that their natural course would not be to abstain from taking part in the division. If, therefore, they depart from the removed attitude on purpose to save the Government and defeat their friends, I do not conceal from you that many of us will feel it deeply & bitterly and I cannot imagine what possible end they hope to serve by doing so.[39]

Davidson calmly replied to this exhortation, just as he had to Salisbury's some days earlier: he had no idea what individual bishops would do, and he had no intention of attempting any leadership 'in a *political* matter, wherein I have no better right to judge than any other Bishop', but he believed that most bishops would abstain, as they had in the motion of censure on the government.[40] The Cecils' arguments had made no impact in swaying the bishops.

Other die-hards endeavoured to pressure the episcopal bench through public statements. At a public meeting in Chelsea, the audience responded with laughter when Lord Halsbury Mockingly suggested that he, the former lord chancellor and leader of the die-hards, 'should abstain from voting for that which he thought to be right, in order that some Bishop or another might not be forced to vote for something or other which that Bishop thought wrong'.[41] Such sentiments did prompt Huysse W. Yeatman-Biggs, bishop of Worcester, to write to *The Times*, stating his intention to vote against the measure. In his view 'if the Empire is to be delivered from Single-Chamber government, the creation of a number of pledged peers will be a scandal which history will never forget, but not

[36] The bishops of St Albans and Southwell who saw Davidson immediately after receipt of Salisbury's letter. Lambeth Palace Library, Davidson Papers, 12, f. 239: Davidson Journal, 1 Aug. 1911.

[37] Cecil Papers (Marquess of Salisbury, Hatfield House, Hatfield, Herts), S(4) 70/126: Selborne to Salisbury, 4 Aug. 1911.

[38] Bodl., Selborne Papers, 6, ff. 106–11: Salisbury to Selborne, 5 Aug. 1911.

[39] Lambeth Palace Library, Davidson Papers, 12, ff. 251–4: Selborne to Davidson, 5 Aug. 1911.

[40] Bodl., Selborne Papers, 88, f. 69: Davidson to Selborne, 9 Aug. 1911.

[41] 'Lord Halsbury and His Supporters', *The Times*, 5 Aug. 1911, p. 5b

so great a scandal as the failure of the House to remain firm to those amendments which it has with much seriousness constructed, for the plain mind of the electorate looks for definiteness in a crisis'.[42]

Yet such efforts did not find their mark. The bishop of Chichester (who did not have a vote in the house of lords) responded to the question posed by Sir Edward Carson to a wavering peer as to the position of the Unionist Party if the bill was carried by Unionist votes, with the rebuke: 'what will be the position of the Unionist Party in the country which, whatever it wants, certainly does not want such an addition [of peers]'. In his mind, clearly, the situation would only be worse.[43] To counter such a perception, no less than Sir Edward Carson, another leading die-hard, suggested that the party would be in a position of 'unparalleled strength, confidence and enthusiasm born of the conviction that straight and plain dealing is right'. Voters simply would not understand the argument implied by the bishop's action that one might have 'To do evil that good may come.'[44] Press debates such as this, or the one initiated by the bishop of Salisbury, did demonstrate the willingness of many on the episcopal bench to enter the political fray. Most – certainly the archbishop of Canterbury – would probably have preferred to avoid being at the centre of a raging political storm, but with the fate of the Parliament Bill so narrowly balanced they did not shy from expressing their views and, ultimately, from acting according to their consciences.

Prior to the debate, the core of the 13 bishops who ultimately entered the government lobby, had already formed. Besides the three who genuinely supported the bill, eight others had already expressed a willingness to do so if necessary.[45] Of these 11, ten voted for the bill. Thus only Davidson and two others – the bishops of Carlisle and Ripon – might be said to have changed their minds on the night. However, the course of the debate hardened pre-existing inclinations.[46]

Early in the debate, Cosmo Gordon Lang, the archbishop of York, expressed a view shared by many of his colleagues that the bill was 'prejudicial to the interests of the House and the country', but the Liberal government had acted in such a determined fashion that the opposition 'could do no more than protest' and he would reluctantly support the Bill. Edward Talbot, the bishop of Winchester, followed, criticizing the crudeness of the measure and the unwillingness of the government to seek a compro-

---

[42] 'Support for Lord Halsbury', letter from Huyshe Yeatman-Biggs, bishop of Worcester, *The Times*, 7 Aug. 1911, p. 5e–f.

[43] 'Unionist Voters and the Bill', letter from the bishop of Chichester, *The Times*, 7 Aug. 1911, p. 5f. One tory MP responded that the party would only 'be strengthened in future elections if the outrage on the Constitution is actually perpetrated': 'The Lords and the Country', letter from J. Fortescue Flannery, *The Times*, 8 Aug. 1911, p. 7e.

[44] 'Unionist Voters for the Bill', letter from Sir Edward Carson, *The Times*, 9 Aug. 1911, p. 6b.

[45] The archbishop of York, and the bishops of Lichfield, St Albans, St Asaph, Southwell, Wakefield, and Winchester. See Appendix.

[46] Several bishops told the archbishop on the first day of the final debate that they 'were clear that if the issue should become close they ought to vote with the government rather than abstain': Lambeth Palace Library, Davidson Papers, 12, f. 258: Davidson Journal, 9 Aug. 1911 (talk with bishops of Lichfield, St Asaph 'and a few others'). The two bishops (Peterborough and St David's) who had been the most persistent episcopal supporters of the opposition through the committee stages of the bill – and Peterborough was the lone bishop to vote against the government in the vote of censure on 8 August – adhered to their earlier pledge to follow Lansdowne's lead and abstained from the final vote.

mise, yet he too would reluctantly enter the lobby in support of the measure.[47] These statements indicated the general sentiment felt on the episcopal bench, but in recognition of the influence which Davidson possessed over his colleagues, the archbishop's speech was awaited with great expectation. One correspondent went so far as to write to the archbishop earlier in the week that:

> I think in the debate on Wednesday speeches may for once turn votes. If you appealed to independent men to save the King I believe you would get a large following. I realize, of course, that there are objections to the holder of your office taking so strong a line, but I cannot help thinking that you are in the position in which the Duke of Wellington was in 1832, people may blame you for a month or two, but after that I am convinced they will come round to think that you acted the part which the Archbishop of Canterbury ought to act.[48]

Certainly the example of 1832 occupied Davidson's mind. The last thing he wanted was for the anglican church to emerge from the debate held in the same odium as had been felt amongst the populace when the votes of bishops had helped block the initial passage of the Great Reform Bill. A second chance to support reform – or at least stand aside to allow passage – was unlikely to present itself, as it had in 1832.

Nevertheless, when he entered the chamber for the final day of debate, Davidson had not made up his mind whether to vote or not. During the course of the evening, however, several considerations caused him to reconsider his intention to abstain and announce his decision to enter the government lobby. Information from Lord Lytton that 20 or 30 Unionists intended to support the government encouraged the archbishop, but also brought home the importance of every vote. [49] Stamfordham's assurance that the king would not again accede to hypothetical guarantees (on, for instance, the question of Irish home rule) comforted the primate against a possible repetition of the present crisis. Lord Morley's statement on behalf of the government that the king would create sufficient peers to ensure passage of the bill against *any* opposition on the next occasion, should it now be defeated (meaning up to 500 new peers and quashing any suggestion of a limited creation) removed any possible doubt that the bill would become law, if not now, later.[50] Finally, as he stated to the House, 'the callousness – I had almost said levity – with which some noble Lords seemed to contemplate the creation of some five hundred new peers', daunted him. He continued: 'we are now told that the issue whether or not these Peers are to be created for the swamping of the House may depend to-night upon a few votes, perhaps a single vote . . . I cannot hold the position of one of those who might have averted that calamity and did not. In face of these facts, I shall, therefore, with a grave sense of public duty, give my vote against adherence to the amendment.'[51]

[47] 'The Great Debate in the Lords', *The Times*, 10 Aug. 1911, p. 6a–b.
[48] Parliamentary Archives, Strachey Papers, S/23/4/11: St Loe Strachey to Davidson, 4 Aug. 1911.
[49] National Archives of Scotland, Whittingehame Papers, GD 433/2/342: Lord Lytton to his mother, 10 Aug. 1911.
[50] Lambeth Palace Library, Davidson Papers, 12, pp. 259–61: Davidson Journal, 11 Aug. 1911; portions printed in Bell, *Randall Davidson*, i, 629–30.
[51] Hansard (Lords), ix, col. 1059: 10 Aug. 1911.

The archbishop's speech had lasted a mere 232 words – 'a few vigorous sentences' according to *The Times* – but had what one commentator called 'a ring of leadership'.[52] Certainly, contemporaries believed it to have influenced both his fellow bishops and other peers into following his lead.[53] Even if the nucleus of those bishops who voted with the government had formed previously, the action of their primate must have consolidated the vote and swayed the two or three who had not indicated their willingness to move in this direction earlier. Certainly, the court, and presumably the king, were relieved. According to the archbishop, his old friend, Lord Stamfordham, 'rejoiced' upon hearing his decision.[54]

The votes of the archbishop and his colleagues did not escape the blame from the political right which had been foreshadowed in the days before the debate. To include the bishops among the 'Judas peers' (as the Unionists who voted with the government would subsequently be known) would have been metaphorical heresy, but this did not prevent the bishops from being heavily criticized by the die-hards and others. To some degree, it was simple astonishment. As the duke of Bedford wrote:

> The vote of the Bishops is extraordinary. The last vote of the Spiritual Peers in the House of Lords before its powers were abolished was recorded in favour of the Government who are pledged to disestablish and disendow the Church. They please the King, the Government and the great leaders of the opposition and don't trouble about their Church. The mental attitude of these holy men is even more puzzling than that of our own party leaders.[55]

George Wyndham too was puzzled: 'I cannot understand [the action of the bishops]. If they could have heard, as I did, the contempt poured on them; by the Radicals on the steps of the Throne, they would have understood that they were selling the Crown and the Church to men who despised them.'[56] This is doubtful. The archbishop and his colleagues were much more focused on preserving the position of the king and not placing the church in a difficult position than with what the Liberals thought of them. The bishops had little concern for the political ramifications of the outcome in comparison to those of the position of the king and the church before the nation.

But, as the condemnations became manifest in the days following the vote, the bishops were staunch in their own defence. Archbishop Lang recorded that he 'was never so sure

[52] 'Parliament Bill Passed', *The Times*, 11 Aug. 1911, p. 6b; A. Wilson-Fox, *The Life of Lord Halsbury* (1929), 273, quoted in Jenkins, *Mr. Balfour's Poodle*, 181.

[53] Lord Blythswood thought 'the violent and at times unreasonable attitude taken up by the "Ditchers" influenced others – among them the Archbishop of Canterbury. He perhaps helped to win some Bishops'. TNA (PRO), Cromer Papers, FO 633/34, ff. 79–80: Blythswood to Cromer, 11 Aug. 1911. Lord Lytton, too, thought the archbishop's words and example, along with that of Lord Rosebery, carried several others into the government lobby. National Archives of Scotland, Whittingehame Papers, GD/433/2/342: Lytton to his mother, 10 Aug. 1911.

[54] Lambeth Palace Library, Davidson Papers, 12, ff. 259–61: Davidson Journal, 11 Aug. 1911.

[55] Parliamentary Archives, Willoughby de Broke Papers, WB/3/17: duke of Bedford to Lord Willoughby de Broke, 12 Aug. 1911.

[56] *The Life and Letters of George Wyndham*, ed. J.W. Mackail and Guy Wyndham (2 vols, 1925), ii, 699: Wyndham to Lady Sybell Grosvenor, 10 Aug. 1911.

that my vote was right. But I did not like it.'[57] Davidson attempted to answer the flow of critical letters addressed to him, by answering one of them through *The Times*.[58] Here the archbishop stressed the inevitability of the Parliament Bill's passage, the only question being whether this should or should not be with the collateral creation of 450 or 500 peers. The former course eliminated even a period of delay to which 'the threatened legislation affecting Ireland and Wales' could be held up.[59]

Despite the spectre of Welsh disestablishment and Irish home rule, the archbishop and his colleagues had had to make the same calculation as Lansdowne, Curzon and the other Unionists who ultimately either stood aside or actively worked to ensure passage: balancing their dislike of the measure with what they perceived as the greater danger of an unfettered Liberal majority in the house of lords. Alongside this political judgment was the honest desire of many of them to rescue the crown from having to submit to such a creation. Two years later, Davidson would regret that the constitution remained 'maimed and crippled' – the Liberals having failed to follow up the Parliament Act with a reform of the composition of the house of lords, which many Unionists hoped would bring about at least a partial restoration of powers – but there was no indication that he regretted the position he took in 1911.[60]

In making these decisions, Davidson and his colleagues were both aided and hindered by their unique standing in the upper House. Unable to look at the question from a purely partisan perspective, the bishops had to balance their own, predominantly Conservative, inclinations, with what they perceived as the greater good (or the lesser evil). But their contribution to both the debate and the tally, both in terms of moral influence and raw numbers, was central to the ultimate passage of a fundamental transition of the British constitution. And not to recur, as both the nature of the house of lords and the episcopacy changed over the 20th century.

[57] Lambeth Palace Library, Lang Papers, 188, ff. 93–4: Lang to his mother, 15 Aug. 1911; Davidson, too, recorded that despite the criticism, 'none the less am I certain that we did right'. Lambeth Palace Library, Davidson Papers, 12, f. 261: Davidson Journal, 13 Aug. 1911.

[58] Lord Sanderson noted that Davidson had received 'a huge pile of denunciatory letters': Cecil Papers (Hatfield House), S(4) 70/142: Sanderson to Lord Salisbury, 17 Aug. 1911.

[59] Bell, *Randall Davidson*, i, 632–3: Davidson to 'a Chichester Churchman', 18 Aug. 1911, *The Times*, 24 Aug. 1911.

[60] Davidson to Lord Stamfordham, 15 July and 28 Nov. 1913, Davidson Papers, quoted in 'Randall Davidson: A Partial Retrospective', ed. Melanie Barber, in *From Cranmer to Davidson: A Church of England Miscellany* (Church of England Record Society, vii, 1999), 399.

Appendix

See	Name	1 Canvas	2 Vote	3	4	5
					Party Affiliation	
Canterbury	R.T. Davidson	A	Y	LU	LU	–
York	C.G. Lang	V	Y	–	–	C
Bangor	W.H. Williams	NR	N	–	C	C
Bath and Wells	G.W. Kennion	A[1]	Y	–	–	–
Birmingham	C. Gore	S	Y	–	–	L
Bristol	G.F. Browne	A		–	–	C
Carlisle	J.W. Diggle	A	Y	–	–	–
Chester	F.J. Jayne	S	Y	C	–	C
Durham	H.C.G. Moule	A		LU	LU	–
Exeter	A. Robertson	A		–	–	–
Hereford	J. Percival	S	Y	L	L	L
Lichfield	A. Legge	A[2]	Y	C	C	C
Liverpool	F.J. Chavasse	A		–	–	–
London	A.F. Winnington-Ingram	A		–	–	–
Manchester	E.A. Knox	NR		–	–	C
Oxford	F. Paget	A	D	–	–	–
Peterborough	E.C. Glyn	A		LU	LU	LU
Ripon	W.A. Boyd-Carpenter	A	Y	LU	LU	LU
St Alban's	E. Jacob	V		–	–	C
St Asaph	A.G. Edwards	V	Y	LU	LU	LU
St David's	J. Owen	A		–	–	C
Salisbury	J. Wordsworth	A	D	C	C	C
Southwell	E. Hoskyns	V	Y	C	–	–
Wakefield	G.R. Eden	V	Y	–	–	–
Winchester	E.S. Talbot	V	Y	L[3]	–[4]	L[3]
Worcester	H.W. Yeatman-Biggs	NR	N	–	–	–

Key:

Column 1. *Response to Davidson/Curzon circular of 26 July 1911.*
S = Supported bill on principle and intended to vote with government.
A = Intended to follow Lansdowne's lead and abstain.
V = Willing to vote with government in order to avoid a creation.
NR = Did not respond.

Column 2. *Vote in debate on 10 Aug. 1911.*
Y = Voted for Parliament Bill on 10 Aug. 1911.
N = Voted against Parliament Bill on 10 Aug. 1911.
D = Deceased.
  F. Paget, bishop of Oxford, d. 2 Aug. 1911.
  J. Wordsworth, bishop of Salisbury, d. 16 Aug. 1911 and was not present at the final debate.

Columns 3–5. *Party affiliation as given in*

  3 *Dod's Parliamentary Companion* (1911).
  4 *Vacher's Parliamentary Companion* (1911).
  5 *The Constitutional Yearbook* (1911).

  Additionally, *The Daily News Yearbook* only indicated Liberals in its list of peers, and only listed J. Percival, the bishop of Hereford.

  The Liberal Yearbook also only indicated Liberals in its listing of peers and did not so designate any bishop.

  L   = Identified as a Liberal.
  LU = Identified as a Liberal Unionist.
  C   = Identified as a Conservative.
  –   = Given no party affiliation.

Notes

1. The bishop of Bath and Wells's letter requesting that bishops willing to vote with the government should meet does not explicitly state that this was his intention, but it may be assumed that his action in circularising his colleagues on this question implies a personal willingness to do so.
2. The earl of Lichfield reported to Lord Cromer on 6 Aug. 1911 that the bishop of Lichfield was now ready to support the government. TNA (PRO), Cromer Papers, FO/633/34, ff. 73–4.
3. E.S. Talbot was translated from Southwark to Winchester in May 1911. As bishop of Southwark he is listed as a Liberal by *Dod's* and the *Constitutional Yearbook*.
4. *Vacher's*, in May, listed Talbot as a Liberal as bishop of Southwark, but the Aug. edition gave him no party affiliation after his translation to Winchester.

Political Ideas and Audiences: The Case of Arthur Bryant and the *Illustrated London News*, 1936–1945

REBA N. SOFFER

Political leaders rely upon particular individuals or party organisations to reach potential constituencies, but they can only guess at the probable effect any agent has on those electors. For politicians anxious to seize and hold power, it is very good news when one of their partisans establishes and maintains a faithful following. The complexities of understanding influence, especially in the 20th century, are compounded by the difficulties of identifying the myriad interests expressed in a variety of contending forums as well as at the polls. While archives of printed, spoken, and viewed materials allow us to recover what political figures said to various audiences, it is very difficult to demonstrate that expressed ideas actually affected political thinking or political conduct. It is a further speculative leap to imagine what audiences actually heard, what they wanted to hear, and what they made of what they believed they heard. In a written or spoken or pictorial effort to transmit ideas, the intention and purpose may be stated explicitly but the contents of the ideas may still be equivocal. Different kinds of audiences and different members of the same audience will find a variety of meanings, often contradictory, in what they read, hear, or see. Arthur Bryant, a popular historian, journalist, and polemicist was remarkably successful in proclaiming the merits of a pragmatic and ideological conservatism to a multiplicity of large, loyal audiences through the end of the Second World War. This essay examines Bryant's remarkable audience in the *Illustrated London News* and the ways in which he engaged and retained them for nearly 50 years.

Keywords: Arthur Bryant; Conservatism; *Illustrated London News*; middle-brow; appeasement; national; tradition; character; rural; peace; left

Within British democracy, a political party's tenure in power depends upon the nature and size of constituencies willing to vote for it. While relying upon particular individuals or party organisations to reach those constituencies, political leaders can only guess at the probable effect any agent has on potential electors. For politicians anxious to seize and hold power, it is very good news when one of their partisans establishes and maintains a faithful following. Among such political spokesmen, Arthur Bryant, a popular historian, journalist, and polemicist was remarkably successful in proclaiming the merits of a pragmatic and ideological conservatism to a multiplicity of large, loyal audiences through the end of the Second World War.

Considerable time, energy, pseudo-science, and wishful thinking have been expended to determine whether political statements – oral, written or graphic – ever reach, let alone affect, the audiences for whom they were intended. The complexities of understanding influence in the 20th century, our own troubling and trespassing past, are compounded by the difficulties of identifying the myriad interests expressed in a variety of contending forums as well as at the polls. More than any other time, the 20th century saw the development of unprecedented and inexplicable events and an enormous expansion and contraction of real and imagined worlds. The erosion and emergence of new kinds of status as well as of mutating religious and secular identities, were mediated by the increasingly rapid manufacture and distribution of images, interpretations, and opinions that became inextricable from the events themselves. The rapidity of change and the confusing barrage of information created unprecedented opportunities for the development and adoption of new ideological movements, which competed for political acceptance and ascendancy. Although often independent of each other, communities of central, local, and regional interests interacted and overlapped at the juncture where political ideas are translated into public discourse.

Archives of printed, spoken, and viewed materials allow us to recover what political figures said to various audiences, but it is very difficult to demonstrate that expressed ideas actually affected political thinking or political conduct. Jonathan Rose is rare among historians in his clever exploration of the ways in which one amorphous group – the working classes – responded to what was said to them in the context of a 'culture' that included all aspects of their experience. Rose's revealing 'audience history' uses library and educational records and opinion polls to check personal testimony in autobiographies and archives of oral histories. In response to the debate about 'whether meaning is inherent in the text or created by the reader' Rose concludes, 'obviously, it is a matter of one working on the other'.[1] Rose's conclusion is useful as a beginning because one of the greatest difficulties in the study of thought, and particularly in the study of political ideas, is the demonstration that ideas actually have influence, either in their own time or in a later period.

It is a further speculative leap to imagine what audiences actually heard, what they wanted to hear, and what they made of what they believed they heard. Even if some individuals really appreciated what they were meant to understand, can we determine the effect upon them of such an understanding? In a written or spoken or pictorial effort to transmit ideas, the intention and purpose may be stated explicitly but the contents of the ideas may still be equivocal. Different kinds of audiences and different members of the same audience will find a variety of meanings, often contradictory, in what they read, hear, or see.

What kind of audiences did Bryant attract and how did he engage them? Bryant set out to persuade as many people as possible about the rectitude of conservatism on both historical and pragmatic grounds. To do that he had to be heard by a public that included an electorate uncertain about party affiliation; policy makers; and those interested in exploring questions about human nature, society, character, nation, empire, and religion. Those to whom he spoke initially were the aristocratic and governing communities into which he was born. For over half a century, his father, Sir Francis Bryant, served the royal households of King Edward VII, George V, and the prince of Wales. Growing up surrounded by royal trappings, Bryant venerated order, place, rituals, historic tradition, and the monarchy as the essential symbol of national unity.

---

[1] Jonathan Rose, *The Intellectual Life of the British Working Classes* (2001), 7.

From his father, he inherited an obligation to serve his country in some meaningful way and an appreciation of, and access to, the wealthy and powerful. Sir Francis did not provide the income that such a life required. Arthur Bryant's wealth, which became considerable by the last decades of his life, was due entirely to his writing and lecturing. There can be no doubt that his views were principled, but he never forgot that he was earning his living by them.

Young men of his class and background went from a public school directly into Oxford or Cambridge university. In Bryant's case, the Great War intervened. From Harrow, Bryant enlisted in the Royal Flying Corps at the age of 18 years to serve in France as a bomber pilot. The war was the definitive experience of his life and it convinced him that future conflict was to be avoided at any cost. Instead of returning to the normal, extended years of university study and then moving into a fellowship in history at one of the Oxbridge colleges, he took the shortened course for ex-servicemen at Queen's College, Oxford, and received a BA in 1920. Then he tried to find a place for himself in a post-war world that ill-fitted his ideas of what England (he only rarely thought 'Britain') ought to be. Starting as a teacher of young boys at a London county council school, he prepared for and was called to the bar. Uninterested in practising law, he accepted an appointment at the age of 23 years as principal of what later would be called the Cambridge Technical College.[2]

Bryant finally found his true vocation in 1926 when he conceived, organised and produced the first of his epic historical pageants to celebrate England's traditional values.[3] Three years later, he extended his educational work by combining it with conservative polemics as a means of serving his country and himself. He became educational adviser at the new Bonar Law College, Ashridge, founded to disseminate 'conservative' rather than Conservative ideas, but with the full backing of the Conservative Party. His first book, *The Spirit of Conservatism* (1929), was written for students of the college, where he later became a governor, and, from 1946 to 1949, chairman of the council.[4] Although he only once held a university appointment, when elected in 1936 to the Alfred Watson chair of American history, literature and philosophy for one year at the University of London, he taught Oxford University extension classes from 1925 to 1936 and lectured to the troops during the Second World War about military history and strategy, political science, and sociology. All of his teaching, as recorded in his papers, repeated his conservative message.

---

[2] King's College London, Liddell Hart Centre for Military Archives, Arthur Bryant Papers [hereafter cited as ABP], C51, MS 3. This autobiographical fragment was apparently meant to introduce the American version, *Pageant of England, 1840–1940* (New York, 1941), of his *English Saga*, meant to bolster morale in Britain and to encourage support in America. I am very grateful to Patricia Metheven, Kate O'Brien and the staff at the archives for their expert and generous help.

[3] The pageant at Greenwich in 1933 had a cast of 2,500 costumed volunteers and an audience of 12,000 with the entire cabinet and the king and queen in attendance for one of the ten nights that it ran. See Julia Stapleton, *Sir Arthur Bryant and National History in Twentieth-Century Britain* (Lanham, MD, 2005), ch. 3. This is the definitive, elegantly written biography of Bryant. See, too, her, 'Sir Arthur Bryant as a Twentieth-Century Victorian', *History of European Ideas*, xxx (2004), 217–40. I am indebted to her for a provocative and very helpful reading of an earlier draft of this essay.

[4] For a brief history of Ashridge and its finances, see Clarisse Berthezene, 'Ashridge College 1929–54: A Glimpse at the Archive of a Conservative Intellectual Project', *Contemporary British History*, xix (2005), 79–93.

There is convincing evidence that contemporaries found his written texts and oral performances compelling and that he was heard by the constituencies for whom the message was intended. Bryant's historical works were best sellers during decades when people actually read the books they bought or took out of libraries, because reading was an important and pleasurable source of education and status, as well as of entertainment.[5] We can estimate the effect of his books by reading what his contemporaries reported about him in book reviews, newspaper articles, letters and memoirs, and we can read his other writings and speeches with the enhanced vision of a retrospective knowledge of the greater context. Some readers and listeners recorded their responses in the local press or as minutes of regional Conservative Party meetings, or in pamphlets meant to solicit support for contentious issues. The survival of a comprehensive body of his historical and polemical writing, including an enormous correspondence with both ordinary people and the politically powerful, permits us to examine his basic assumptions and values, his political commitments, the audiences for whom he spoke and wrote, the contemporary problems he addressed, and the activities he pursued.

While fiction was often read to enter alternative existences, readers of non-fiction, whether in the form of history or political argument, may have had a greater interest in understanding and even contending with the real world. Bryant believed in the existence of this kind of reader and he attempted to capture and retain them through his vivid historical and polemical writing. Bryant produced 40 books that sold over two million copies during his long lifetime. In 1931, his reputation as a historian was established by his *King Charles II*. Thirty-seven years later, the journalist, David Grosvenor, could still describe Bryant accurately as 'probably the most widely read – and readable – historian writing in Britain today . . . a rarity: a popular historian whose meticulous research wins favour with scholars' and even with Labourites such as Lord Attlee and the prime minister, Harold Wilson.[6]

Remarkable for his prolificacy by any standard of measurement, Bryant wrote, spoke, traveled, organised, and flattered – shamelessly and consummately – those who furthered his influential career. Audiences were created and maintained through a strenuous schedule of lectures all over Britain, to political clubs, self-betterment groups, and any assembly able to pay and willing to listen to him. There was no end to those able and willing. As the King's College archives amply demonstrate, Bryant was flooded with invitations that he had no time to accept because he was already filling so many.[7] Through his leaders and daily, weekly, or regular columns for major and minor newspapers and journals, Bryant addressed a significant proportion of readers. When he lectured to groups throughout the nation, it is reasonable to infer that he was heard by those present and that his speeches, printed verbatim in the local and national press, were read by even more people. Casting an even wider net, he spoke to the BBC's then captive audience as well as serving on the BBC's talks advisory committee. When the Second World War began, R.H.S. Crossman, although admitting to be a 'vituperative' critic of Bryant before the war, asked him to take part in the home publicity division

---

[5] See Rose, *Intellectual Life of the British Working Classes*.

[6] David Grosvenor, 'The British: What Makes Them What They Are', *Daily Express*, 14 Sept. 1967.

[7] Pamela Street, Bryant's secretary, further documented the frantic pace of her employer's life in her eulogistic *Arthur Bryant: Portrait of a Historian* (1979).

of the ministry of information because of the crucial part he played in 'forming public opinion'.[8]

In addition to his faithful, popular following, Bryant was close to the party elite, including Stanley Baldwin, Neville Chamberlain, 'Rab' Butler, Sir Joseph Ball, Sir Horace Wilson, Douglas Hacking, Lord Davidson and Lord Halifax, as a Conservative Party spokesman through the Second World War.[9] To strengthen his educational ends at Ashridge, Bryant wrote, edited and produced books for the National Book Association (NBA) from 1936 to 1939 in an unsuccessful attempt to create a conservative readership to rival the 50,000 subscribers to the Left Book Club.[10] As part of the Conservative Party's policy apparatus, Bryant prepared material for Baldwin and Neville Chamberlain, burnished the defence of Munich, became Chamberlain's intermediary with the BBC, laboured consistently for the Conservative Party's policy of appeasement, and prepared war aims for the government in 1939.[11] Bryant also worked closely with media moguls such as Lord Kelmsley, proprietor of *The Sunday Times*, *The Sunday Graphic*, and eight morning, nine evening, and six other Sunday papers, as well as eight weeklies throughout England, Scotland, and Wales. In addition to his gentlemen's agreement with the Kelmsley Press from the late 1930s through the late 1960s, not to write for rival newspapers, he maintained a working friendship with A.J. Garvin, editor of *The Observer* and Bruce Ingram, editor of the *Illustrated London News* (*ILN*).

The *ILN*, that unique, large format weekly, supplied Bryant with an aspiring, literate, middle-brow, middling, and upper-class audience who read his 'Our Note Book' column for 50 years, beginning in the summer of 1936. One of the few pieces of text in a journal that conveyed its information largely through drawings and photographs, his leader was the first thing seen by readers when they opened its pages. A header portraying a scene from a fanciful, prosperous, content medieval England, introduced 'Our Note Book'. Although designed for G.K. Chesterton, Bryant's predecessor, it was especially fitting for his romantic view of that historical period. From every possible pulpit, including the *ILN*, in prose that his enormous, receptive public found addictive, he preached pride in national character and in the exceptional English virtues expressed through patriotism, duty, rural life, social justice, Conservative leadership, the church, the empire and the monarchy.

Launched in 1842 by Herbert Ingram, a Lincolnshire printer's apprentice, the *ILN* was the first illustrated newspaper in the world. A century later Bryant recalled that as a small boy his 'greatest happiness' was to lie on the floor in his father's library with a volume

---

[8] ABP, C50: R.H.S. Crossman to Bryant, 10 Oct. 1939. Bryant accepted Crossman's offer in his response on 13 Oct. 1939.

[9] See ABP, as well as the Davidson Papers and the Beaverbrook Papers in the Parliamentary Archives and the Conservative Research Department Papers in the Bodleian Library. I am indebted to R.S. Harrison, archivist at the Parliamentary Archives for his assistance.

[10] The membership of the NBA never exceeded 5,000, and the project was abandoned when war was imminent and Baldwin resigned as president. For further discussion see Reba N. Soffer, *History, Historians and Conservatism in Twentieth-Century Britain and America, 1914 through the 1960s* (Oxford, 2008); E.H.H. Green, *Ideologies of Conservatism* (Oxford, 2002), 135–56; Stapleton, *Sir Arthur Bryant*, 107–17.

[11] See, e.g., ABP, C41, National Book Club correspondence with the Conservative central office: Bryant to Douglas Hacking, chairman of the Conservative Party, recounting Baldwin's request and Bryant's agreement to prepare Baldwin's speech for him, 9 Nov. 1937. Bryant's extensive correspondence with the Conservative Party elite testifies to his remarkable influence.

of the *ILN*, 'the Aladdin's lamp to a wonderful world' which reflected 'almost every side of national life'.[12] That description continued to be accurate through Bryant's lifetime, although his audience diminished after the Second World War.[13] While Bryant always paid attention to what he perceived as national crises, the weekly obligation to prepare the *ILN* column focused his attention more sharply on daily events as they unfolded. The responses that he made reveal his own idiosyncrasies as well as the prevailing attitudes characteristic of Conservative thinking generally during the period from 1936 to 1945.[14]

The *ILN* brought national and international events into people's homes, often in vivid and memorable colour drawings, engravings and photographs provided by intrepid reporters. Bryant's 'Our Note Book' explained the importance of those accumulating conflicts, offered remedies, and predicted their outcome. The image of himself that he wanted to convey was that of a professional historian equipped to analyse and explain both mundane and extraordinary events, as well as to propose solutions for current problems. Bryant believed that his grasp of the meaning of historical processes licensed him to speak with authority about what needed to be done in the present, as well as in the future. If we begin with his fundamental beliefs, we can understand better the messages that his columns intended to convey.

Bryant's suspicion of the regrettable unreliability of most people was shaped largely by the aristocratic and governing communities in which he moved by birth and, above all, by choice. Society was necessarily hierarchical because people were inherently unequal in character, aptitude and intellect. Winston Churchill, 'cadet of the bluest blood in England', was instinctively the people's choice as prime minister in 1940 because of his 'moral courage, unrelenting will and the readiness to take responsibility without thought of self, fear or reelection'. The working classes, through no fault of their own, lacked the 'social background for leadership'.[15] Bryant's appraisal of ordinary people fluctuated between admiration and paternalistic distrust. British politicians knew that 'good government in a world where human beings are left free to express their own foolish preferences is unattainable'. It was difficult to 'secure the consent of some millions of fools and at least a proportionate number of knaves . . . to the complicated business of legislation'.[16] During the successive years, Bryant reiterated his conviction that democracy would always be flawed because 'the unavoidable weaknesses of human

[12] *ILN*, 16 May 1942, pp. 566–7. Bryant reported that there were 200,000 subscribers during the mid Victorian period. The artists and engravers included Sir John Gilbert, George Cruikshank and W.J. Linton.

[13] In the 1960s, when Bryant's popularity diminished, his column was moved to the back pages. Unfortunately, there are no circulation figures for the *ILN* before June 1963, when it was 73,210, which dropped to 59,012 in Dec. 1968: Stapleton, *Sir Arthur Bryant*, 9.

[14] For a discussion of Conservative historiography, see Reba N. Soffer, 'The Historian, Catholicism, Global History, and National Singularity', *Storia della Storiografia*, xxxv (1999); Soffer, 'The Long Nineteenth Century of Conservative Thought', in *Singular Continuities: Tradition, Nostalgia and Identity in Modern British Culture*, ed. George Behlmer and Fred Leventhal (Stanford, 2000); Soffer, 'British Conservative Historiography and the Second World War', in *Traditions, Perceptions and Transfers. British and German Historiography from the Eighteenth to the Twentieth Centuries*, ed. Benedikt Stuchtey and Peter Wende (Oxford, 2000); Soffer, 'Catastrophe and Commitment: Conservatism and the Writing of History in Twentieth-Century Britain and America', in *Anglo-American Attitudes*, ed. Fred Leventhal and Roland Quinton (2000).

[15] *ILN*, 8 Feb. 1941, p. 166.

[16] *ILN*, 25 July 1936, p. 136.

nature . . . make themselves felt in every institution, however rationally devised'.[17] Given these constraints, he proposed strengthening the ordinary person's exercise of their traditional English liberty through civics education and voluntary forums where they could learn how to co-operate while leaving the direction of those things they did not know to the more qualified.[18] Bryant combined his paternalism and his idealisation of ordinary people by arguing that instinct led every Englishmen to establish a parliament in permanent session in every pub and street corner.[19]

Bryant, who consistently presented himself as a 'realist', wanted ordinary people to know that politics was the art of the possible.[20] The standards for Bryant's realism, whether in policies or principles, were drawn from his ideological convictions. It was realistic to re-arm in 1937, but not to consider war. By 1945, he was pleased that the war had transformed Britons into 'realists'. Rejecting abstractions, they had learned that social justice was essential both spiritually and materially.[21] It was also realistic to recognize that in 'politics the right action is scarcely ever practicable: the via media almost invariably is the wise solution'.[22] A brief for pragmatism over speculation led him to combat what he believed to be an unholy trinity of enemies. The first was an 'intelligensia', whose theoretical constructs and professional activities were divorced from the real world. The political left was dismissed because it dreamed untenably of a utopian, egalitarian society that would be sustained by a distribution of wealth that Bryant was convinced would destroy any opportunity for prosperity for all classes. And finally, he despised a selfish commercial, financial, and industrial nexus characterised by greed, materialism, and social irresponsibility as well as other powerful, privileged groups indifferent to public good.

In his rebuttal to the 'higher intelligence' and the left, he maintained that England was historically indifferent to a 'philosophic conception of freedom' and her 'Statue of Liberty' was 'the parish pump'. Equity and the well-being of the community evolved 'dispassionately and rationally' following England's 'best advantage' arrived at through instinct.[23] He often ridiculed the urban-bred and exclusively-educated civil servants, as well as the 'endowed University dons and the dividend-supported men of higher education' who lacked real experience of life.[24] After the Great War, 'a few, but gifted with unusual powers of expression and persuasion' went to college common rooms and 'a life of ceaseless talk and shuttered contemplation of abstractions'. Those who, like himself, fought in that war learned 'that scarcely any abstract cause is worth the human wastage, torture and degradation that arise out of modern war'.[25] The left, in common with university dons, suffered from 'dogmatism', unlike the 'commonsense' Conservatives

---

[17] *ILN*, 24 July 1937, p. 146; see, too, 4 May 1940, p. 578.

[18] *ILN*, 28 Oct. 1939, p. 634; see, too, 24 July 1937, p. 146; 25 Sept. 1937, p. 508; 30 June 1945, p. 686.

[19] *ILN*, 15 Nov. 1941, p. 632.

[20] The title of Lord Butler's 1971 autobiography, *The Art of the Possible* (Boston, 1972), echoed a recurrent Conservative theme.

[21] *ILN*, 6 Mar. 1937, p. 378; 28 Apr. 1945, p. 446.

[22] *ILN*, 25 May 1940, p. 646.

[23] *ILN*, 1 Aug. 1936, p. 180; 13 Mar. 1937, p. 426.

[24] *ILN*, 27 Mar. 1937, p. 520.

[25] *ILN*, 5 Mar. 1938, p. 372; see, too, 13 Apr. 1940, p. 472.

who understood the historical evolution of everyday life in England.[26] In September 1936, he defended Franco's attack on the legitimate Spanish communist government because that communist government had obliterated 'civil rights' in the name of abstract theories.[27] At home, he found a bias to the left 'widespread among our ruling classes'.[28] Bryant's quarrel with the left was not 'with what they condemn, but with what they condone'. Moscow's attack on Finland on Christmas day 1939 typified, to Bryant, the left's advocacy of an atheistic society. Consistently, he opposed the left as threatening traditional security, class harmony, morality, and the economic and political liberty that he vested in private property.[29]

Repudiating what he scorned as nebulous ideology and soulless materialism, Bryant imagined a paternalistic pre-industrial aristocracy who, together with ordinary people, revered God, self-discipline, hard work, love of country, and a rural life close to nature. 'Deep down, for all our city breeding', Bryant proclaimed, 'we are all countrymen at heart. That . . . is the secret of England.'[30] In 1933, Bryant's series of broadcasts for the BBC, published as *The National Character* (1934), found the origins and merit of exceptional English character in country-bred men. From 1936 through the end of the Second World War, his *ILN* columns urged an agricultural resurrection, even though England had become increasingly industrialised as a result of war, and her agriculture could not meet the demand for food. Bryant often complained that food was produced insufficiently because of poor farming and faulty processing, driven by financial exploitation of the soil and livestock.[31] Although aware that food consumption had outstripped production, he advocated a post-war employment of more men on land in smaller units as a means of solving both unemployment and the import of food.[32] Bryant persistently romanticised 'digging in English earth, and the sweat that flows from such digging, and the natural and living growth that such digging begets in a calming and temperate climate'.[33] That perspective on farm labour was enjoyed best from the window of Bryant's country house.

Rural life was synonymous for Bryant with national character and its expression as patriotism. He understood very well that a discontented and exploited population, unemployed, without decent housing, and ill-fed, does not make the staunchest patriots. Ever since surviving his years in the Great War, he campaigned for making people 'better'

[26] ABP, C48, general correspondence c.1936–9: National Book Association meeting of committee, 14 July 1938. The subscription form describes the policy of the NBA as 'the Golden Mean, the practical way of commonsense, preserving the traditional values natural to our country and seeking improvement the whole time by evolution. We present all the necessary facts and realities in a good humoured way to counter the intellectual foreign suppositions and dogmatic catchwords of the Left.'

[27] *ILN*, 19 Sept. 1936, p. 464.

[28] *ILN*, 23 Jan. 1937, p. 120; ABP, C65, BBC correspondence: between 4 and 26 July 1938: Bryant went through 13 of Harold Nicolson's 'Past Week' broadcasts to identify what he perceived as pro-Czech, anti-German, anti-Chamberlain and anti-Munich agreement bias and then asked R.C. Norman, chairman of the BBC, to correct that bias.

[29] *ILN*, 18 Sept. 1937, p. 464; 13 Jan. 1940, p. 34; 17 Feb 1940, p. 194.

[30] *ILN*, 4 Sept. 1937, p. 374.

[31] See, e.g., *ILN*, 31 Mar. 1945, p. 334.

[32] *ILN*, 18 Oct. 1941, p. 482.

[33] *ILN*, 22 Aug. 1936, p. 304; see, too, 29 Aug. 1936, p. 340; 9 July 1938, p. 52; 29 Oct. 1938, p. 770; 15 Apr. 1939, p. 610; 29 Apr. 1939, p. 708; 4 Oct. 1941, p. 418; 18 Oct. 1941, p. 482.

by improving their material as well as spiritual conditions. When he began his conservative career, he put social justice at the heart of the 'conservative creed'. The 'poor man's health and recreation are held to be forms of property', he wrote in *The Spirit of Conservatism* (1929), 'as sacred as the rich man's dividends'.[34] During his first year at the *ILN*, he insisted that the poor must have 'a high standard of bodily living; good beef and ale, warm blankets and woollen clothes, the maintenance of the aged, impotent, or unemployed poor, not as a charity but as a right'.[35] When the war began, and the standard of living of ordinary people suffered even more, he cautioned his readers against nostalgia for the inter-war years, because they had failed to eliminate war, poverty and unemployment. Bryant had no doubt that the 'ordinary Englishman (of all classes) wants a home which he can call his own and which no other man can take from him, security in his employment, pride in his work, a decent chance for his children to do better than himself, and, in at any rate a very large number of cases, a bit of land to sweat and ruminate over and in which to grow flowers and vegetables'.[36]

The two other major problems that confronted Bryant were appeasement and the 'jewish question'. On both of these issues his *ILN* columns did not always reveal either his thinking or his activities. That departure was most conspicuous in his *Unfinished Victory* (1939), a last-minute plea to avert a war that Bryant believed would accelerate the precipitous decline, which began for Britain with the Great War. While his *English Saga* (1940) continued Bryant's signature story of British greatness and exceptionalism, *Unfinished Victory* set out to explain, very sympathetically, why the defeated, demoralised and economically ravaged Germany of 1918 became the prosperous, proud, and ordered Germany of 1939. Bryant expected that the Third Reich, 'despite many revolting cruelties and the unjustified sufferings of the persecuted minority in exile and concentration camps', might still produce 'a newer and happier Germany in the future'. The Nazis described German jews as asset-gatherers who had benefited parasitically from Germany's economic crisis in the inter-war years. Although comprising less than 1% of the population, the jews supposedly controlled national wealth, power, and the artistic and learned professions to the detriment of German values and well-being. Illogically, Bryant accepted that description while condemning the 'revolting and sickening' destruction of jewish shops and synagogues and the organised Nazi beating of defenceless jews, as well as Hitler's 'mystical and irrational hatred of all Jews'.[37]

Bryant had close friends who were jews, including the historian, Lewis Namier, and he supported Zionism despite the growing unpopularity of that concept with

---

[34] Arthur Bryant, *The Spirit of Conservatism* (1929), 7.

[35] *ILN*, 5 Sept. 1936, p. 380.

[36] *ILN*, 7 Sept. 1940, p. 294; see, too, 30 July 1938, p. 182; 5 Oct. 1940, p. 422; 12 Oct. 1940, p. 455; 19 Oct. 1940, p. 486; 4 Apr. 1945, p. 390; 21 Apr. 1945, p. 418; 28 Apr. 1945, p. 36.

[37] Arthur Bryant, *Unfinished Victory* (1940), pp. xiv, xx, 136–52; see, too, *ILN*, 10 Dec. 1938, p. 1086. Andrew Roberts's 'Patriotism: The Last Refuge of Sir Arthur Bryant', in his *Eminent Churchillians* (1994), although clever and witty, often cites quotations from Bryant partially, selectively, and out of context. Roberts accurately reports Bryant's undeniably egregious anti-semitic rants, but he never mentions Bryant's condemnation of the Nazis for attacks on helpless jews. Richard Griffiths's very interesting *Patriotism Perverted: Captain Ramsey, the Right Club and British Anti-Semitism* (1998), tends to accept Roberts's reading of Bryant, esp. 210–11, as does his 'The Reception of Bryant's *Unfinished Victory*: Insights into British Opinion in Early 1940', *Patterns of Prejudice*, xxxviii (2004), 18–36; see, too, R.A.C. Parker, *Chamberlain and Appeasement: British Policy and the Coming of the Second World War* (New York, 1993), 88, 317–18, 266.

Conservatives after 1937. On 25 July 1937, Bryant wrote a leader in the *Observer* accepting the royal commission report that, in response to the Arab revolt of 1936, promised the Arabs part of Palestine. At the same time, he reminded the government that the jewish 'right to a place in Palestine rests not only on history and a British promise but on their own achievement'.[38] In the *ILN*, he reproached Nazi 'intolerant prejudices about Jews' nearly nine months before the brutal and bloody barbarism of Kristallnacht on 9–10 November 1938.[39] After Kristallnacht, Bryant protested that the jews in Germany were 'subject to poverty, humiliation and violence', just as the 70 million Germans had been after the war. Although protesting, he still believed with wilful naïvety that Hitler, 'the great leader' who knew so much suffering himself, could be persuaded to behave more reasonably. The 'Jewish leaven is no longer a menace to Germany and the Children of Israel in her midst are poor and powerless and without protection.' History teaches, he concluded, that the ultimate blow 'is on the head of the persecutor'. Bryant accused the German government, rightly, of 'wreaking vengeance on hundreds of thousands of its own Jewish nationals, already long subject to a cruel persecution'. Acknowledging his consistent efforts to advocate peace with Germany, Bryant admitted, 'this savage outburst against the Jews is like a blow between the eyes'. Britons could not ignore the fate of the jews, Bryant maintained, because Christ was born and lived as a jew and the Old Testament was most responsible for 'all that is finest and most idealistic in the English character'. Moreover, in modern times, jews, including the creator of contemporary political Conservatism, contributed nobly to British life. If the Germans insist that Karl Marx was a jew, 'we can reply that so too was the author of "Coningsby" and "Sybil" '.[40]

Bryant defended 'our' jews who were an integral part of the British nation, such as Disraeli, although he shared the suspicion, often repeated by prominent Conservatives, that jews were linked either to a global economic conspiracy designed to undermine national governments or to left-wing and revolutionary movements designed to over-throw them.[41] Praising the cultural, commercial, and military successes of the Germans, Bryant regretted that they did not have their just role in the world. Simultaneously, he lamented their inability to see themselves as Britons were seeing them: 'Leaving aside the sickening cruelty inflicted on poor sentient fellow creatures whose only fault has been to be born Jews as Germans are born Germans, the persecution of a helpless minority already down and out can do nothing but alienate those with whom a great power would most wish to be on friendly terms.'[42]

In spite of his avowed sympathy for the jewish plight in Germany, evidence of Bryant's support for Nazi Germany, especially from 1938 to early 1940, is undeniable. Among the Conservative upper classes, who were Bryant's most immediate friends and patrons, Hitler was admired for his successful and prosperous nationalism.[43] Anti-war

---

[38] Arthur Bryant, 'Judgment of Solomon. A Tragic Dilemma. The Peace of Jerusalem. The Rights of Two Historic Races. Imperial Necessity for Order', *Observer*, 25 July 1937.

[39] *ILN*, 19 Feb. 1938, p. 286.

[40] *ILN*, 26 Nov. 1938, p. 968.

[41] Harry Defries, *Conservative Party Attitudes to Jews, 1900–1950* (2001), 5.

[42] *ILN*, 26 Nov. 1938, p. 968.

[43] Ian Kershaw, *Making Friends with Hitler: Lord Londonderry and Britain's Road to War* (2004), 143.

support for appeasement crossed political lines to include many who prospered from business with Germany as well as those who regretted the Versailles settlement as unjustly punitive, those who knew Britain's military inadequacy, and committed pacifists. In Bryant's early *ILN* columns in 1936, mindful of England's dependence upon trade, he rebuked the British athletes at the Berlin Olympics for not giving the Fuhrer the Nazi salute as the French did because 'it helps to oil the wheels of international goodwill'. He also used the column to praise Hitler for his miraculous resurrection of Germany.[44] In September 1938, one month before Hitler took the Sudetenland, Bryant wrote in the *ILN* that 'it would seem a far lesser disaster to mankind that the Sudeten Germans should for ever languish under what they consider tyranny or that Czechoslovakia should vanish altogether under the hammer-blows of Hitler's army, than that men of every race in the world should be pitted against one another in an all destructive and, for most of the victims, utterly meaningless conflict'.[45] Bryant's horror at having been part of the destruction of a whole generation of young men during the Great War led him to a 'realistic' acceptance of Hitler's conquests of Austria, Memel and Czechoslovakia. Germany had rightfully, if too brutally, regained lands unjustly stripped from her at Versailles; the 'Austrian people regarded themselves as Germans' and had wanted union with their fellow Germans and 'three and a half million Germans . . . subjected against their will' to seven million Czechs, were now reunited with their countrymen.[46] Memel had been taken from Germany by Lithuania under 'peculiar circumstances'.[47]

In April 1939, Bryant secretly visited Ribbentrop to urge Hitler to mitigate the hostility of British feelings that, he argued, would then become friendlier to Hitler and his just aims.[48] Most appeasers throughout the political spectrum repudiated peace with Germany after the Nazi invasion of Poland on 1 September 1939. Bryant persuaded himself that the Poles, like the other peoples who had come under Hitler's rule, might be better off for being compelled to join Germany Although Bryant wrote a letter to *The Times* on 1 April 1939, supporting the British unilateral guarantee of Poland, his support was for the government's policy to seek peace by peaceful and mutual means. He repeated his often-stated argument, that before Munich, German militarism was the only method 'available to Germany to affect revision of an unjust status quo'. Germany was not to have anything she wanted but the British must be aware that the Germans, 'like ourselves a strong race, are so constituted that they can never respect arguments that seem based on fear and weakness . . . A realization in both countries of what will inevitably produce war, coupled with a readiness to seek an adjustment of existing

[44] *ILN*, 15 Aug. 1936, p. 26; see, too, 19 Feb. 1938, p. 286.

[45] *ILN*, 10 Sept. 1938, p. 432; 8 Oct. 1938, p. 643; 15 Oct. 1938, p. 679; 14 Jan. 1939, p. 46; 4 Feb. 1939, p.160; 25 Mar. 1939, p. 456; 13 May 1939, p. 812.

[46] ABP, C69, MS, 13, 15. Written by Bryant, at the request of Sir Horace Wilson in late July 1939, to appear in a German newspaper under Kelmsley's name. Approved by Kelmsley and the prime minister, it did not appear 'owing to the situation'; pencil note by Bryant on front page. Although this was clearly meant to appeal to a Nazi audience, it is very close in language and substance to Bryant's *Unfinished Victory*, which he was working on simultaneously.

[47] *ILN*, 13 May 1939, p. 812.

[48] ABP, C66, MS Bryant, pp.1–4, visit to Berlin on 15–18 Apr. 1939: some notes and impressions following conversations with the foreign minister 'Ribbentrop' and others sent to the foreign office. Bryant apologised for attending Hitler's birthday party, but felt that it would have been rude to refuse.

differences by every other means, is now attainable.' In January 1940, he ruminated in the *ILN* that going to war over Poland may not have been the best course because that country had a blemished record of tolerance of its minorities and aggression towards its neighbours.[49]

Readers of the *ILN* never knew that even after Britain declared war on 3 September 1939, and Bryant condemned Germany in his columns, he had not abandoned his determination to secure an accommodation with Hitler that would halt a world war.[50] That determination was shared and encouraged to at least February 1940 by 'Rab' Butler, then under secretary of state for foreign affairs, and an opponent of the British treaty with Poland; Sir Horace Wilson, the liaison to the prime minister; and Halifax, the foreign secretary. From 1939 until Hitler unleashed his Blitzkrieg in the spring of 1940, Bryant was involved in a movement for 'peace without destruction' led by Lord Brocket who, through the British delegation in a 'neutral country', was trying to sound out peace possibilities with Goring. This was known to Halifax, who approved it on 20 February 1940.[51] By 25 May, when Germany invaded Belgium and Holland, 'England's front door', Bryant repudiated his efforts at appeasement somewhat obliquely by asserting that it was no longer time to evaluate whether immediate past actions were wise. Now, he contended, 'it is him or us'.[52]

Bryant wrote consistently in the *ILN*, and in all his other publications, about national character and its contributions to British exceptionalism. National character, although limited by the imperfections of human nature, was presented as irresistibly triumphant because English people were pragmatic in their expectations and resolute, courageous, generous and kind in their conduct. The making of national character depended, for Bryant, on the historically essential and interdependent roles of the monarchy, religion, and paternalist leaders in sustaining a harmonious, hierarchical society that dealt fairly with the condition of the working classes whilst recognizing fundamental inequalities due to intelligence, education, talent and merit. The best English qualities were rooted in the countryside, while the worst were derived from financial and commercial cupidity.

Did Bryant change anyone's understanding of politics or their political activities? Most readers of the *ILN* were probably drawn to the publication because they agreed with its Conservative, middle-brow emphasis, its insistence upon maintaining normality in the most abnormal circumstances, and its appeal to their considerable disposable income. A subscription to the *ILN* was 1*s*. per week while the daily pay of a commissioned acting pilot officer, an elite RAF position, was 8*s*. 3*d*.[53] What Julia Stapleton rightly calls the 'culture of deference' may have led to a broad readership, but the *ILN*'s target audience

---

[49] Bryant to *The Times*, 1 Apr. 1939; *ILN*, 20 Jan. 1940, p. 68; David Childs, *Britain Since 1939: Progress and Decline* (1995), 45–6, has a counterfactual scenario which suggests that if Britain had not entered the war over Poland in Sept. 1939, the country would have been saved from bombing and from a severe economic decline, and fewer jews would have died. That speculation does not appear persuasive when tested by the reality of Hitler's European plan for conquests and his final solution for jews and other 'undesirables'.

[50] *ILN*, 16 Sept. 1939, p. 412; 11 Nov. 1939, p. 698; 27 Apr. 1940, p. 541; 25 May 1940, p. 686, all damned German policy and conduct.

[51] ABP, C69 Appeasement & War Aims Correspondence, 1938–1942: Brocket to Bryant, 18 Feb. 1940. The intermediary in these negotiations was a Dane named Bengt Berg.

[52] *ILN*, 25 May 1940, p. 686.

[53] Recruiting advertisement in *ILN*, 9 Sept. 1940, p. 607.

was clear from its weekly features as well as from its advertisements for luxury goods.[54] In October 1939, while trenches were dug in London, school children were evacuated, and the war office appealed for 25,000 women as motor drivers, clerical staff and for other general duties, the *ILN*'s 'Of Interest to Women' page showed glamorous women modelling elaborate fur coats and 'amusing' hats.[55] Each edition also contained essays and images about the arts, music, architecture, archaeology, literature, science, technology, and primitive and sophisticated peoples. Special and extended coverage was given to the royal family. Bryant's column preceded these pages because his message was considered more important – he gave the *ILN*'s readers a historical context and satisfying romantic and psychological justifications for their assumptions, prejudices, and judgments.

Sonya Rose's, *Which People's War? National Identity and Citizenship in Wartime Britain, 1939–1945* (2003), argues successfully that, despite proclaimed insistence upon wartime unity, there was no agreement upon what citizenship meant or who were full participants in the fight against a common enemy. For the readers of the *ILN*, Bryant made the meaning and content of citizenship clear and compelling. In return for the deprivations of the war, he held out the hope to his, generally, affluent readers, of a better and more satisfactory tomorrow that would provide social justice without altering the historical structure of traditions, institutions, and classes. Bryant provided historical and rhetorical validity for a unifying myth of one people and one shared, heroic, self-sacrificing imperial destiny. Every week, from 1936 to the end of the war, Bryant's column reassured his audience that the England they loved would survive every trial, and emerge victorious in a world based more on an imagined past than an unknown future.

[54] Personal communication.

[55] *ILN*, 8 Oct. 1939, p. 658.

Index

Gascoyne-Cecil, James Edward Hubert *see* Salisbury, marquess of
Gash, Norman xxi, xxii
Gaskell, William 133
Gathorne-Hardy, Gathorne 21
general elections:
 (1832) 102
 (1835) 106
 (1847) 9
 (1852) 9
George, prince of Wales 88, 89
George III, king 88, 89
George V, king 144, 147, 150, 151
Giffard, Hardinge Stanley *see* Halsbury, earl of
Gilwell Park, Essex xxiii, 2, 19–29, 55, 56, 120, 137
Glasgow, Dunbartonshire 130, 134
Glasgow, university of 135
Glenelg, Charles Grant, baron 124
Gordon Riots (1780) 84
Gore, Charles 51
Goring, Herman 166
Graaf Reinet 114
Grahamsown 4, 112, 113
Grant, Charles *see* Glenelg, baron
Green, John Richard 33
 Thomas Hill 2, 43–8, 51–6
Gregory, Arthur 107
Grenville, William Wyndham Grenville, baron 87
Greville, Sir Charles 102–4
 Henry Richard Greville *see* Warwick, earl of
Grey, Charles Grey, 2nd earl xxiv, 97, 98, 100, 104, 105
 Sir George 120
Grosvenor, David 158
Guizot, Francois 49
Gwynn, Denis 83

Hacking, Douglas 159
Haggard, H. Rider 64
Haldane, Robert Adam Philips *see* Camperdown, earl of
Halifax, Edward Frederick Lindley Wood, 1st earl of 159, 166
Hall, Hubert 38, 39
Halsbury, Harding Stanley Giffard, 1st earl of 148
Hamburger, Joseph 97
Hanham, H.J. xxi, xxii
Hansard 90
Hartley, David 132
Hawker, Thomas 8, 12, 14, 16
Hay, William Anthony xxv
Hegel, G.W.F. 50, 53
Helmholtz, Richard xix
Hempton, David 122
Henry VIII, king 34
Herbert, George Augustus Herbert, styled lord 85
Hexter, J.H. xviii, xix
Hicks-Beach, Michael Edward *see* St Aldwyn, viscount
Hilliard, Henry 134

Hipisley, Anne 84
 William 84
Hippisley, Sir John Coxe, 1st bt 3, 84–95
Hirst, David xviii
Hitler, Adolf 163–5
Hobhouse, L.T. 45
Holyoake, George Jacob 134
Holland, Henry Richard Fox, 3rd baron xxiv
Holland, Henry Scott 51, 52
Hoskyns, Edwyn, bishop of Southwell 147
Howard, Bernard Edward *see* Norfolk, duke of
Hughes, Hugh Price 52
 Thomas 49
Hume, Joseph 100

Inglis, Sir Robert 127
Ingram, Bruce 159
 Herbert 159

Jacks, L.P. 137
Jackson, Thomas 87
Jacobi, Friedrich Heinrich 50
Jaggard, Edwin 4
Jeal, Tim 63
Jekyll, Joseph 84, 90
Johnston, Andrew 125
Joliffe, Sir Willam 7, 9, 14–18
Jones, H.S. 46, 48–50, 56
 Thomas 85
journals *see* magazines, newspapers and perodicals
Jowett, Benjamin 48
Jupp, Peter 117

Kat River Settlement 4, 109, 110, 113
Keble, John 121
Keeney, Barnaby xviii
Kelmsley, James Gomer Berry, baron 159
Kennedy, Padriac 2
Kennison, George, bishop of Bath and Wells 147
Kenrick, J. Arthur 136
 John 133
 William 136
Kenyon, John 38
Kerry, bishop of *see* Moriarty, David
Kilkenny, Co. Kilkenny 22
King, Edward Bolton 100, 102, 103, 106
Kingsley, Charles 49
Kitchingman, James 112, 114–16
Knollys, Francis, baron 143, 144
Kok, Adam 111
Kumar, Krishan 46, 47
Kuruman 112

Lamb, William *see* Melbourne, viscount
Lambton, John George *see* Durham, earl of
Lancashire 20
Lang, Cosmo Gordon, archbishop of York 149, 151